Freshwater Aquariums

FOR

DUMMIES®

2ND EDITION

by Maddy Hargrove and Mic Hargrove

WILEY

Wiley Publishing, Inc.

Freshwater Aquariums For Dummies,® 2nd Edition

Published by
Wiley Publishing, Inc.
111 River St.
Hoboken, NJ 07030-5774
www.wiley.com

For general information on our other products and services, please contact our Customer Care Department within the U.S. at 877-762-2974, outside the U.S. at 317-572-3993, or fax 317-572-4002.

For technical support, please visit www.wiley.com/techsupport.

Wiley also publishes its books in a variety of electronic formats. Some content that appears in print may not be available in electronic books.

Library of Congress Control Number: 2006927727

ISBN-13: 978-0-470-05103-0

ISBN-10: 0-470-05103-5

Manufactured in the United States of America

10 9 8

2B/QR/QZ/QW/IN

WILEY

About the Authors

Maddy and **Mic Hargrove** are both contributing writers for many aquatic magazines, including Tropical Fish Hobbyist and Aquarium Fish magazine, and are also the authors of several aquarium books. They have both been in the writing industry for over 30 years.

Maddy's interest in fish began when she was five years old. She often dreamed of keeping fish at home as she watched the local fishermen bring in their daily catch in her hometown. She began keeping aquariums at age seven and began breeding fish at age ten. She built her aquarium collection by selling and trading her newborn fry to local aquarium stores in exchange for aquariums and equipment as she was growing up.

Her passion for aquarium fish continued on after she finished her college degree in journalism and began writing aquarium-keeping articles for print and online aquatic magazines. Eventually, she wrote several aquarium columns and began writing fishkeeping books to help other hobbyists enjoy keeping aquariums at home as much as she did. Her love of fish has also appeared in her greeting cards, cartoons, and other artwork.

Mic has kept aquarium fish for almost 30 years. He was one of the first sailors to develop a tank system that could keep aquarium fish alive onboard Navy vessels. His love of fish began when he saw many different species, aquatic traditions, and other hobbyists while on his worldwide military travels.

Both authors enjoy breeding fish, traveling, scuba diving, cooking and creating exciting new recipes, collecting old records, and computer games.

Dedication

This book is dedicated to the memory of Maddy's father who taught her the true beauty of the natural world in which we live. Thanks, Dad, wherever you are.

Authors' Acknowledgments

We would like to thank our editor Corbin for dedicating himself to making this book great. We would also like to thank Claudette for her moral support when it was needed most. And we would also like to thank our two dogs who persistently reminded us that we needed to stop playing with fish and go out for a good brisk walk now and then.

Publisher's Acknowledgments

We're proud of this book; please send us your comments through our Dummies online registration form located at www.dummies.com/register/.

Some of the people who helped bring this book to market include the following:

Acquisitions, Editorial, and Media Development

Project Editor: Corbin Collins

Acquisitions Editor: Michael Lewis

Copy Editor: Corbin Collins

Technical Editor: Carol Sindelar

Editorial Manager: Michelle Hacker

Editorial Supervisor and Reprint Editor: Carmen Krikorian

Editorial Assistants: Erin Calligan, David Lutton

Cover Photos: Maximilian Weinzierl / Alamy

Cartoons: Rich Tennant (www.the5thwave.com)

Composition Services

Project Coordinator: Patrick Redmond

Layout and Graphics: Andrea Dahl, Joyce Haughey, Stephanie D. Jumper, Clint Lahnen, Lynsey Osborn, Alicia B. South, Erin Zeltner

Special Art: Color photos courtesy of Aaron Alcantar

Proofreaders: David Faust, John Greenough, Leeann Harney, Aptara

Indexer: Aptara

Publishing and Editorial for Consumer Dummies

  Diane Graves Steele, Vice President and Publisher, Consumer Dummies

  Joyce Pepple, Acquisitions Director, Consumer Dummies

  Kristin A. Cocks, Product Development Director, Consumer Dummies

  Kathleen Nebenhaus, Vice President and Executive Publisher, Consumer Dummies, Lifestyles, Pets, Education

  Michael Spring, Vice President and Publisher, Travel

  Kelly Regan, Editorial Director, Travel

Publishing for Technology Dummies

  Andy Cummings, Vice President and Publisher, Dummies Technology/General User

Composition Services

  Gerry Fahey, Vice President of Production Services

  Debbie Stailey, Director of Composition Services

Contents at a Glance

Table of Contents

Part II: Fish and How to Care for Them 79

Chapter 7: Fish Anatomy 81

Introduction

Welcome to the wonderful world of freshwater aquariums! *Freshwater Aquariums For Dummies,* 2nd Edition, is a handy reference guide for those who want the basics of setting up and maintaining an aquarium system. Everything you need to know to get started on your very own freshwater system can be found right here in this book.

In this book we tell you about tank styles and equipment, disease prevention and cures, aquarium decoration, maintenance routines, species of fish and their habits, test kits for your water, and tips on working with plants. And much, much more. You're likely to encounter all sorts of equipment and different fish species in pet shops, but all you need is the information contained in this book to get you started on the road to successful fishkeeping. After you master the basics, you will be able to venture into new areas of aquarium keeping with confidence.

So sit back and journey into the fascinating world of freshwater aquariums, gathering the basics of keeping your fish healthy and happy the easy way. Your new aquatic pets will love you for it.

Why a Book for Dummies?

You may have heard horror stories about your neighbor's aquarium. Or maybe your best friend told you that his new aquarium that was in his second floor apartment is now decorating the downstairs tenant's apartment. Okay, problems happen, but these rare aquarium misadventures can be avoided with a proper knowledge of the basics.

About 99 percent of all potential aquarium problems never occur if hobbyists take the time to learn a few simple fishkeeping basics. Wet floors can be mopped, and tanks can be repaired. Aquarium keeping will still move forward, despite the occasional setbacks encountered from time to time.

It's really very easy to become a successful fishkeeper. All you need is a little bit of help to get you going, which is exactly what this book provides. *Freshwater Aquariums For Dummies* 2nd Edition gives you good, basic information and the ammo you need to battle any problems that may occur as you live with your aquarium.

What We Assume About You

If you're an absolute beginner, never owned an aquarium before, or never even fed a goldfish, then this book has all the information you need to get started. We assume that you have no prior knowledge of how to set up an aquarium or take care of fish.

However, if you do know a little something about fishkeeping, you'll find this book to be a great resource as well. You'll discover how to keep your aquarium cleaner and how to make your fish healthier. This book is for just about anyone who's the least bit interested in aquariums.

How to Use This Book

This book is a reference, not a tutorial. You don't have to read it from Chapter 1 to the Appendix if you just want to get a glimpse of the hobby before you get down to the basics. Just use the Table of Contents or Index to find the topics that interest you and go from there. If you want to check out some cool fish, turn to the freshwater species chapter first. If you want to look at a few plants, there are chapters for those as well. Start with your needs and interests.

How This Book Is Organized

Even though this book is a nonlinear reference, we did go to the trouble of organizing the chapters in a logical fashion. Here's how things break down:

Part 1: Aquarium Basics

The chapters in this part present all the information required to get an aquarium started. From choosing and finding a good location for a tank and equipment to adding artificial plants and substrate, you'll find everything you need to create a safe home for your fish.

Part II: Fish and How to Care for Them

In addition to telling you what makes fish tick, we run through all kinds of fish species, detailing their behavior patterns, eating habits, and much more. On top of all that, we offer some helpful tips on finding the right dealer from whom to purchase your fish.

Taking care of your fish involves more than just sprinkling flakes into the tank every morning on your way out the door. We explain what food options are available, how to feed your aquatic pets properly, and tell you how to identify, treat, and prevent many common illnesses.

Part III: Water, Chemicals, and Plants

A freshwater aquarium can really be outstanding with the addition of live plants. Two chapters in this part give you the lowdown on plant species that can make your aquarium more beautiful and also more hospitable for your fish. You will check out some popular and beautiful plants and find out what they need to stay healthy.

You also find out about how to make water safe for your aquarium, how to set up your system, how the nitrogen cycle affects your new tank, and what to do if you have a problem with your aquarium. We all have problems now and then, but this is where you find solutions.

Part IV: Breeding and Other Fun Stuff

What do the birds and the bees have to do with fish? The chapters in this part tell the breeding story. If you're interested in getting your fish to mate, this is where you find out how. You also learn how to keep track of your fish, photograph them, and enter your aquatic pets into fish shows.

Once you have mastered the freshwater basics, we give you a quick glimpse into the world of marine fishkeeping so that you will have other exciting avenues to explore.

Part V: The Part of Tens

This part consists of several fun lists. It's sort of a way for us to squeeze a bunch of extra information at the back of the book in as succinct a way as possible. Here are some really cool and helpful aquarium gadgets, a few useful aquatic New Year's resolutions, and some often overlooked scientific fish laws.

Icons Used in This Book

If you've flipped through this book at all, you've probably noticed little pictures, called icons, in the margins. Here's what they mean:

TIP

This icon indicates good advice and information that will help you keep your fish healthy and safe.

WARNING!

When we discuss a task or procedure that might be problematic, we use this icon. It also points out things that might be dangerous to you or your fish.

TECHNICAL STUFF

This icon flags information that's, well, technical, and you can go ahead and skip that paragraph if you want to.

REMEMBER

When we make a point or offer some information that we feel you should keep with you forever, we toss in this icon.

We hope you enjoy reading this book as much as we did writing it. Sit back, read, and then start your own aquarium adventure!

Where to Go from Here

If you don't already own fish and don't know how to set up an aquarium, start with Part I. If you have a little more background in fishkeeping, maybe you want to check out the species guide in Part II. Or maybe the chapter on live plants in Part III has caught your fancy. Go ahead and skip around. That's what this book is for.

Part I
Aquarium Basics

In this part . . .

*I*t's time to enter the world of freshwater aquariums. The first six chapters of this book provide an overview of aquariums and aquarium equipment such as heaters, pumps, and filters. These chapters provide the mechanical and technological foundation necessary to bring your tanks to life.

Chapter 1

Tanks for the Memories

*W*e think some of the most pleasurable moments in our lives life have involved aquarium keeping. There is a special excitement that comes with owning a beautiful tank full of wonderful fish and plants. Most people have either owned an aquarium, lived in a house with a fish tank, or dreamed of putting one together.

Maddy remembers the first time her fish had babies. Her little heart was ready to burst with excitement and pride! She stayed up all night watching the new fry adjusting to their new world. She also remembers getting a $20 gift certificate for her 10th birthday that she could redeem at the local fish store. She walked to that store feeling like she had just won the lottery. (Okay, she admits that she is older than dirt, and $20 bought a lot in those days.)

She can still remember entering the store the day after her birthday and just feeling like she was in a whirlwind of new and exciting discoveries as she saw isle after isle of equipment and tank after tank of fish. Sound like fun? Well it is more than fun; aquarium keeping is hobby that can bring joy throughout your entire lifetime.

Many people think aquarium fish are harder to keep than other pets. This is simply not true. Everyone pretty much knows how to feed, water, and walk a dog, but many tend to shy away from setting up an aquarium because they worry about the minor details too much. Never fear, this book will show you how simple fishkeeping can really be so that you can start building your own memories.

You can be successful at any hobby you choose by simply understanding the basics:

- ✔ In this book you will learn the basic building blocks of an aquarium system such as tanks, gravel, equipment, plants, and fish.

- ✔ In this book you will learn how to make choices that will suit your needs and ideas so that you can make the perfect aquatic world that will bring you years of enjoyment and pleasure!

- ✔ In this book you will find many ways to expand your aquarium-keeping hobby.

Well, now that you are ready to get started on your new adventure into the wonderful world of fishkeeping, let's get going and see what else you are going to learn as you read this book.

If you have other immediate family members living with you, such as children, don't forget to get them involved in the aquarium decisions as well. By involving others, you will be able to share your new hobby from day one with those you love.

Seeing the Big Aquarium Picture

If you look at an aquarium from all sides and from the top, you will quickly see that it is just a glass, plastic, or acrylic box with a bunch of things added to it. It is as simple as that.

You may be asking yourself a few questions: What is the function of all this equipment, and how does the tank use them to run? Does it matter which fish and plants I choose? Is there a special type of water in the tank? How do I feed and care for my fish and plants?

These are all very good questions, and you have come to the right place for answers. Let's take a brief look and preview some of the main aquatic questions that people have when they are figuring out how to set up an aquarium.

Where do I put my tank?

People wonder where they should place an aquarium in their home. There are good places and bad places. Tanks should be placed away from direct sunlight and drafts. There are also household traffic issues and electrical considerations to take into account as well.

In Chapter 3 you learn how certain places in a room can affect the water temperature of your tank. You will also learn about how high-traffic areas have an impact on your fish, how close your water source needs to be to your tank, what electrical supply is required, and how much space will be ample to set up the tank that you want.

Every home has numerous spots to put an aquarium, and after reading Chapter 3, you will know exactly where to put your tank so that your fish will be safe and happy.

What type of tank and stand should I buy?

There are many sizes and shapes of aquariums and stands on the marketplace, and you may be wondering if you should start out with a small tank or a large tank. In Chapter 4, you learn that starting out with a larger tank will provide a more stable environment for your fish.

In that chapter you also learn the difference between glass, acrylic, and plastic aquariums. You will be given the information needed to purchase an aquarium stand that works best for your needs. Chapter 4 also shows you how to correctly move an aquarium if you ever decide to set your tank up in a different location or in a new home.

What do I put inside my aquarium?

When you look at different aquariums, you will see that they contain many different combinations of rocks, decorations and interesting objects such as driftwood. No big mystery here. Some items are necessary for your tank to run properly, and others are not.

In Chapter 5, you learn that gravel and/or other substrates are necessary for your aquarium. You also learn that the type and number of decorations in an aquarium come down to matter of individual taste (though some species do well with certain additions such as rock caves), and that this is an area that you can really let your creativity, decorating skills, and good taste shine.

Chapter 5 shows you what types of substrates there are and gives you good information on the types of decorations available. The chapter also gives you a good excuse to spend your "mad money" on cool-looking stuff.

What does all this aquarium equipment do?

Most new hobbyists get very confused when it comes down to deciding what equipment to purchase. As you find out in Chapter 6, there are many different options to choose from.

Chapter 6 explains filters, heaters, lighting, pumps, airstones, thermometers, tubes, valves, and hoods. In that chapter you will also learn the most important rule when it comes to purchasing equipment: Always buy the best that your budget will allow.

When it comes to setting up an aquarium, there are no shortcuts. You can't rush your down to your aquarium store, buy a bunch of stuff, and expect to have fish swimming around in your new tank within an hour. If you take the time to set up an aquarium properly, you will have fewer problems later on down the road.

Caring for Your New Aquatic Pets

Once you have read through the chapters that show you how to set up an aquarium system, you need to start thinking about what other things you will need to take care of the fish you will be purchasing. You will also have to get a general idea of what type of fish you will be purchasing so that you know what types of plants you will need and how to set up water conditions that are just right for the species you choose.

Why are so many fish so different?

A fish's physical makeup (fin shape and size, body shape, color, and so on) is important when determining what type of fish and what type of aquarium is needed for that particular species. For example, long, thin, streamlined fish such as danios tend to be speedy horizontal swimmers and love a tank that is long and not tall.

Chapter 7 explains the physical makeup of aquatic species so that you can understand what system your fish will enjoy most. This chapter also allows you to quickly see if there is a problem such as stress or disease by observing any deviation from your fish's normal body shape, fin shape, and swimming patterns.

Knowledge is not only power, it is also the best preventative method on earth for diagnosing aquarium problems before they get out of hand.

What type of fish is best for me?

There are so many choices in aquarium fish; you may wonder, where is the best place to start? Chapter 8 gives you a good selection of popular aquarium fishes so that you have a many good options to choose from right off the bat.

Of course, there are numerous other fish not listed in that chapter. It would take volumes to describe all the species available. Chapter 8 offers excellent choices for beginning hobbyists. These fishes are inexpensive, easy to find, forgiving of beginner mistakes, and will help get any aquarium off to a good start.

What should I look for when buying fish?

The best way to start out as a beginning fishkeeper is to develop a good relationship with a local pet store. A quality vendor can help you make decisions on the best way to set up or improve your system. They can also make good suggestions on fish compatibility and lend a hand if your fish become ill.

Chapter 9 helps you learn how to choose quality dealers and develop good relationships with them. This chapter also shows you how to select healthy fish for your new aquarium by providing information on how to evaluate the physical attributes and behavior of fish in a store.

The World Wide Web is a great place to find fish, plants, and equipment for your new aquarium, but nothing beats the wonderful feeling of walking through a tropical fish store and seeing everything up close with a helpful dealer at your side.

What should I feed my fish?

We all know that you can buy canned fish food. But nutrition goes beyond pre-manufactured dry food. Many species of fish have different nutritional requirements.

Chapter 10 helps you understand basic aquatic nutrition and shows you what and how to feed your fish properly.

A well-balanced diet for you fish can include prepackaged, frozen food, live food, and in some cases fresh vegetables.

What if my fish get sick?

Despite having the best setup possible, fish *will* eventually contract disease from time to time. This is usually not a cause for alarm because most fish illnesses can be cured.

Chapter 11 helps you identify stress, spot common problems ahead of time to prevent disease, treat common illnesses, set up a hospital tank to treat disease, and understand the importance of a quarantine tank to avoid introducing sickness into your main tank with newly purchased fish.

Never buy ill fish with the noble idea of taking them home and nursing them back to health. This practice will endanger your other fish and risk upsetting your current system.

Understanding Water, Chemicals, and Live Plants

In Part III, you learn many important new concepts:

- ✔ Chapter 12 shows you which water is safe to use in your aquarium.
- ✔ Chapter 13 helps you to understand what chemicals you can use to improve your aquarium conditions.
- ✔ Chapter 14 explains the nitrogen cycle and water testing so that your aquarium water will be perfect for your fish and plants.
- ✔ Chapter 15 describes the steps that are necessary to set up examples of a freshwater, coldwater, and indoor mini pond.
- ✔ Chapter 16 helps you understand the nature of live plants and what is required to keep them healthy and happy in a home aquarium.
- ✔ Chapter 17 offers some good examples of plants that are great choices for beginning aquarium keepers.
- ✔ Chapter 18 is a quick guide to fixing the most common aquarium problems.

Cool! A lot of great new stuff to learn!

Expanding Your Aquarium Hobby

Setting up and maintaining an aquarium is only the beginning. If you want to expand your hobby, you can do many fun and interesting projects.

Can I breed my fish?

Many hobbyists love to breed their fish for fun and profit. If you become really good at breeding, you may even come up with a new color or pattern for the world to enjoy. Chapter 19 helps you find the right water conditions, feeding schedule, plants, and equipment for breeding fish. It also tells you how to help coax your fish into mating. When you get to Chapter 20, you will learn how to decide which fish to breed, how to select strong breeding traits, the best way to care for fry and protect them from other fish, and how to succeed in this wonderful and challenging aspect of the hobby.

How do I keep track of all my fish?

Many hobbyists are concerned about remembering every fish and the problems and success they have had with each species. Chapter 21 helps you cut through the clutter by teaching you how to accurately record fish data and photograph your fish for fun, education, and potential profit.

How do fish shows work?

Like dog shows, fish also have their own competitions. Fish shows can be a lot of fun. Chapter 22 explains how to get your fish in top form, the best way to transport your aquatic friends to a show, how to set up once you arrive, and the standards by which your species will be judged.

Is there another type of aquarium system?

Once you have mastered the basics of freshwater fishkeeping, Chapter 23 gives you a brief overview of the marine (saltwater) side of the hobby. This chapter also shows you where to find good information on setting up an aquarium for those oh-so-beautiful marine species of fish and invertebrates.

Now that you know what this book has to offer, let's move on to Chapter 2 so you can get started.

Chapter 2

The Practice of Aquarium Keeping

*W*elcome you to the world's greatest hobby! We have always loved fishkeeping, and know that you will, too. This book can help you achieve your goal of setting up and maintaining a successful freshwater aquarium. Aquarium keeping is one of the fastest growing hobbies in the world, so get ready to dive right in.

Imagine: It's eight o'clock at night and you're just getting home from the office, where you spent the final half hour listening to your irate boss rant and rave about problems beyond your control. Your ears are still ringing, your head is pounding, and your mood is ugly. You walk in the front door of your home, plop down in your best easy chair, and let the healing therapy begin.

Directly in front of you is your beautifully maintained 55-gallon aquarium. In your private underwater world, you can see bright green plants waving softly in the gentle current. The clear water soothes your tired eyes as it swirls endlessly through the tank. A frolicking mix of brightly colored guppies and platys dart merrily though a hole in a piece of driftwood. The smooth pebbles on the aquarium floor gently reflect the dazzling array of fish colors. The faint soothing bubbling from the filter reminds you that there is always a place you can go to relax and get away from it all right in your own home.

Hey, your aquarium sounds fantastic! Can we come over?

The Benefits of an Aquarium

Okay, it's time to snag a comfortable chair and travel with me through the marvelous world of freshwater aquarium keeping. There are a lot of great reasons for having aquatic pets in your home. Fishkeeping is a hobby that the whole family can participate in and enjoy together. A fish tank is a great way to teach children the responsibility of animal care as well as the biological principles that go hand in hand with their own species' daily survival. The older generation can also benefit as well — scientific research shows that aquariums can help lower stress and prolong life.

Another advantage of keeping an aquarium is that the tanks don't require a lot of space, and are perfect for apartment dwellers who may be prohibited from owning larger, roaming pets, such as dogs and cats. You can match an aquarium to almost any space that you have. You can get a tank that takes up an entire wall in your home, or one small enough to fit on your desk — and every size in between. And speaking of desktops, an aquarium in your office is a great way to spend a little bit of time goofing off each day without your boss finding out. Besides, your coworkers will think you're cool if you have a tank that they can come look at.

Other advantages to keeping aquariums are that fish don't bark at the neighbors, caterwaul at the moon, chase the letter carrier, make unsightly messes on the floor, or whimper all night. You probably will never have to bail an escaped renegade goldfish out of the local pound, either.

If you need to go on a vacation, fish are the perfect pets to leave home alone. As you will learn later on in this book, there are many ways to feed and maintain your fish while you are away. No need to find daily petsitters for your aquatic friends, because today's aquarium technology allows you to spend your time enjoying your vacation instead of worrying about your fish.

An aquarium encourages your artistic side to run wild when it comes to aquatic decorating, and you won't find another hobby quite as soothing — nothing compares to dipping your tired arms into nice cool water to do a little underwater planting or rearranging. It beats periodically putting a new collar on your dog any day. Aquariums are great because aquascaping allows you some real hands-on interaction with your aquatic pet's amazing environment.

Daily care and maintenance of a home aquarium is fairly simple, and really doesn't require a great deal of time or money. You can set up a complete aquarium system with a relatively little investment, as long as you don't go overboard at the beginning and are content to add to your system as you go along. But if you're like me, you may find yourself paying off several charge accounts at your local pet shops.

Aquariums of old

The ancient Egyptians are generally believed to be the first "true" aquarium keepers. Historical evidence suggests that Egyptians kept fish in ponds as a source of food, and smaller species in their homes to impress their friends. (We don't know if they had pyramid-shaped aquariums back then, but we kind of doubt it.)

High-ranking Roman officials are rumored to have kept ponds full of hungry eels. If an eel-keeping official happened to have a politically uncooperative neighbor . . . well, the neighbor may have gotten a fish-eye view of their good buddy's aquatic pets.

From Rome, fishkeeping began spreading in the Far East. Oriental aquarists became so fascinated with the common goldfish that they went into aquatic hyperdrive and started selectively breeding them at a rapid rate. Needless to say, they came up with a bunch of cool-looking goldfish!

Public aquariums began to show up in Europe in the late 1800s. Those first aquariums were quite a bit different that the ones we have today and displayed only a few different species. Later on, expensive glass aquariums were manufactured for the elegant homes of the rich and famous. Unfortunately, because they were heated by open flames or oil lamps, these primitive tanks were unsafe. Often, members of high society with aquariums ended up with a very large pile of ashes where their mansions once stood (and a fish fry dinner).

During these early, dark days of aquarium keeping, hobbyists had to make do with makeshift equipment and scary potions. The situation finally began to improve in the 1900s when fish shows and aquarium societies (fish nerds gathered together in one place) emerged to help the increasing number of hobbyists maintain their tanks.

Today we have the best of the aquarium-keeping world. Top-of-the-line equipment, caring breeders, and expanding species availability allows anyone to keep a home aquarium with ease. Technology has made it easier than ever to keep our aquatic pets healthy and happy.

Setting up and maintaining an aquarium is simply a matter of learning and following basic rules. That is what this book is for. Knowledge is the key to success, and you're making a good start by buying this book. But you can also keep current on future fishkeeping trends by joining local fishkeeping societies, and from many other sources, such as libraries, magazines, and the World Wide Web. A little research can go a long way and make all the difference between complete success and unnecessary failure. Do your homework well and you'll be prepared to handle any aquatic situation.

What Kind of Aquarium Do You Want?

You are starting out in the freshwater side of the hobby, which is why you purchased this book. Good choice! This book focuses on freshwater systems, but the following gives a good glimpse of what you might want to dive into after you have mastered the basics of freshwater fishkeeping.

The aquarium hobby has three general types of systems to set up: saltwater, freshwater, and brackish. Individual types of fish, tanks, equipment, and plants vary dramatically from system to system. Here is a brief overview of each type of setup to give you a better idea how space considerations, initial financial outlay, difficulty level, and availability of species may effect your decision to try other systems after freshwater.

Freshwater systems

The most popular type of aquarium is a *freshwater* system. It's the most practical system for a beginning aquarist for several reasons:

- ✔ **A freshwater system is not quite as expensive to set up as a saltwater system.** (Saltwater systems require larger tanks and extra equipment; see the "Marine systems" section later in this chapter.)

- ✔ **Freshwater fish are generally less expensive than marine fish.** It's much better to work with less expensive fish when you're just starting out, and still learning the ins and outs of the hobby.

- ✔ **Freshwater fish are readily available at most aquarium shops and come in a wide variety of colorful species.** Many hardy species, such as guppies, platys, and swordtails, are very easy to keep and do not have difficult special requirements. Marine fish are much more sensitive to water conditions and don't tolerate mistakes as easily.

- ✔ **Many varieties of freshwater fish breed quite easily.** Breeding freshwater fish may provide you with opportunities to sell your overstock (don't quit your day job, though) and a chance to experiment with new breeds.

- ✔ **You can have more fish.** You can keep significantly more freshwater fish than marine fish in the same amount of space.

Freshwater systems come in either tropical or coldwater varieties. Each has slightly different equipment requirements and houses different types of fish.

Freshwater tropical aquariums

Freshwater tropical aquariums house the majority of retail freshwater fish. If you choose a tropical system, you can set up a *community aquarium* with a variety of species that can coexist peacefully. Or you may decide to try a *species tank* for a more aggressive fish family, such as cichlids. A freshwater tropical aquarium offers a huge number of choices in livestock and plants to suit everyone's individual taste.

Most tropical freshwater fish are inexpensive and pretty easy to keep, which is why this is the best system for a beginning hobbyist. You can also purchase an aquarium system at many superstores and pet stores in kit form. A kit generally includes a tank, hood, filter, net, food, instruction book, and the heater necessary for a tropical tank. A kit often doesn't include gravel, plants, or decorations that must be purchased separately. Always read the box label so that you will know what extras you will need to buy to get the tank up and running properly. Pet stores and large retail stores are great places to find these starter kits, which are a good buy for the money.

Popular species of tropical freshwater fish include these:

✔ Platys

✔ Guppies

✔ Mollies

✔ Neons

✔ Swordtails

✔ Angelfish

✔ Bettas

✔ Tetras

✔ Barbs

And that's just to name a few.

Freshwater coldwater aquariums

A *coldwater aquarium* usually houses species such as these:

✔ Goldfish

✔ Sunfish

✔ Shiners

✔ Bitterlings

In their native habitat, these fish normally live in lower temperatures than their tropical counterparts. Large koi are often kept in coldwater ponds. The equipment you need for a coldwater aquarium is similar to that for a tropical aquarium, except that coldwater tanks don't require a heating system. Larger tanks are better for this type of system because coldwater species are generally bigger than most tropicals and consume more oxygen.

Special consideration must be taken when choosing plants for a coldwater system because many plants can't survive the lower temperatures. Room temperature is a factor in coldwater aquarium setups as well, because many homes are kept very warm which can affect the temperature of your tank.

Aside from goldfish, coldwater fish can be difficult to obtain in many areas of the country. Setting up a coldwater system drastically reduces your choices of fish and live plants, unless your local dealer can special order them if he does not have them in stock. The World Wide Web is an excellent place to purchase coldwater fish, as you can see in Chapter 9.

Marine systems

Marine or *saltwater systems*, not surprisingly, require saltwater. You see marine fish on scuba and underwater nature programs. The most popular of these fish includes the coral reef species often found living in close proximity to various *invertebrates* (animals without backbones, such as anemones), and are often very colorful and quite beautiful. But don't fool yourself, beauty has its price. Saltwater fish and invertebrates that go in their aquariums can be very expensive.

The saltwater used in a marine system is usually obtained by mixing fresh water with a manufactured salt mix. A good filtration system is important in marine tanks to keep the oxygen levels high and the ammonia levels low. Marine fish have a lower tolerance to ammonia (a fish waste product) than freshwater species do, and an inadequate filter soon leads to disaster in a saltwater tank.

Gaining a little experience with a freshwater tropical or coldwater system is a great way to prepare yourself to enter the marine side of the hobby. Don't get me wrong. A beginner can maintain a successful marine tank, but the lessons you learn can be very expensive. We see many new hobbyists become disheartened with fishkeeping because they start out with a marine setup that's just too much for them to handle. If you have a close friend who is experienced in marine systems, ask her for advice—she may be able to help you get started successfully. And check out *Saltwater Aquariums For Dummies,* 2nd Edition by Greg Skomal (Wiley Publishing, 2006).

Brackish systems

The *brackish aquarium* is the least popular of all the three systems, simply because the fish are generally difficult to find in many local pet stores and are usually more expensive than freshwater tropical fish. The water in a brackish aquarium lies somewhere between fresh and marine in salt content.

Here are some popular species for a brackish system:

- Monos
- Archers
- Puffers
- Scats

The equipment for a brackish system is similar to that for a freshwater setup, but only specific plants can tolerate a brackish system.

Organization Is the Key to Success

One of the keys to success in almost any project is organizing your goals and ideas. If you're like me, you own one of those all-purpose planners that weigh about as much as the family car. This would be a good time to start using it. If you don't have a planner, and your earliest memory goes back to yesterday's breakfast, then you should probably begin your aquarium project by making a simple list. Even if you have a good memory, go ahead and make a list anyway.

A good list provides you with a set of short- and long-term goals to help you set up and maintain your new aquarium system. For example, your short-term goals may include purchasing your tank and equipment and picking out a few starter fish. Long-term goals may be breeding your fish and trying different types of systems. By setting a few goals, you give yourself a plan to follow. You can begin your own list of goals as you read through this book.

A little knowledge can spell the difference between success and ultimate failure. We realize that "research" may bring up frightening memories of school librarians, but there are other practical ways to gain knowledge. With the advent of the Internet, aquarists can access current information on the aquarium hobby. Here are a few good places to start:

- www.aquaria.info
- www.aquariuminfosite.com
- freshaquarium.about.com
- www.aquahobby.com/links/

It is important to keep researching the type of system you're interested in, even after you have it set up. By researching a fish's natural environment and finding out how and where it lives in the wild, you arm yourself to provide your fish with the best aquarium conditions and environment possible. A natural, stress-free environment promotes long and healthy lives for your wet pets.

As mentioned previously, this book focuses on freshwater systems so that you can gain a strong foothold on the basics of keeping a successful aquarium. After you have mastered the basics of freshwater aquariums, your choices will become unlimited, and you may want to continue your adventures in the hobby by trying other types of setups.

Chapter 3

Finding a Good Location

*W*hen you are looking for a good place to set up your aquarium, keep in mind that physical aspects of your home can have a major effect on its success or failure. Carefully inspect the area where you plan to set up your aquarium to check for a few easily avoided hazards. A little good judgment and patience goes a long way.

To start you off, we examine a few common physical problems that can occur when aquariums are placed in inadequate spots. (Check out Chapter 4 for some of the psychological aspects of tank placement.) We know, you're probably like us and are bound and determined to put an aquarium on a flimsy breakfast bar no matter what the cost. Well, after a few days of poached eggs floating around in your tank and greasy fingerprints all over the aquarium glass, not to mention that the breakfast bar is sagging under the aquarium's weight, you probably will be forced to change your mind. So start your aquarium in the right place from the very beginning and save yourself a bunch of migraines later on.

Room Temperature and Its Effects

Most aquariums need a stable water temperature. Extreme changes in temperature can lower your pets' immune systems and increase their risk of contracting disease, and even cause your fish to die in a tropical tank. Heaters can keep your water temperature high enough to prevent your fish from becoming floating fishcicles. But if you place your aquarium in a room where the temperature is 20 below zero, your heaters are going to go south for the winter, and your aquarium is going to be an ice sculpture. The point is, your heaters can only handle so much.

Starting out right

Nothing is more frustrating than having to move an aquarium because you put it in a place that just isn't working out for one reason or another. Aquariums are very heavy when fully loaded and must be drained to be moved to a new location. Don't spend a lot of time setting up a tank if you're not completely sure about its location. It's better to take a day or two and look over your options than to just put up the aquarium without any forethought. Start out on the right foot if you want to be successful.

Too high of a water temperature can also cause death. Poor water conditions such as fluctuating temperatures can cause another problem: As water temperature rises, the water loses oxygen. After a short period of time in a hot tank, your fish start gasping at the surface and can eventually die of asphyxiation. Extreme temperatures can damage their scales, fins, and other physical aspects as well. One piece of equipment designed to keep water temperature down is a *chiller,* but this can be very expensive.

The most important thing to remember is that your room should not change the temperature of your aquarium more than a few degrees from the norm (normal temperature depends on our species of fish and is covered later in this book).

So now you know not to put your aquarium in an area that is too cold or too hot. You may be thinking, "But my house is well insulated." And you're probably right, but two things in even the best-insulated homes can cause temperature fluctuations: Windows and doors.

Wicked windows

Windows may seem innocent enough, but an aquarium placed near one is going to have several problems. When normal, direct sunlight shines on an aquarium, the water temperature can reach lethal levels in a period of just a few hours if the windows have thin curtains or blinds. Heavy drapes and thick blinds can help to block out enough light to prevent this problem if you have nowhere else to put your tank.

Placing your aquarium near a window may also promote a tremendous overgrowth of algae. I'm not talking about a little algae — we're talking about your aquarium looking like a golf course. Once algae begins to overrun your aquarium, it can be really difficult to get rid of.

The opposite is also true. In colder areas of the country, drafts and chilly air can seep through windows and lower the temperature of your tank. The best thing to do overall is to avoid placing an aquarium by a window.

Keep an eye on your window for a day during normal sunlight hours to get a good idea of just how far and brightly the sun's rays reach inside your window. Place your aquarium beyond the outermost limits of the sun's potentially lethal grasp. Putting the aquarium in an area with good air circulation and ventilation will help to avoid hot or cold spots in the tank as well.

Deadly doors

There are two types of doors in most homes: Interior doors that connect rooms and exterior doors that lead outside. Both types can wreak havoc on your aquarium in different ways:

- ✔ Exterior doors can be very drafty. Every time someone opens a door in wintertime, cold air seeps in. It doesn't take long for an aquarium to chill under these conditions. Place your tank well away from any outside doors to avoid drafts.

- ✔ Interior doors may be safe from cold drafts, but they can be deadly if they hit your aquarium. It seems that most doorknobs are at a perfect level to slam into the glass on many tanks. We have seen many expensive aquariums broken by a door that has been hastily flung open. If you must place an aquarium near a door, open the door a few times to make sure that it has plenty of room to safely clear your tank.

High Traffic Areas and Children (Spell D-I-S-A-S-T-E-R)

High-traffic areas are those places in your house where the carpet is constantly dirty or worn. (I have two teenagers, so unfortunately that's about 90 percent of my house.) Anyway, high-traffic spots such as hallways, entranceways, kitchens, and so on are not good places for your aquarium. Constant movement along the tank's glass also tends to keep many species of fish continually spooked. Fear leads to stress. Stress leads to disease. Disease leads to death. This is a very simple but all too frequent pattern.

To avoid freaking your fish out all day, place them in a nice quite spot such as a corner in the living room or den. These types of rooms give your fish an opportunity to get used to people occasionally moving around them, without overloading them with constant traffic 24 hours a day.

Children are another major problem for aquariums. Children can tend to get a little wild sometimes. If you have children, we haven't told you anything you don't already know. Even if you don't have children living in the house, you may have neighbor kids or nieces and nephews who come over once in a while. Aquariums can be great learning tools for children, but youngsters need to be reminded that the fish have needs and wants that have to be considered in the overall scheme of things.

When you have young children in your home, you childproof rooms by locking up chemicals, putting away sharp objects, and hiding anything that can harm them. You need to do the same thing with your aquarium. If you have young children, place the aquarium where the kids have a hard time getting at it, such as on top of a large cabinet-style stand in an area you're in frequently. Make sure your aquarium is on a solid stand that will not move easily if someone bumps into it. If your family spends most of its time in the family room, that's a great place to have the aquarium so that you can keep a close eye on it when your children are near.

A few examples of childhood play that can be devastating to your aquatic friends include the following:

- Tossing a Nerf ball back and forth in front of the tank (guaranteed to give your fish whiplash)
- Floating toy boats on top of the aquarium water
- Practicing finger painting on the tank's glass.

Now, if you were a fish, what would you think of all these situations? A fish may likely think that it's about time to check out and visit that great fishbowl in the sky as it is gasping at the UFO in your home. Give your fish a break by teaching your children to respect their aquatic pet's privacy. Remind them that fish are like all other animals on earth and need a little bit of relaxation to wind down.

Water Sources

One important thing to remember when placing your aquarium is the availability of a water faucet. Nobody wants to spend hours of backbreaking work hauling water around. You have to have water to fill up your tank when you first set it up, and you also need to top off your tank from time to time as the water evaporates. And don't forget those weekly water changes. All that water lugging gets old quickly.

It's best to use a faucet that other family members don't use very often so you don't inconvenience them by using the tap all the time. A faucet in a spare bathroom is an excellent place to work from.

Checking the source

Make sure that the water you are going to use is free from heavy metals and other hazardous content. For example, if you are using water from an old well or any other source that may contain large amounts of iron and other metals, take a sample to your local water company or university and see if they will test it for you to make sure that it is safe for not only your own consumption but for your fish as well.

City water has chlorine, but that can all be removed using dechlorinator from your local fish store.

Using a Python

Don't panic — we're not talking about a snake here. A *Python* is actually an amazing aquarium vacuum that can be found at most fish stores. It's a long, clear water hose with one end that connects to your sink faucet. (Depending on your fixture, you may have to purchase an adapter.) The other end of the Python has a large plastic tube that suctions up water and gathers debris from around the *substrate* (gravel or other aquarium floor covering). The faucet end has a little gadget that you push up or down to direct the water to either go from the faucet to the end of the hose or to suck water from the other end so that water spills into the sink.

Pythons are usually available in many lengths at pet shops. Get one long enough to hook one end up to the sink and suck the water out of the aquarium with the other. To replace the water, reverse the python's plastic switch, put the other end in a clean bucket by your aquarium, and fill it up. After adding dechlorinator, pick up the bucket and slowly pour the water into your aquarium. This method is much easier than hauling water back and forth across your home. Make sure the water you are adding is the same temperature as the water in the tank by using a thermometer.

Other Considerations

There are a few other things to keep in mind when deciding where to place your tank.

Furniture and space

Make sure you have enough space in your home to add your aquarium without having to sell any furniture. If you do find the need for more space, casually suggest to your spouse that the loveseat and couch are looking kind of shabby and need to be replaced. While your spouse is hauling the furniture away, set up your tank. Talk up how great the new aquarium looks and hope your mate doesn't have the heart to make you move it after you've gone through all the trouble of setting it up.

An easier method is to just make sure that you have enough room for the tank you buy. Measure the intended spot carefully so that you know exactly what size tank you can purchase before you buy.

Electrical

Check for electrical outlets near the place you want to set your tank. Nothing is more frustrating than setting up a tank only to find out that you have nowhere to plug in your aquarium equipment. Make sure that electrical outlets (you will probably need more than one) are in good working condition and are close to the tank so you don't have extension cords lying around, which can short out, look messy, are difficult to clean around, and can cause people to trip. And make sure your outlets are up to code. If necessary, get a professional electrician to install a new outlet; or use a multi-outlet strip.

Cleaning

Once in while, you have to do a little cleaning and maintenance on your aquarium. Leave enough room around the tank so that you can easily reach all sides of it without pushing against the tank itself. Trying to squeeze in behind a tank that is too close to the wall is flirting with disaster.

Even aquariums with tight-fitting hoods tend to have drips and dribbles every so often. So one way or another, you have to get behind your aquarium at some point. Make sure when you are setting up your tank that you have plenty of space to take care of any problems that may occur.

Chapter 4

The Tank and Stand

The two largest items that you will purchase for your aquarium system are the tank and the stand. Many different styles, shapes, and sizes of aquariums are available on today's market. The quality of the construction of these modern acrylic and glass tanks is much better than that of the old steel-framed aquariums that were around when the hobby began. Even if you have a very small space to work with, you will be able to find an aquarium that fits perfectly.

Aquarium stands have also come a long way over the years. The old, ugly, heavy iron stands have now been replaced with beautiful cabinets and fancier wrought-iron varieties. Now aquarium keeping is truly an art form in itself. With all the variety and colors of stands to choose from, you will be able to easily find one to match your décor.

Before You Buy a Tank

The first step in setting up your new aquarium system is purchasing a tank. But before you go out and actually buy one, take the time to look at a few of the variables that may affect your purchase. Your aquarium has to fit into your individual situation. You have to match your tank to its surrounding environment and to any of your special space needs.

Stop for a moment and think about the purpose of your tank. Are you setting it up in a common area so that everyone in your family can enjoy it? Or do you want to have it in the privacy of your own office or bedroom? A freshwater *community* tank (one with several species in it) may be more suited to family viewing than a *species* tank (one devoted to one species) would be. If this were the case, you would not want to purchase a 2-gallon tank for your living room, because that would be too small for a thriving group of community species. A tank of that size would not make a very good conversational piece either. For your crowded office, maybe a *portrait* tank would be best Different types of aquariums are covered later on in this chapter.

After you decide where to put the tank, take a measurement of the intended space so you don't end up with an aquarium blocking the refrigerator or being used as a doorstop. Add 6 to 8 inches on to the back measurement so that you have plenty of room for aquarium equipment such as filters, heaters, and pumps. Add at least a foot on to the sides of larger aquariums as well so that you will have room to move around the tank for cleaning.

Water is heavy

To determine the weight of a proposed aquarium, multiply the total number of gallons by 10 pounds. That's right, a 100-gallon aquarium weighs around *half a ton*. Take weight into consideration when choosing your aquarium setup. This method provides a good, rough estimate of the total weight of an aquarium with the tank, water, rocks, equipment, and decorations all figured in. Here are a few common aquariums and the weight you will need to take into consideration on average:

- ✔ 10-gallon tank, 100 pounds
- ✔ 20-gallon tank, 200 pounds
- ✔ 55-gallon tank, 550 pounds
- ✔ 100-gallon tank, 1,000 pounds
- ✔ 125-gallon tank, 1,250 pounds

As you can see, you really need to make sure that your floor can handle the weight of heavier tanks. If you are unsure, call a contractor.

Watching the tendency to overspend

Before you go shopping, check to see how much money you have available, taking into consideration that even though your aquarium is probably the largest piece of fishkeeping equipment you'll ever own (and the one with the largest price tag), the cost of all the other hardware — filters, pumps, gravel, chemicals, and heaters — adds up quickly. A larger tank is not only more expensive to start with, it requires more equipment. You don't want to purchase a 125-gallon aquarium if that leaves you five bucks to spend on equipment. It's better to purchase a small tank and have more than enough money left over for substrate, plants, equipment, and other essentials.

Checking out starter kits

One easy option is to purchase a starter kit. A starter kit is a system-in-a-box that usually contains the following:

- ✔ Tank
- ✔ Filter
- ✔ Food
- ✔ Hood
- ✔ Lights
- ✔ Heater
- ✔ Fish net
- ✔ Thermometer
- ✔ Water conditioner
- ✔ A beginning aquarium book

Not every kit contains exactly the same things, so read the label carefully. If you purchased the kit in the previous list, all you would need to buy afterward is gravel and a few plants to get the tank up and running, plus a stand (unless you're using furniture instead). Many starter kits don't have gravel, decorations, plants, or stands, so they're not really complete.

Don't be nickel-and-dimed to death

If you're not careful, you can go broke purchasing "extras" for your tank. Skip the fancy decorations when you first set it up and use your money instead to purchase the aquarium you really want and the equipment you really need to keep it running properly. Make sure you figure in the price of filters, lights, gravel, chemicals, hoods, plants, air hose, nets, pH test kits, heaters, medications, and of course, your fish — which you will be buying later on, *after* the tank is set up and ready.

Aquariums are really a good value in the long term, and generally cost quite a bit less than many other expensive hobbies such as skydiving and bungee jumping. The money you invest in a beautiful aquarium now will pay you and your family back with years and years of pleasure.

Finding free space

Okay, you finally decided where you want to put your aquarium, but now you want to know what size tank won't require a two-foot shoehorn. If your home is small, you'll want an aquarium that you can enjoy without cramping your living space. If you find yourself sleeping on the sofa the following week, you probably miscalculated your free bedroom space.

To avoid space hassles and a significant other's fury, use Table 4-1 to gauge minimum space requirements (length by width by height) for various sizes of several standard aquarium tanks. These are *minimum* requirements — the space that extra equipment takes up and the room needed to clean around the aquarium is not figured in.

Table 4-1	Space Requirements for Tanks
Tank Volume	**Inches Needed**
10 gallon	Regular: 20 x 10 x 12
	Long: 24 x 8 x 12
	Hex: 14 x 12 x 18
15 gallon	Regular: 24 x 12 x 12
	Long: 20 x 10 x 18
	Show: 24 x 8 x 16
20 gallon	High: 24 x 12 x 16
	Long: 30 x 12 x 12
	Hex: 18 x 16 x 20
25 gallon	Regular: 24 x 12 x 20
29 gallon	Regular: 30 x 12 x 18
30 gallon	Regular: 36 x 12 x 16
	Breeding: 36 x 18 x 12
40 gallon	Long: 48 x 13 x 16
	Breeding: 36 x 18 x 16
45 gallon	Regular: 36 x 12 x 24
	Hex: 22 x 22 x 24

Tank Volume	Inches Needed
50 gallon	Regular: 36 x 18 x 18
55 gallon	Regular: 48 x 13 x 20
75 gallon	Regular: 48 x 18 x 20
100 gallon	Regular: 72 x 18 x 18
125 gallon	Regular: 72 x 18 x 22
200 gallon	Regular: 84 x 24 x 25

Taking people into consideration

The people living with you are another important part of your tank placement decisions. Face it, your aquarium is going to make some noise, even if it is outfitted with the most up-to-date equipment on the market. Sure, it won't bark, meow, chirp, croak, hiss, or growl, but it probably will do a little bit of bubbling, rattling, and/or humming once in a while.

If your friends or family are like ours, they will actually enjoy all the neat little sounds that an aquarium makes. They may even find them relaxing. But other people may think your little aquatic setup is downright annoying. We usually get rid of the people before the tank, but if that's not practical for you, your placement options may be limited quite a bit.

Children are another important factor in considering the type of system you purchase. If you have small tots in the house, a tank full of piranhas will probably go over with your spouse like a lead balloon. A community tank filled with friendly fish such as guppies and platys may be more appropriate for younger children.

Deciding where to buy

You have a few choices when it comes to where to purchase an aquarium:

- ✔ **Your local pet shop:** This is an obvious choice. The advantages of buying from a dealer are numerous. Dealer tanks usually have a warranty of some kind, depending on the store's policy, and are in good condition. If you have any problems with your aquarium, you can often return it for a replacement or a refund. A dealer can also give you advice and help you pick out your equipment and livestock. The drawback of purchasing from a pet shop is that the prices are usually higher than at retail superstores.

- ✔ **Retail superstores:** These usually carry a small line of aquarium equipment, but you don't generally find a whole lot of specialty items such as odd-sized hoods. The employees are usually trained in the basics of aquariums at best, so you may end up with bad advice on more complicated systems. Also, we find that the quality of livestock in this type of store is not the greatest. (In fact, it's downright scary!)

- ✔ **Garage sales:** This is a really fun and practical way to purchase used equipment at rock-bottom prices. But keep in mind that the aquarium equipment is used and may have some problems.

- ✔ **Newspaper ads:** These can lead you to a nice set-up at a nice price, although reservations about buying used equipment apply. Buying through an ad, however, may give you a chance to see the tank up and running before you purchase it.

- ✔ **Online stores:** There are many good dealers on the World Wide Web that sell standard and custom aquariums. Enter **aquariums for sale** into Google's search box to get started. Online shops are mentioned in Chapter 2, and buying fish on the Web is talked about in Chapter 8.

Before you buy a used tank, carefully inspect it for leaks, glass cracks, and worn silicone. Fill it up and see if it drips. Check to see that the silicone seal (the goopy-looking stuff in the corners and seams) is not cracked, peeling away, or missing in some areas. A small break in the silicone can cause the aquarium to leak. Look at each individual piece of glass in the tank to ensure that it does not have any cracks or broken glass. If the aquarium has any of these problems, don't buy it.

If this is your first aquarium, avoid buying used equipment such as pumps. An old pump could have frayed or worn wires that might pose an electrical hazard. Once you get a comfortable with how your aquarium equipment works, then it might be okay for you to take a chance on used equipment.

Ask the person selling used equipment if you can try the stuff out. If he or she is uncooperative, simply look at your watch with a worried expression and then burn rubber to the nearest pet shop.

What Aquariums Are Made Of

The high-quality aquarium products now offered by manufacturers is quite mind-boggling compared to the old glass aquariums of the '60s and '70s. The original metal frame tanks were very heavy and not very pleasing to the eye. Fortunately, nonmetallic materials were developed that eventually replaced heavy-metal frames and inadequate seam adhesives. This breakthrough in aquarium construction was a direct result of complaints filed by fishkeeping enthusiasts who demanded better products — ones that could be used for all types of systems.

Figuring water volume without a Ph.D.

If you happen to run across an older tank at a local garage sale or auction, the seller may not know how many gallons the aquarium holds. Although aquarium tank sizes today are standardized, many older tanks were not. A good formula for obtaining an on-the-spot total for the gallon capacity of any rectangular or square-shaped aquarium is as follows:

Multiply the length (inches) × width (inches) × height (inches) and then divide by 231. The result is the capacity of the tank in gallons.

Glass aquariums

The all-glass aquariums on today's market are the most popular of all available tanks. These tanks are constructed of plate glass and sealed with a non-toxic silicone. The glass in these aquariums is either *tempered*, meaning it's stronger, lighter in weight, and shatters into pieces when it breaks, or *plate*, meaning it's heavier and thicker but only cracks when it breaks.

The frames on glass tanks are usually plastic, come in a wide variety of colors, and are glued onto the rim. Glass tanks do not scratch easily and provide a good viewing area because all of the walls are flat.

Some plate glass tanks can be purchased pre-drilled, which means that they have holes drilled in them for equipment and hoses, allowing you to hide hoses and equipment inside a normal cabinet without having to route everything on the outside of the tank. However, pre-drilled tanks can be quite expensive and are intended more for experienced hobbyists. Having drilled holes is not necessary for any aquarium setup.

One disadvantage of glass aquariums is that they can be formed into a limited number of shapes — basically, rectangles or squares. If you really want a tank with an unusual shape, you won't find much to please you in the glass department.

Glass aquariums are also heavy because the glass used in construction gets thicker as the tank gets larger. This can be a real problem if you want a big tank and have weak floors in your home, or if you attempt to move the aquarium. Glass aquariums can break or shatter and leave you with a lot of dead fish and a huge mess to clean up. If you want to purchase a larger tank, play it safe and have a contractor look at the floor where you want to place the tank to see if it can hold the weight.

Testing and repairing a leaker

One way to test an aquarium for leaks is to fill it with water and let it stand on a piece of newspaper for 24 hours. If the newspaper gets wet, the tank leaks (make sure you aren't fooled by condensation drips). You should always test new *and* used tanks for leaks. To repair a leak, dry the tank, remove the old silicone with a safety razor (please be careful!). Gently wipe the area with a soft, clean cloth to remove any oils from your hands to ensure a good seal. Replace the old sealer with new aquarium sealer. Let the sealer dry for 48 hours before you add any water to the tank.

Acrylic aquariums

Acrylic tanks have made a big splash in the aquarium marketplace in the last few years. These lightweight tanks are available in an amazing number of shapes and sizes such as bubble, half spheres, L-shaped, tubular, triangular, and convex. With acrylic, the shape possibilities end only with the designer's creativity. There is an acrylic tank somewhere out there to please almost anyone's personal taste and desire.

Acrylic advantages

There are a few advantages of acrylic:

- **Lighter than glass:** Acrylic tanks are easier to move and produce fewer hernias. If your aquarium is upstairs, acrylic may give you the option of having a larger tank.

- **More stylish:** Many acrylic tanks come with colored backgrounds, which can be quite stunning with the proper tank decoration. The modern look of acrylic tanks you just cannot find in a standard glass aquarium. You also get more choices in colors and styles to match the interior of your home or office. An acrylic tank gives any room an upscale appearance and generally looks more expensive than glass tanks.

- **Much stronger:** It takes an exceptional blow with a blunt instrument to shatter an acrylic aquarium.

- **Cool shapes:** Acrylic can be shaped into cool bubbles, tube shapes, and other unusual but fantastic-looking aquariums.

Acrylic disadvantages

Acrylic does have a few drawbacks:

- **Distortion:** Unfortunately, acrylic tanks have small amounts of visual distortion because of the way the material is bent during construction. They are generally made out of one large piece of acrylic that is heated and bent to shape; this method produces a seamless look that is really outstanding. These transparent corners allow you to view your fish from almost any angle with ease.

- **More expensive:** Acrylic aquariums are a lot more expensive, if you get into custom styles, than their glass counterparts. These babies can cost some serious bucks, but they are well worth the investment. (Good ones run $500 to several thousand dollars.) These tanks are top of the line as far as quality and workmanship and beauty are concerned. If you have the budget to afford one, you won't be disappointed.

- **Scratching:** Acrylic aquariums are quite easily scratched. Be careful when cleaning with rough algae pads, for example, to avoid leaving scratches or smears. Moving gravel around can also damage the surface, and pay close attention when you are moving or adding decorations to the aquarium. There _are_ good scratch remover kits available through your local pet shop or the Internet that can handle most simple blemishes caused by carelessness.

Plastic aquariums

Plastic tanks can usually be found collecting dust on superstore shelves. These types of aquariums are very inexpensive. Not surprisingly, they have more serious drawbacks than any other type of aquarium and really are not worth purchasing. Plastic tanks are now almost obsolete (kind of like the computer we purchased last year) and for several good reasons:

- **Scratching:** They scratch easily, and there is really no way to repair the scratches.

- **Discoloration:** They often take on a yellowish cast as they age.

- **Limited sizes:** They're available only in small sizes (usually between 2 and 5 gallons) which doesn't provide enough water volume and surface area to insure a biologically stable environment.

- **Distortion:** They suffer major distortion problems due to their odd shapes.

- **Prone to melting:** They can buckle when they come in contact with any heat source, including their own hood and light! Whoever designed these tanks needs to have his or her little (and we do mean little) gray cells examined.

Different and Unusual Aquarium Styles

Along with different materials used for aquarium construction, there are also many different styles of construction as well. If you don't want a simple box-shaped aquarium, you have other options to choose from.

Portrait aquariums

Acrylic portrait tanks are aquariums that are mounted on the wall of your home, and do not require a stand; they mount on a wall stud just like a picture. These tanks are great if you have small children at home. You simply hang the tank out of their reach, so they can't pull the tank off the wall. Wall tanks are also very handy if you do not have a lot of floor space but still want an aquarium. These tanks are so beautiful we'd want one even if we lived in a 12,000-square-foot mansion, which we don't.

Portrait aquariums come in a variety of sizes, often ranging from 4 to 6 feet wide. These wall hung tanks also offer a good choice of scenic backgrounds and frame colors. When you look at your portrait aquarium, it is kind of like looking through a window into an underwater menagerie.

Feeding your aquatic pets in your portrait tank is a breeze, because these tanks have a feeding hole. Remember that these tanks have a small surface area and are very thin, so you won't be able to keep huge fish or large amounts of fish in them.

In-wall tanks

These tanks are flat like portrait tanks but are actually mounted inside your wall and are supported by wall studs (see Figure 4-1). If you want to put up one of these models, it is best to find a contractor to install it properly. Make sure to ask them to run the lights to a light switch in your room so that you can simply turn them on and off with the flick of a switch. These tanks are also used for desktop aquariums because their small width doesn't take up a lot of working space.

Wall tanks are not hard to clean because access is left open on one side of the wall, or the top trim piece can be installed to flip open. Follow manufacturer's instructions and get a contractor if you are not familiar with carpentry.

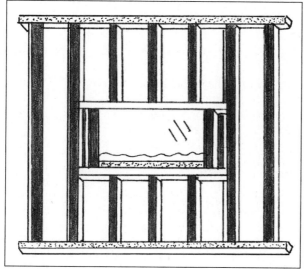

Figure 4-1:
Building an aquarium into your wall is one way to solve the problem of not enough space.

Furniture aquariums

If you would like to combine a piece of furniture with an aquarium, then a furniture aquarium may be just what you are looking for. These tanks are built into pieces of furniture such as coffee tables, headboards, end tables, nightstands, lamps, and clocks. Often these dual-purpose tanks can be expensive, but are well worth the money if you can spare it. Use caution when purchasing one of these tanks if you have small toddlers in the house who can easily break or fall onto them.

Tower aquariums

Tower aquariums are simply tanks that are built into the shape of a tall column or tower. These tanks are great for corner spaces and add a contemporary look to any room. The disadvantages to towers is that they can be expensive, and it may be difficult to find tall enough plants to make them look realistic without buying specially made tall plants from the manufacturer.

Indoor pond barrels

Indoor barrels can make miniature versions of outdoor coldwater ponds inside your home or on your porch. Great care must be taken when considering the overall weight of a small indoor barrel, so once again consult with a contractor to see if your floors can withstand the strain.

Choosing the Right Tank

There are many issues you need to address when you're preparing to actually purchase your aquarium. Size, water volume, and shape have a lot to do with the type of aquatic creatures you can actually put in it. As you have already read, there are many different tank sizes and styles to choose from. If you start off with a tank that meets the needs of your individual project or system (a large tank if you want a huge community of fish, for example), you have one foot in the door of success.

Tank size

If you plan on setting up a freshwater system, you should purchase at least a 10-gallon tank to make sure your new fish have an adequate area to provide stable water conditions. A smaller tank is harder to work with, can turn your fish into instant sardines, and will eventually bring you disappointment and heartache. Smaller aquariums are more prone to foul water conditions, which can damage your fish's health. A small tank also does not leave much room for adding decorations or extra fish.

Always buy the largest tank that your budget and space limitations allow, because increased surface area means better overall biological stability. A large surface area provides good oxygen absorption and carbon dioxide exchange.

Small tanks can be a real problem if you have a power or equipment failure. Due to the small amount of water the tank holds, the temperature can drop very quickly. An extended period of lost filtration (usually after several hours depending on your aquarium size) can also foul the water to lethal proportions.

Tank shape

Although it is cool to have an oddly shaped aquarium, be aware that a few drawbacks go along with these tanks. The shape of an aquarium helps determine the amount of oxygen its water contains.

Vital gas exchange (carbon dioxide for oxygen) occurs at the water surface. A tall, thin tank, such as a tower aquarium, with a small water-surface area, has less gas exchange going on than a shorter tank with a longer, and therefore larger, surface area.

Another factor to take into consideration is that odd-sized tanks, especially if they are really tall and narrow, can be hard to clean or decorate without scuba gear. There may even be areas near the bottom that are totally unreachable. You may also find yourself having a hard time locating equipment such as filters and hoods to fit a tank that isn't a standard size if the original part happens to break. (Even if you do find a good match, it probably costs twice as much as the same piece does for a standard-sized tank.)

Carrying capacity

The *carrying capacity* is simply the total number of fish you can keep in your aquarium safely without their going belly up. If you choose to buy a tank that is very tall and narrow, you can't keep as many fish in it as you can in a tank with a larger surface area. It's as simple as that. We'll say it one more time: If you get a fancy tank that has a small surface area, don't count on having a whole bunch of fish.

Choosing the Right Stand

Choosing a good aquarium stand can be just as important as picking the right aquarium. A stand needs to be sturdy and strong and look cool at the same time. The one thing that you *don't* want to do is use Granny's antique table as an aquarium stand, because any unforeseen water leaks will quickly ruin that heirloom. A heavy tank can warp the wood on your regular household furniture, too. It is always best to use a manufactured aquarium stand built to support a tank's weight and designed to be perfectly level.

Make sure your aquarium fits its stand correctly. If the edge of the tank hangs over the stand, the stand is too small and eventually can cause the aquarium to warp or break.

Manufactured stands are generally made out of iron, steel, or wood. All three materials make great stands, so it is just a matter of individual preference as to which one you decide to buy. (Okay, okay, we give you a few hints: Just read on.)

Wooden cabinet stands

Stands that include a built-in wooden cabinet are enclosed on the bottom so that you can hide equipment and hoses that generally spoil the overall look of your aquarium system. Chemicals, test kits, nets, and other paraphernalia can be conveniently stored behind closed doors

Such a cabinet also allows you to buy a bunch of expensive aquarium junk and hide it from your spouse. The only problem with wooden stands is that they can warp under extreme weight (placing tanks on it that are too large and hang over the sides), and they tend to bend if they become wet. They tend to cost a little more than standard iron stands. Make sure that the aquarium you choose matches the stand that you buy to avoid these problems.

But despite the drawbacks, wooden cabinet stands are the best stands that you can buy because they look good, will not tip over easily, and often contain shelves for storing items.

Angle and wrought iron stands

Iron stands are made of either *angle iron* or *wrought iron*. Angle iron stands are welded together and have a bulky look to them. They would look great in a medieval castle. Angle iron stands can also leave nasty marks on your floor (if water gets on the metal and then sits stagnant on the floor under the stand) or carpet (the weight of the tank pushed onto small legs instead of spread out over the entire length of a cabinet stand, can leave indentations in the carpet that are almost impossible to remove).

Wrought iron stands are made of thinner metal than angle iron and are a little bit fancier.

Do-it-yourself stands

There are a few stands that you can purchase and build yourself, assembling them easily with a few household tools. The pieces are usually made of pressboard and include at least one shelf. These stands are not as strong as manufactured ones and may warp or buckle if they get wet.

One option is to head down to the hardware store, buy some good hardwood lumber such as oak, and build an aquarium stand yourself. You may find out that a homemade stand costs as much as or more than a manufactured one. But if you have the know-how, an interesting idea, cool tools, and the energy to turn off the TV and head out to the garage, go for it. Make sure the stand you make is firm enough to support the weight of the tank. You can test the stand by adding books or other heavy materials to it. Add enough books to equal the total weight of the aquarium that will be sitting on it (see earlier in this chapter for aquarium weight estimation).

Material-based stands

Material based stands are made of any man-made material that is not metal or hardwood. Examples include fiberboard and acrylic stands.

Mixed-media stands

Mixed media stands are made for those people who want to combine an aquarium system with storage shelving. These stands usually have an area for the tank and extra shelves for displaying your CD player, books, and so forth.

Bow-front stands

A bow-front stand has a semi-circular shape in the front to properly support bow-front shaped tanks (tanks that are convex in the front). We personally love the shape of these stands, but it all comes down to personal choice.

Placing the Stand Correctly

As we mentioned, the first step in setting up your aquarium system is finding a permanent place to put it. Set the stand in an area away from drafts and direct sunlight to keep the water in your tank from overheating or chilling. Don't put your tank in a garage or basement unless the room is insulated or heated. Placement near doors, windows, and other drafty areas where the temperature can change unexpectedly is a no-no.

Checking floors and walls

Make sure the stand is on a solid surface. Check the floor carefully so that your new aquarium doesn't end up decorating the downstairs neighbor's apartment. Remember that a 100-gallon tank weighs somewhere in the neighborhood of 1,000 pounds fully loaded!

Do not place the stand directly against a wall. You need room back there for hanging equipment.

Looking for power

When determining where you want to place your aquarium, keep in mind that your system requires a few electrical outlets in order to run. A friend of ours once set up a complete aquarium system — water and all — and then realized that there was no electrical outlet anywhere near the tank! (He was a couple sandwiches short of a mental picnic anyway.)

Use an electrical outlet that is not connected to a wall switch. You don't want anyone to hit the switch and unknowingly shut off your aquarium equipment.

Moving an Aquarium

Never try to move an aquarium all by yourself, no matter how small it is. Any aquarium should always be lifted by a minimum of two people. You can cause yourself physical injury, and damage the silicone and frame of the tank if you attempt to haul your tank around by yourself.

(A good way to get help moving an aquarium is to put on a dirty apron, throw some flour on yourself, call your couch potato neighbors, and tell them you want them to try out an exciting new recipe. When they arrive, tell them that your aquarium is blocking the way to the food supply. Works every time.)

When you're ready to move your tank, make sure to unplug all equipment and then remove it from the aquarium. Don't remove the heater until 15 minutes have passed to avoid shattering it. Fill a plastic bucket with water from the aquarium and place the fish in the bucket. Drain the rest of the water. Before you lift the aquarium, remove any large rocks or other heavy decorations, which can shift positions and break the glass.

Never lift your tank by grabbing the top of the frame. Lifting an aquarium by its top frame can damage and break the sealer or glass, eventually causing water leaks. The proper way to lift an aquarium is to place your hands (and your hungry neighbors' hands) beneath the bottom corners of the tank.

Chapter 5

What to Put and What Not to Put in Your Tank

*A*quascaping is a fancy word that means decorating your aquarium with different types of rock, wood, plants, and substrate. Arranging the gravel, sand, and other aquarium floor coverings can be a lot of fun and gives you a good chance to show off your personal creative talents. We can think of no greater joy than creating a pleasing arrangement of rocks, plants, and substrate (material that covers the bottom on your tank) for our fish to enjoy. Your fish will appreciate a proper setup as well.

Designing the inside of your tank can be one of the most enjoyable aspects of the aquarium hobby. Imagine beautiful plants swaying gently in the water as colorful fish dash playfully between shimmering rocks and uniquely shaped pieces of wood. What an exciting sight! Your aquarium is your own little personal aquatic world that is just waiting to be shaped into an amazing underwater scene by your creativity.

But although aquascaping can be a real blast, certain types of substrates, rocks, and wood are suitable only for specific aquarium setups. You need to know what to buy before you begin randomly throwing things into your aquarium. This chapter can help you make good choices that will keep your fish happy and healthy.

Many hobbyists choose to set up heavily planted tanks with few fish. Others prefer a simplistic layout with many aquatic species. The choice is yours, of course. If you use your imagination and follow the few simple aquascaping rules that we present in this chapter, you'll quickly realize that the possibilities are endless.

Just remember that you want to create an environment that is good for your fish and pleasing to the eye as well.

Taking Clues from Your Fish's Natural Environment

The first thing to do when aquascaping any aquarium is to take a close look at the native environment of the fish you're planning to keep in your tank. For example, freshwater fish are much happier in an aquarium full of plants, driftwood, and rock than they are in one with coral and shells — which you generally use in a marine setup. Different types of systems have different aquascaping elements.

We find that it often helps to sit down and draw out a plan on paper before adding any substrate or decorations to a tank. That way you get a better overall feel for the layout you want. You don't have to draw anything really fancy, just plot out a simple schematic for where you want to place everything and adjust it as you go along. Save your final schematic in case you ever have to completely break down the tank for moving or other reasons.

Take the overall size of your tank and fish into consideration when making your plan. You want a layout that is filled with life but not overcrowded. Fish need open spaces as well as hidden areas so that they can feel secure and have a place to exercise.

The following list gives you a few good ideas about which substrates and decorations are most often used in different types of systems:

- **Freshwater tank:** Pebbles, igneous and shale rocks, live plants, artificial plants, driftwood, with sand and standard fish shop gravel for substrate.

- **Brackish water tank:** Pebbles, shale, stratified rocks, plants, driftwood, pea gravel, and small amounts of coral sand for substrate.

- **Marine tank:** Live rock (rock that has invertebrates attached), tufa rock, and dolomite with coral sand and live sand (pre-cultured sand that contains biological organisms for filtration) for substrate. Select algae, such as grape plant, for decoration. Invertebrates such as anemones and tubeworms are common in many marine tanks.

All About Substrates

Substrates come in many different shapes and sizes to suit the needs of each type of aquarium. You can find substrates in grades from fine to coarse and in different shapes such as smooth or chipped. The actual size of substrates can often vary from vendor to vendor, so for the sake of this chapter, we'll say that a *fine* gravel is small like sand, a *medium* gravel is what is found in most prepackaged bags at retail stores, and a *coarse* gravel is similar in size to a dime.

The substrate you put into your aquarium plays a very important role in its overall biological cycle. In time, beneficial bacteria start growing on top of and throughout the substrate bed and help break down waste in the aquarium water. Substrate is also quite useful for anchoring live plants and for holding down various types of artificial plants, live plants, and decorations.

Choosing the proper substrate gives you a good start on maintaining a healthy aquatic system for your fish. So you're probably wondering how to find your way though this substrate mess. Well, read on.

Gravel

Manufactured gravel is usually the best bet for a freshwater or brackish tank. It is easily cleaned and widely available in pet stores and super centers by the bag or the pound. Gravel also comes in many different colors and levels of shininess. As you will learn, some gravels are better choices than others. Most manufactured gravel is lime-free (so it doesn't change the water chemistry by raising the pH and hardening the aquarium water) and very inexpensive, which makes it one of the most popular substrates.

Of course, gravel is a completely inanimate substance and does not provide any type of nutrition for living aquarium plants. So, if you decide to use live plants in your freshwater or brackish setup, you have to supply extra nutrition for them by using plant plugs or liquid food. (Say what? Chapter 16 explains all that, we promise.)

Substrates and pH

Putting the right substrate in an aquarium setup is just as important as providing the correct water conditions. One important point to remember is that some substrates can affect the pH of your aquarium water, so make sure to buy the correct type for the species that you own (check with your local dealer on what substrate works best for the fish and plants you are going to choose). Many live plants also have requirements in gravel size, so check with your dealer to find out what is right for the species you plan on putting in your tank. You will also find helpful setups at the end of this chapter.

For example, marine dolomite raises the pH of aquarium water to an alkaline level, and therefore is unsuitable for most freshwater tanks that contain fish who prefer more neutral pH levels. If you put dolomite in your freshwater tank, your fish will do the backstroke permanently. Standard aquarium gravel doesn't affect the water's pH, and therefore isn't suitable for a marine setup which requires a consistently higher pH level.

If you're not sure how much calcareous material (such as snail shells and seashells) a substrate contains, perform this simple test: Add a few table-spoons of vinegar to the test pile of substrate and if it has calcareous (that is, containing calcium) material, it will fizz. If it fizzes, don't put it in your fresh-water tank, or you will end up with hard alkaline water.

Crushed coral (pieces of dead coral gathered from coral beaches) and shells raise your water's pH values as dolomite does and should not be used in a freshwater setup (with exceptions like African cichlids who like the higher pH and hardness produced by coral).

Substrates to avoid

Get all substrate materials from a reputable fish dealer so that you know that it's pure.

No matter which substrate you choose for your aquarium, make sure that it's safe for all the fish in your tank. Sharp edges on gravel can damage your fish's body. Jagged surfaces can be especially injurious to bottom-dwelling species that continually dig in the substrate. If your bottom dwellers look like dart-boards, check your substrate carefully and remove any pieces that look like they have sharp edges.

Never use marbles

Several types of familiar items sometimes found in a beginner's freshwater aquarium are not really suitable for a fish's natural environment. Never use marbles, glass flakes, or other such materials to cover the bottom of any aquar-ium. Marbles are quite large and allow debris to become trapped between their surfaces, which can eventually lead to water fouling and diseased fish.

Stay away from disco gravel

Brightly colored or neon gravels take away from the natural beauty of your fish and should be avoided if it all possible. Neon gravel tends to make your fish look like they're in a made-for-TV movie about a bad night on a disco floor. Neon gravel also tends to reflect a lot of unnecessary light upward into the water, which can be an annoyance to your fish and cause their colors to look washed out.

Keep an aquarium's colors simple and natural looking for the best results. You can get away with a few cool plastic decorations such as treasure chests and scuba divers, but shocking-pink gravel is too much of an eyestrain for both you and your fish (if you wake up one morning to find your fish sporting sunglasses, you know you need to tone down your gravel). Neon gravels may also keep your fish from spawning and make them shy away and hide in corners.

Gravel size and the perils of sand

Choose the size of your gravel carefully to avoid water fouling. Avoid the larger-shaped materials because they allow food and waste to fall between the pieces, where they can cause serious water problems in a short time because they are hard to vacuum out and reduce water flow. If you use an undergravel filter (you can read all about them in Chapter 6), choose a medium-size substrate (the size of regular bagged aquarium gravels) so that the plastic plates don't get clogged with gravel that is too fine. If using sand, a hang-on-tank powerfilter would be a better choice.

Gravel with a particle size of ⅛ inch works best for most setups.

Larger granules also have a cumulatively smaller surface area because of their shape, and don't allow space for the growth of the proper bacteria for biological filtration. Let us put it this way — if you think you can break a window at 10 feet with a piece of your aquarium gravel, then it is too large for your tank, and might be better used to pave your driveway.

Small-grained substrates such as sand quickly clog the water flow in your aquarium if they slip down into the undergravel filter plate and can subsequently cause a rise in waste. So if you decide to use sand in your aquarium, lay it down in a very thin layer or have a mesh plate beneath it to stop it from falling through into the filter.

If you can't find the right size of substrate at your local pet store, either order some on the Internet or wait until it becomes available from your dealer. A little bit of patience can definitely save you many headaches in the future.

Here are a couple good Web sites where you can purchase gravel:

✔ www.aquariumguys.com/aquarium-gravel.html

✔ www.customaquatic.com/

Adding substrate to your system

Before adding gravel to a freshwater system, clean it thoroughly by rinsing it under fresh water. As you clean, carefully check for and remove defects such as extremely large clumps, foreign matter, and sharp pieces in the gravel.

The amount of substrate required for a freshwater tank varies not only with the size of the aquarium, but with the type of filtration used as well:

- ✔ If you have an undergravel filter, you need a 2- to 3-inch layer of substrate in order to create a proper bacterial bed.
- ✔ If you're not using an undergravel filter, use only an inch of substrate to cover the bottom of the tank.
- ✔ If you plan on using live plants, you may need to add a bit more substrate to make sure that the plants stay anchored and do not float up to the top of the tank.

On average, a standard, rectangular aquarium needs about a pound and a half of substrate per gallon of water. It should be obvious that this rule doesn't work for a tank two inches wide and eighteen feet tall. You'd end up with a column of gravel that would look great as a pillar on your front porch. Use common sense when adding gravel depending on your tank's shape.

Slope the gravel by making it slightly higher in the back, so that debris will tumble down and collect toward the front glass. This makes it easier to vacuum up and keep clean. A few well placed rocks or plants will help to keep the slope from flattening out as it slowly slides forward.

Rocks, Wood, and Artificial Plants

Using rocks, wood, and artificial plants is a great way to add a natural-looking environment to your aquarium. Normal, everyday rocks that come from a quarry are generally used for freshwater setups. Rocks and hardwoods also provide hiding and spawning areas for your fish, and artificial plastic or silk plants can easily be found at most retail pet stores to add that realistic touch to your aquarium

Rocks for freshwater tanks

Rocks can help break up the total bottom space into individual territories. Establishing territories often prevents fighting among fish. Squabbles often break out during spawning or feeding times. Some individual fish may also be more aggressive than others, so it never hurts to have a few rocks in your aquarium that can provide shelter if needed.

You can purchase several varieties of rocks including granite at your local aquarium store that are safe to put into any tank. These rocks are pre-cleaned and won't crumble. You can also pick up a little slate while you're at the store. Rocks such as slate, granite, and red lava rock will not change the water conditions in your aquarium and promote a pleasing and natural layout. Another good place to find natural, worn rocks is along riverbanks and streams. Make sure you thoroughly clean any rocks you find with hot water and allow them to dry in the sun before using them.

When adding rocks to your tank, make sure that you try to distribute them throughout the substrate. While adding rock is rarely a problem, your glass can become stressed and prone to cracks if you pile a very heavy load of rocks on one side of the tank. Natural riverbeds have small rocks strewn around the bottom and small clusters of larger rocks on the sides.

Wood for a freshwater tank

Wood is a wonderful way to add a natural look to your home aquarium. Most retail fish stores sell driftwood, branches, and small hollow logs. These may be real wood that has been sealed or artificial pieces that usually look as good as the real thing. In today's market the choices seem almost endless.

Keeping wood from floating

If you have not bought a pre-sealed piece of wood from a retail store and have found some nice-looking driftwood, you may run into a floating problem. Nothing is more aggravating or unsightly than a big chunk of wood floating all over your aquarium. Plus, floating chunks of wood may cause aquarium and equipment damage, and put dents in your fish, and they will hate you for it. This can be fixed in some cases, so don't toss that beautiful piece out simply because it is bobbing to the top of the water.

If your driftwood tends to float, pre-soak it in water until it's saturated. Saturated wood usually stays down on the bottom of the tank. If wood still floats after being submerged for a 24 hours, you can try attaching it to a rock.

You can use plastic suction cups to attach driftwood to a rock in your aquarium. Simply add the cups to the wood using aquarium-safe silicone. Anchoring wood keeps it from floating or being knocked around by the fish in your tank. You can buy suction cups at most hardware and aquarium stores.

Once you have the wood attached to a rock (slate often works best for this) in the substrate to anchor the wood arrangement in place. Use gnarled branches whenever possible, because they look cool and provide nifty little mazes for your fish to swim around in.

If all else fails, remove the wood and look for another good piece that is less buoyant.

Don't lean rocks against the back glass of the aquarium, as this can cause "dead areas" on the rear surface. These tightly enclosed areas do not allow for proper water circulation in the tank and will contribute to uneven heating and water fouling.

Buying wood

Although driftwood is very beautiful and helps create interesting scenes in your aquarium, it can be very expensive if you buy the stuff from the retail store. There are always other options such as finding your own wood as previously mentioned.

We've found that woodworker's shops often carry small pieces of driftwood at much more reasonable prices. Other good places to check for driftwood are second-hand shops and yard sales. Often people have a piece that they picked up while on vacation sitting around for years just taking up space and then decide to sell it for cheap once they tire of storing it.

Safely sealing wood

Because several types of wood (*bogwood*, for example) contain tannins which produce acidic conditions, not all woods are suitable for every type of system. Bogwood (which produces a golden-colored water) lends itself best to systems that contain species that prefer soft conditions that are slightly acidic (tetras.)

If you're not sure how a particular piece or type of wood will affect your aquarium conditions, the safest thing to do is to seal it with polyurethane varnish. Use at least three coats of this sealer, allowing each coat to dry before applying the next. The varnish keeps wood from releasing any products that can affect your water conditions. You can seal an interesting piece of wood from the wild with polyurethane varnish as well.

Plastic plants

The appearance and variety of artificial aquarium plants have really improved in the last ten years. You can easily find plastic plants in all different colors and sizes to suit your aquarium size and layout. If you don't want to crowd the appearance of your tank, buy small plants for the front of the tank and larger plants for the back.

Many artificial plants are now manufactured with attachments such as caves and rocks. These types of decorations may incorporate hanging gardens, substrate caves, and interesting bundles that are bound together in large groups. Most of the time, these combo decorations do not cost much more than single plastic plants.

There are many advantages to artificial plants:

- **Easy to clean:** If you have algae problems or water that is accidentally fouled, plastic plants can be cleaned simply by running warm water over them and then gently wiping them with a moist cloth. That little sprayer attachment on your sink works wonders for this job as well.

- **Easy to care for:** Many people don't have a lot of extra time to spend trying to keep live plants in good condition, so plastic plants are a great substitution for those who are constantly on the go. Artificial plants do not require sunlight, so if you have a busy schedule you don't have to worry about the amount of light they receive. This is especially helpful if you don't have timer-based lighting that turns your lights on and off automatically at pre-set intervals.

- **Live forever:** Artificial plants do not die or affect the chemistry of your tank. Dead plants can make a mess quickly, so plastic plants are a saving grace to many. Young children often benefit from use of plastic plants in that they can devote their time to learning how to care for their fish first. All artificial plants tend to show wear in time, but most will last years.

- **Won't be eaten:** Plastic plants cannot be easily eaten or torn by more aggressive species of fish. Nothing is more heartbreaking that to have your beautifully planted tank destroyed by your beloved aquatic pets. If you have species that are natural nibblers or havoc seekers, consider artificial plants so that you don't have to purchase new live ones on a regular basis, which can quickly get expensive.

- **Easy to move:** Artificial plants can be easily moved around when it comes time to clean or redecorate your tank. Just gently remove them from the substrate by the base and don't worry about tearing the leaves or damaging the plants. Most artificial plants have a hard plastic base that aids in keeping them under the gravel.

- **Wide variety:** There are more choices of colors and sizes if you use artificial plants because not all fish stores carry live plants on a regular basis.

There are also a few disadvantages to artificial plants:

- **Can look fake:** If you buy poor quality plants, they can look fake and ruin the look of your tank. Always buy the best quality plants that your budget will allow.

> ✔ **Expensive:** Artificial decorations can cost more than the real thing.
>
> ✔ **Fish may not like them:** Many species that like to nibble on plants will not like your artificial ones.

As you can see, it's up to you to decide what is best for your particular lifestyle, budget, and aquatic species. Plan before you buy.

Other Aquarium Decorations

Okay, we have to admit that we have been tempted once or twice to take a few frog statues, oversized rocks, and other decorations out of our yard and put them in an aquarium. But this isn't really a good practice.

Unsafe decorations can cause problems

Stuff from your yard often contains all sorts of parasites and other nasty things that can cause disease in your tank and foul the water. And it may not be safe to use non-aquarium rocks, wood, plastic sunflowers for standard aquarium use because many contain harmful dyes and paints or fall apart once they sit in water. Despite the fact that the small rotting wagon wheel would make a great centerpiece in your 250-gallon cichlid tank, it's not worth the trouble.

Your best bet for safe decorations is to purchase pieces from a reputable aquarium dealer or other retail store. We can't emphasize this important point enough. Unsafe decorations can kill your fish, ruin your aquarium conditions, and cost you a lot of money and heartache.

Statuettes and toys that you find around the house may contain internal parts made of metal, which can cause destruction in a tank. Dyes and other surface materials can produce ill affects on freshwater fish and other species.

Plastic divers and other oddities

Plastic divers (Figure 5-1), dead pirates, bobbing turtles, treasure chests, mermaids, sunken ships that bubble, castles, nasty looking skeletons, and mutant oysters may be fine and dandy in the safety department, but you need to *exercise a little control* when buying these items or your aquarium may end up looking like a scene from *Toy Story*.

Figure 5-1:
A toy diver
is a true
classic, but
it won't help
your fish get
in the mood.

Manufactured decorations sold in aquarium shops are quite safe for freshwater tanks, but they tend to become a little unsightly if you cram your tank with lots of them, and will turn your naturally behaving fish into Toys "R" Us kids in a heartbeat.

There is nothing wrong with incorporating one or two of these pieces into a tank if you surround them with plants or small rocks to make them blend into the scene. Just use a little common sense and don't overdo it.

Artificial items like plastic scuba divers do not help much when you are trying to get your fish into the spawning mood, either. Be honest, would you feel romantic with a larger-than-life man with a knife standing over your favorite make-out spot? We didn't think so. If you really want to see a ton of these toys floating, diving, and bobbing up and down, set up a small aquarium just for decorations and leave the fish out of it.

Aquascaping Tips and Tricks

As you decorate more and more tanks, you will eventually learn to see what looks good and what doesn't. Practice makes perfect as they say.

Aquascaping can turn a bare tank into a real showpiece. Aquascaping will provide a feeling of safety for your aquatic friends, help to cover up bare spots and equipment, and will enrich the overall look of your aquarium. Creating a beautiful tank will also help to educate family and visitors on species and their natural environments, and provide your fish with a natural looking habitat that they will flourish in.

Here are some tips that will help you understand the basics of good aquascaping:

- **Keep it clean.** Keep your water and aquarium glass clean so that your aquascape will really shine. Nothing ruins a good scene quicker than dirty water and particles floating all over the place.

- **Don't make everything symmetrical.** If you looked at the natural environment of your fish, you would not find stones set exactly 2 inches apart, or a lake with only one type of plant grouped in bunches of three for miles.

- **Make rocks look natural.** Pile a few small stones together and then put one off to the side as if it had tumbled down from the pile over time. Use stones that are similar in the extent that they have been worn over time by water movement. For example, avoid putting one craggy looking rock in the middle of a bunch of smooth stones.

- **Pay close attention to color.** Not all rocks in nature are the same color, because they have been bleached out by water and sunlight. Add a few odd-colored stones to enhance the appearance of a grouping.

- **Plan, plan, plan.** If needed, sketch out your overall layout before you begin setting it up as mentioned previously, so that you have a good idea where everything will look.

- **Add the water first.** Don't aquascape a tank without water, because once it is added, plants will spread out and look different. Try filling the tank halfway to aid in determining how something will really look.

- **Research.** Check library books for pictures of your species' geographical environment to give you ideas on how a setup can be aquascaped to look natural.

✔ **Have a focal point.** Try to have at least one main point of interest in your aquascape such as an unusual, beautifully shaped rock or a stunning plant. Group other objects around to highlight the point of interest and guide your eye toward it naturally. Take advantage of a point of interest by using it to tell illustrate a natural area. For example, a hollowed out log can make a great point of interest for natural breeding if it is surrounded by broad-leafed plants that shelter it.

✔ **Think natural.** Try to use wood and stones from the same region for aquascaping. Don't mix apples and oranges. Keep it natural instead.

✔ **Think outside the box.** Why not use aquarium-safe silicone to add small stones to the back wall of the tank in the shape of a rock hill? (Make sure the rocks are close together to avoid dead spots in water flow.) Let your imagination run wild. Try turning your true creative talents into a reality by experimenting with different techniques.

✔ **Avoid crowding.** Don't cram your tank with so much aquascaping that food will become trapped and foul the tank. Leave enough space to vacuum the tank as needed. Keep in mind that your plants will need to grow as well. Leave enough room for them to flourish naturally.

✔ **Suit aquascaping to species.** Some species such as many cichlids can quickly tear up and destroy a beautifully aquascaped tank. Make sure the plants and rocks you choose match the personality of your fish. For example, large fish such as pacus do not seem to like large plastic objects such as divers and will pull them up. Goldfish may eat live plants. Plecos will dig up plants that are not buried deep in gravel.

The natural tank

When aquascaping, keep your fish's natural habitat in mind. A natural tank shows the beauty of your fish in a better light and allows them the freedom to act more naturally. Many native decorations such as plants, rocks, and wood have a lot to do with the successful spawning of many freshwater species.

By providing natural conditions in your aquarium, you can enjoy the environmental interactions that make aquarium keeping so fascinating. For example, a guppy weaving its way in and out of dense plant leaves is much more exciting to watch than an oscar trying to make lunch out of a plastic diver's helmet.

Providing a balanced aquatic system for your fish shows your children basic biological principals that they can apply to other scientific areas in the future. The delicate balance between plant and animal life in a freshwater tank is easily illustrated in an aquarium ecosystem.

Chapter 6

Equipment and Other Technical Stuff

*I*n the wild, a fish's environment functions without equipment for one basic reason: Mother Nature takes care of everything. You know the old saying: Don't upset Mother Nature. Well, unfortunately we have done just that by placing our wet pets in a small, enclosed aquarium environment. That's why at home we need to replace the natural systems that we have taken away by placing fish in captivity. Now that you have your aquarium tank and stand, you need some equipment to keep it running smoothly. An aquarium's equipment is the lifeblood of the whole system.

In nature, ocean, river, and pond waters are heated and regulated by the sun and seasons. In your home aquarium, you duplicate these effects by using a heater, thermometer, and artificial lighting.

In the wild, currents remove fish waste and rain replenishes the water. Natural bacteria help eliminate waste, plant debris, and other undesirable materials. At home, you accomplish these necessary tasks with filters, water changes, and other specialty equipment.

As you will see, aquarium equipment is vital to the health of your fish. It also helps keep your water crystal clear so that you can enjoy the view.

Taking the Mystery out of Filters

Filters play an essential role in performing mechanical, biological, and chemical functions in your aquarium. Some filters cover only one function; others may do two or three.

The three main functions of a filtration system are to

- Promote the nitrogen cycle (which removes unwanted ammonia and nitrites from your system) by providing a medium for bacteria growth
- Remove debris and waste from the water
- Aerate the aquarium's water by producing water flow and bubbles. By adding these bubbles, oxygen goes into your tank, and eventually CO_2 is removed at the surface through gas exchange.

When you check out the astounding number of filters at a pet shop, you'll probably want to reach for the aspirin by the time you get to the second or third shelf. But don't worry, filters really aren't as complicated as they may first seem.

There are three types of aquarium filtration, and whatever system you decide on needs to incorporate all three of them:

- Mechanical
- Biological
- Chemical

You accomplish this balance by combining different filters, or by using one that performs all three kinds of filtration.

Mechanical filtration

Mechanical filtration removes solid wastes and debris suspended in the water by passing it over materials, such as synthetic foam or nylon fiber floss, which captures small particles. Basically you are removing dirt and other bad floating materials from the tank with mechanical filtration.

In time, this same filter can perform biological filtration when the surface area of the filter medium (the foam or floss) becomes covered with beneficial bacteria. The medium is usually contained in a small cartridge that slips inside of a power filter unit, or is added in bulk form from a bag or box, as with a corner filter.

Popular mechanical filter types include

- ✔ Canisters
- ✔ Power filters
- ✔ Corner filters

Mechanical filters come in many different sizes to accommodate the many different tank sizes. When you go shopping for filters, we suggest purchasing Penguin, Ehime, or Whisper products, because in our opinion they are the cream of the crop.

A good filter cycles your tank's water volume at least eight times per hour. Mechanical filters are rated on the number of gallons of water that flow through them every hour. If you look carefully at a filter box, you can usually find a GPH (gallons per hour) rating. Manufacturers generally indicate on the label which size tank the filter is designed for.

If you have a tank larger than 10 gallons, you may want to have more than one filter running even if your filter covers all of the requirements for taking care of your water. You could for example have two power filters, or a canister filter and a power filter. There is nothing wrong with mixing two different types of filtration system, or having multiples of one type. As a general rule, we always have at least two filtration systems on each of our tanks just in case one fails.

Biological filtration

The main purpose of biological filtration is to provide a home for the bacteria that changes ammonia into nitrates and then nitrates. The function of nitrifying bacteria is to convert deadly ammonia (produced by fish waste) and food debris into less harmful *nitrites,* and then into even less harmful *nitrates* which can be removed with water changes. This amazing biological purification process is also known as *detoxification* or the *nitrogen cycle.* Chapter 14 talks a lot more about it.

The bacteria are everywhere naturally (air and water) in small amounts. By adding fish and food, the bacteria have the nutrition required to establish a larger colony. The filter medium provides the perfect "nesting" place for them to multiply.

Large filters don't necessarily mean better biological filtration. What counts is the amount of surface area on the medium. The larger the total surface area of the medium, the more bacteria your system and fish have to use in the fight for good water quality.

Filters that have alternative media, so that you can replace one part without losing it all, are better than the completely disposable type where you lose the whole bacteria colony when you throw the only source of filter medium away.

The filter box or instructions indicate which parts of the filter you need to replace and when to replace them. For example, a power filter with bio-wheels (see the section "Power filters," later in this chapter for more on bio-wheels) would be better than a power filter that only has compact floss and carbon pads that have to be replaced when the pad becomes clogged or the charcoal is no longer active. The reason for this is that the bio wheels will retain beneficial bacteria even though you are replacing the pads.

Chemical filtration

Chemical filtration takes place through mediums such as *activated zeolite* and *activated charcoal,* which absorb chemicals and dissolved minerals as water passes over them. Proper chemical filtration helps keep your aquarium water clean and sparkling.

You generally find activated charcoal in corner, undergravel, replaceable uplift tube heads — and power filters. Replace the filter medium according to the manufacturer's instructions. You should replace the medium once a month in most cases.

Sifting Through Filtration Systems

Once you understand the importance of filtration systems and what they do, you need to know what types of filters are out there and how they work. The many types of filters on the market fall into several categories as far as function and purpose are concerned. Technology is advancing rapidly, and a few new systems combine the best aspects of several different filters.

Undergravel filters

An undergravel filter is one of the best systems for almost any type of aquarium setup and has been around for a long time. We recommend starting with an undergravel filter and building up from there. You can combine a good mechanical/chemical filter combo (such as a power filter) with an undergravel unit and have a complete setup. You can use an undergravel filter with any type of system, and it's an excellent tool for creating good biological filtration.

Undergravel filters have one or more perforated plastic base plates that sit on the bottom of the aquarium with a gap between the bottom of the plate and the bottom of the tank. The base plates have holes for the insertion of plastic uplift tubes (which allow air to flow up from beneath the filter plate) containing an airstone which connects to an air pump.

Airstones come in many shapes including globe, circular, and rectangular. An airstone can be made out of many different materials including porous wood, fused glass, plastic, and refined ceramic. An air-line tube attached to a pump forces air into the stone which releases it in the form of unified bubbles for greater aeration.

An undergravel filter pulls water down through the gravel and the slots in the plates and returns it to the tank via the airlift (uplift) tubes. During this process ammonia is broken down as the water passes over a colony of beneficial bacteria living on the substrate's surface and in the space beneath the plates. Debris is trapped along the substrate bed, making it easy to vacuum away. Periodic vacuuming is a must with this type of system to keep the bed from becoming clogged. (If you don't vacuum, eventually your substrate bed looks as if a mudslide hit it.)

Undergravel filters are one of the oldest systems around; many hobbyists do not use them much anymore. We still believe they are a good building block for aquarium filtration. Many pre-packaged kits come with undergravel filters included. As long as you have it as part of the package, you might as well use it.

Undergravel filters are great for systems that do not have big rocks or decorations to block large sections of the gravel bed. Blocked plates create dead spots on the filter. A regular, store-packaged gravel substrate is best for this system — because smaller substrates will fall through, and larger ones can hide big chunks of debris (your lost golf balls, your child's hidden leftovers). Set the undergravel filter in place before adding the substrate (usually gravel).

Sponge filters

A sponge filter provides biological filtration. This type of filter is simple in design and, when attached to an air pump, draws aquarium water though a large sponge that acts as a medium for bacteria to gather on. Sponge filters are good to use in quarantine and hospital tanks because they have no chemical filtration that can ruin the effectiveness of medications you may be using.

Sponge filters are also useful in fry tanks and aquariums with small fish because they eliminate the danger of youngsters getting sucked up into standard filtration units. However, sponge filters only take care of biological filtration and are inadequate for use in large tanks. One other problem with a sponge filter is that it makes your aquarium look kind of like the junk shelf underneath your kitchen sink, because it takes up room inside of the aquarium.

One good use for sponge filters is to quickly build up a biological bacteria medium for new aquariums.

Corner filters (submersible filters)

Corner filters function primarily as mechanical filters but also provide biological and chemical filtration. This is one of the oldest filtration systems known to the aquarium hobby. Corner filters were originally designed for the small aquariums that were the staple of aquarium-keeping years and years ago. Generally, the original clear plastic filter was shaped like a small square box and contained an airstone that pushed water through a layer of charcoal and floss with the help of an air pump.

Fortunately, corner filters have really come a long way in the last decade. The newer corner filters are much quieter; many come with swiveling spouts to change flow direction and water flow adjusters to change the power of the water flow. You can also find corner filters that have a clogging indicator that will show you when the filter media needs to be maintained.

The old corner filters rested on the gravel bed inside the tank (if you could manage to keep it from floating all over creation and back by weighting it down with small pebbles or gravel). There are corner filters today that can hang vertically and horizontally on the glass walls. The downside is that they still take up room in the tank and can only be hidden using strategic placement of plants and other aquarium decorations.

Power filters

Power filters are cool because you can use them for mechanical, chemical, *and* biological filtration. A power filter runs on electricity (with an internal motor so a pump isn't needed) and usually hangs on the outside of the aquarium. Power filters are box-shaped and come in a variety of sizes to meet the needs of different-sized tanks (see Figure 6-1). These units usually have one or two slots on the inside of the unit that hold removable fiber-coated filter pads. The inside of these pads usually contain charcoal.

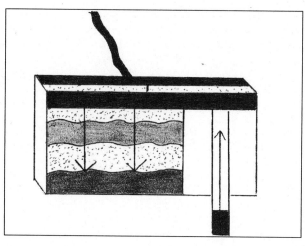

Figure 6-1:
A power filter draws water in, passes it through charcoal, and returns it to the tank.

A power filter hangs on the back of an aquarium and sucks up tank water through an intake tube, which hangs inside the aquarium. The water passes over the filter pads and filter media (which house biological colonies that provide biological filtration) and then returns to the water surface. The charcoal in the pads work as chemical filters, and the fibers pick up debris before it clogs the media.

Clean the pads on these filters by rinsing them with dechlorinated water and replace them every month so that you have fresh charcoal. Unfortunately, replacing the pads destroys the biological colony, but there is enough remaining in the aquarium and other parts of the filter to repopulate quickly.

Some power filters contain *bio-wheels,* which rotate so that they come into contact with both the water and beneficial oxygen in the air, and never really need to be replaced unless they break. This wheel keeps the bacteria colony alive even if you change the internal pad. Bio-wheels combos are the best type of power filters to buy.

You can use power filters in any type of system.

Powerheads

A *powerhead* is a cool piece of equipment that isn't really classified as a filter, but it can help increase an undergravel filter's output and efficiency by drawing water up through the tubes at a faster rate than most air pumps with attached airstones can. A powerhead is nothing more than an electric motor-driven pump sealed in hard plastic which you can insert into the top of the uplift tubes of an undergravel filter system. You can also hang them on the tank (or buy a fully submersible model) to provide good circulation in your aquarium. Some models come with internal filter pads as well.

The really neat thing about powerheads is that they have adjustable valves to regulate the speed of the airflow (thus increasing or decreasing the speed and force of the water flow). This little valve is convenient (not to mention fun to play with) in smaller tanks when you want to cut down the flow to keep the tank's inhabitants from being blown all over the aquarium or permanently embedded in the glass walls. Powerheads also have a rotating outflow that you can turn to direct the water flow to a specific area in your aquarium. (Or turn the outflow straight up and have your whole family shower at the same time.)

Canister filters

A canister filter provides biological, chemical, and mechanical filtration. This type of unit is very popular with hobbyists and is often used in larger aquarium systems because they do such a wonderful job of keeping water in good condition. A canister filter contains several media compartments (baskets) that usually contain sponges/foam blocks, carbon (charcoal), and some type of ceramic medium. The aquarium water is drawn through the filter via hoses attached to a high-pressure pump.

Canister filters are capable of turning over several hundred gallons of aquarium water per hour and have an internal motor to accomplish this task. Most canister filters sit on the floor beneath the aquarium, but some models attach to the back of the aquarium glass ("hang on tank," also know as H.O.T.). You can adjust the filter's output to any part of the tank that meets your personal desires. A canister filter can be very large, bulky, and unsightly, so make sure you have a place to hide it in the aquarium cabinet or behind the stand so that your house doesn't look like a water-processing plant.

Fluidized bed filters

A *fluidized bed filter* is one of the best biological filters on the market. The only drawback is that they can be very expensive and require a pre-filter to remove particles. But if you happen to make a few extra bucks selling some fry, it's well worth the investment to purchase one of these units.

Fluidized bed filters are extremely compact and use sand as a filter medium. The sand is continuously kept wet by water flowing through it and has a huge surface area where a large colony of nitrogen cycle beneficial bacteria can grow and multiply, as mentioned earlier in this chapter. This type of filter improves oxygenation because the sand is constantly tumbled in a stream of water that creates what is known as a *fluidized bed*. Sand grains move with the water flow to create a high-quality transfer between the water and the bacteria present.

Another important feature of fluidized bed filters is that they respond quickly to any rise in the aquarium water's ammonia levels.

A fluidized bed filter really only covers biological filtration, so if you use one you must *also* have mechanical and chemical filters working in conjunction with it in order to balance your overall cleaning system.

Fluidized bed filters are great for planted tanks because they do not remove as much CO_2 (carbon dioxide) from tanks as many other filters do.

Diatom filters

This type of filter uses *diatomaceous earth* to filter aquarium water to a very clean and "polished" state. It can capture even the smallest of dirt particles. Due to the super clean water this equipment produces, it will help to lower diseases such as fin rot, velvet, ich, and other problems caused by microorganisms. This type of filter can be hung on the tank or placed on the floor.

The only drawback to diatom filters is that they are expensive compared to many other filters made for the same size aquarium. But if you can afford them, they are well worth the money.

Wet/dry filters

As the name suggests, wet/dry filters use a mixture of water and air to clean the water. In the first step, waste is removed from the water after it is passed through an initial filter. On the second step, a filtering chamber aerates the water and passes it through another filter.

Pond filters

Most pond filters are just glorified canister filters in box form. Some pond filters are even disguised as flowerpots. Some models go directly in the pond, whereas others rest on dry land. These filters turn over massive amounts of water, which is essential for a healthy, well-planned pond system. The only problem with a pond filter is that you have to have a pond to put it in. (Putting a good pond in your backyard will probably be on the same wish list as the swimming pool you always wanted.) You can, however, buy a small pond kit that fits into a barrel, which can be placed in your home or on a porch.

A wet/dry filter requires more maintenance, because the media must be replaced to avoid build up of wastes, and it has a higher rate of evaporation. This filter is mainly for biological and mechanical filtration, so you will need an additional type or combination filter to take care of the chemical filtration in your aquarium.

Natural filtration with plants

Long before artificial filters appeared on the market, as mentioned at the beginning of this chapter, nature had its own special way of taking care of everyday cleaning. That way is called *plants*. Plants act as natural filters and complement the manufactured units in your home aquarium.

Freshwater plants help biological and chemical filtration in the home aquarium. These aquatic marvels remove ammonia, nitrates, and carbon dioxide from the water with relative ease. In aquatic systems, plants take in inorganic molecules and carbon dioxide from the aquarium water and return oxygen and organic molecules for your fish's benefit as long as the plants have enough light to carry out the process of photosynthesis during daylight hours.

Gauging Heaters and Thermometers

If you plan to set up any type of tropical freshwater system, you need to have at least one heater.

The three main types of heaters you can purchase at a fish shop are

- ✔ Submersible heaters
- ✔ Non-submersible heaters
- ✔ Undergravel heating cable

Reducing the noise

All aquarium equipment will make a bit of noise now and then. Thankfully, today's aquarium equipment is much quieter than the stuff from the early days of the fishkeeping hobby.

If your filter equipment is making too much noise, you may need to replace it or have the motor (if it has one) fixed by a professional at an aquarium store. Save the directions that come with the filter, because many models have parts that you yourself can easily replace by following the manufacturer's instructions.

Submersible heaters

As their name suggests, you completely submerse these in the aquarium water. Ideally, you should place them in a diagonal line across the rear piece of glass, so that heat flows evenly throughout the tank.

A submersible heater has a watertight glass tube containing an electrical element wound around a ceramic core. A small red or orange light lets you know whether the heater is on or off. At the top of the heater is a temperature adjustment valve you use to raise or lower the heat. Submersible heaters usually have an internal thermometer that you can see through the glass tube. You simply rotate the adjustment valve so that the temperature line moves to the temperature you want to set for your species Other models have temperature lines (similar to markings on a measuring cup but in degrees) built in with the control knob. The heater automatically maintains the temperature you choose.

Make absolutely sure that the heater is a submersible model before you put it completely underwater!

Non-submersible heaters

Non-submersible heaters hang on the outside aquarium frame, with the glass tube hanging in the water. The adjustment valve sits above the water line. This type of heater generally does not have an internal thermometer. You make adjustments in small increments by turning the valve and repeatedly checking the temperature. This is the older style of heater.

How to heat your aquarium

The safest arrangement is to keep two heaters operating at the same time just in case one unit happens to fail. If one does fail, disaster can be adverted by the second heater, which can keep the water temperature from dropping while you replace the failed unit.

The rule for determining which size heater your aquarium needs is to allow 5 watts of heater per gallon. For example, a 50-gallon aquarium needs at least a 250-watt heater.

Never remove a heater from the aquarium without letting the whole system sit for at least 20 minutes *after* unplugging the heater! Likewise, never turn a heater on for the first time in an aquarium until *after* you let it sit in the water for at least 20 minutes!

If your heater does not have a built-in thermometer, you can purchase one separately. Extreme fluctuations in water temperature can cause disease or death, so it is important to closely monitor the thermometer readings. You can find a ton of good information on what temperature is correct for many species in Chapter 8. Thermometers are very inexpensive and come in several varieties:

- ✔ **Hanging thermometers** hang from the aquarium on the inside of the aquarium glass. This style of thermometer is composed of a capillary tube containing mercury that moves up and to display the temperature.

- ✔ **Stick-on thermometers** are flat and adhere to the outside of the aquarium glass. Degree panels light up as the temperature changes, displaying the current water temperature. The two disadvantages of stick-on thermometers are that they're permanent (can't be moved from place to place) and they can be hard to read in rooms with low lighting.

- ✔ **Floating thermometers** slowly cruise around the aquarium and display the current temperature with a mercury line like home thermometers that hang on the wall. (Unless you are used to watching tennis, you may get whiplash trying to read one of these.)

- ✔ **Digital thermometers** run on batteries and measure the water temperature with a probe that can be attached inside the tank with a suction cup. Many models also display the room temperature.

- ✔ **Wireless thermometers** use a radio wave signal to send the water temperature from a remote sensor to a unit with a digital readout. Some models allow you to have several sensors sending information to one display unit.

Making Bubbles with Airstones and Pumps

One of the big advantages of having an aquarium is that it makes a bunch of cool sounds. Air bubbles produce a great tone and can be very soothing. After you get your filter system all figured out, it's time to have a little fun and create a few cheerful bubbles.

You can do this in a couple of cool ways:

- ✔ **Air pumps** (used to run some filters and decorations) usually have some kind of bubble or current outflow that is fun to watch.

- ✔ **Airstones** can create mega-bubbles, which will impress your friends and neighbors.

Air pumps

An *air pump* is kind of a jack-of-all-trades. They can power filters, airstones, and several types of plastic decorations. Air pumps are available in both vibrator and piston models. When added to an undergravel filter, a pump drives air though the airstone in the uplift tubes via tubing. The air is then broken up into small bubbles as it passes through an airstone and up the tube. See Figure 6-2 for a typical air pump.

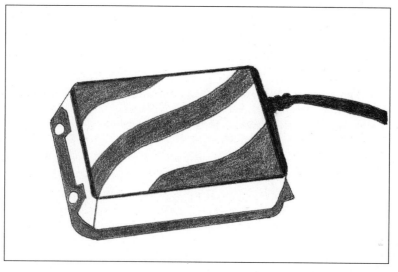

Figure 6-2:
An air pump adds bubbles to the water, helping gas exchange at the surface.

An air pump should always sit above the midpoint level of the aquarium to avoid water backflow (which can ruin your pump) if electrical power is lost. For example, if your aquarium is 12 inches tall, the pump should sit higher than 6 inches measured from the bottom of the tank.

However the easy solution to this problem is to buy a checkvalve. The *check-valve* is a small plastic cylindrical object that allows water or air to flow in only one direction, so that any backflow of water will not damage your pump. The check valve is added to the air-line tubing.

Air pumps come in a variety of different sizes to suit almost any filter. (All filters are driven either by an air pump or an electric motor.)

There are two main types of air pump:

- ✔ **Vibrator pumps** are great for the home aquarium because they are not as expensive as piston pumps, and don't require a whole lot of mechanical maintenance. Vibrator pumps do have one big drawback: They can be very noisy, especially if you purchase a poor-quality model.

- ✔ **Piston pumps** are much more powerful than vibrator pumps and are often used on very large or multiple systems. The disadvantage to piston pumps is that they are hard to find, need to be oiled, and require traps to keep oil from getting into the aquarium system.

Airstones and circulation

An *airstone* is a neat little tube-shaped artificial stone used to split the air supplied by the pump into small bubbles. These bubbles help increase water oxygenation. Airstones are generally made of ceramic or perforated wood-based materials. Airstones can be short and round or tall and thin. The tall stones tend to emit a finer stream of bubbles than the shorter ones do. Airstones are very inexpensive, and should be replaced when they become clogged.

You attach airstones to one side of standard air-line tubing, and attach the other end of the tubing to the air pump. You can use airstones in undergravel filter tubes, and corner filters or just put them in the tank.

To create a big bubble stream in your aquarium, you can purchase a *bubble disk*. A bubble disk is a large airstone that looks like a plastic flying disc. You simply connect the disk to an air pump with tubing and then slip it into the tank. The disk makes a large stream of bubbles, which can aid in water circulation. Bubble disks may become clogged with algae (usually this takes quite some time), but you can clean them by rinsing them gently under clear water. Fish love swimming in and out of the bubbles.

Try to stay away from *bubble wands*. These delicate little stones are shaped like rods and usually have suction cups attached to the back of them so that they can be mounted on glass. The problem with bubble wands is that they can become clogged and stop functioning quite quickly. Bubble wands break easily, so you may end up trashing half the decorations in your tank trying to remove one for cleaning.

Connecting Tubing, Valves, and Tees

Air-line tubing functions like the veins and arteries in the human body. Without your veins and arteries, your internal organs would just kind of lie there, lifeless, because they have nothing connecting them — nothing keeping the lifeblood flowing. So it is with air-line tubing and your aquarium equipment; therefore, a supply of good air-line tubing is an absolute must.

We need to mention some of the other important elements of your aquarium system. At first, you may think that some of this equipment is unnecessary, but everything has its place. Even if you don't use everything, some of these extra gadgets are nice to have lying around just in case of an emergency. Besides, the more fish junk you have, the better you look in the eyes of other hobbyists.

Air-line tubing

Air-line tubing connects equipment such as corner filters, airstones, decorations such as divers and moving ships, and bubble disks to an air pump. Tubing is really a necessity — not an option. Even if you have nothing in your aquarium that runs off of tubing connected to air pumps, it is always a good thing to have on hand.

Older tubing (the standard clear stuff you purchase at your local pet store) is semi-rigid. Standard tubing has a few drawbacks: It tends to crack as it ages, turns yellow, and bends out of shape (even when it is still new, right out of the package) when you set it over equipment connections. Because it is rigid, older tubing also tends to pinch and kink easily, which can diminish or completely cut off the airflow to your equipment. Working with old air-line tubing can be as frustrating as untangling a cheap garden hose.

Fortunately, a new rubber type of tubing manufactured from a silicone/rubber-based material provides greater flexibility and is much easier to work with. Rubber tubing is blue-green in color and blends in nicely with the natural tint of the aquarium water. Rubber tubing is easy to bend, simple to maneuver around decorations, and does not crack easily when it begins to age.

You can purchase tubing in different lengths. The diameter of most tubing is standard; however, you can purchase mini tubing with connectors (that will connect mini tubing to standard tubing) because a few aquarium decorations have very small connections in the back that are too small for standard tubing.

You can also buy air-line suction cups which attach to the inside of the aquarium glass. You simply push your air-line tubing into the plastic clip on the suction cup and it will keep your tubing in place so it doesn't float in the tank.

Gang valves and tees

Valves and tees help you split the air from an air pump in several directions. You use *gang valves* to run several pieces of equipment or decorations off of one air pump. A valve usually hangs on the back of the tank, and is made out of plastic or brass. The air-line tubing from the pump hooks into one side, and the tubing directed toward decorations and equipment is connected to one of the multiple outlets on the valve. You can adjust the strength of the airflow coming out of the valve for each piece of equipment simply by turning the individual shut-off nozzles.

Tees are usually made of plastic or copper, and are shaped like the letter T. A tee splits a single air source in two opposite directions.

Creating the Best Lighting

Unless you can see in the dark like the movie version of Catwoman, you need a little bit of lighting for your aquarium. Your fish probably were not born in a black hole either, and will be much happier if you provide them with a little daylight. Without light, your fish can't see their food or each other and may miss the mark by a fraction of an inch when they spawn.

Live plants in an aquarium require light in order to photosynthesize, manufacture their own food, and expel oxygen beneficial to your fish.

Some *hoods* (a top that fits over the upper edge of the tank) have a built-in light (full hoods); others don't. If you purchase a unit that has a light built in to it, you can change the bulb when it burns out or put in a bulb that better suits your needs. Check the manufacturers' instructions so that you don't end up with a meltdown due to excessive heat build-up. Also make sure that the hood fits the tank correctly to prevent water loss from evaporation and the escape of any high-jumping fish.

If your light is not connected to the hood, such as a *strip light,* and sits on top of a glass cover (called a *canopy*), you can experiment a little bit by moving the light around to see which position illuminates the tank best. The main advantage of strip lights is that they provide you with the freedom to add more lighting later on; full hoods do not.

Make sure the lighting system is unplugged when you put it on top of your tank. Do not plug the unit in until you're sure it's stable! You (and your fish) can be electrocuted if lighting falls into your tank.

Looking at bulb types

You have several bulb options to consider:

- ✔ **Tungsten (incandescent)** lighting is used in household lamps. Tungsten lighting is not good for aquariums because it is too hot, burns out quickly, produces excess algae, has a limited spectrum, doesn't show your fish's colors very well, and distributes light unevenly. You may see colored tungsten lights in your pet store, but avoid them. You will often find these in all sorts of 1960s disco colors including red, blue, and green.

- ✔ **Actinic blue** bulbs produce long-wave ultraviolet radiation. This type of lighting is great for plant growth but also produces an abundance of algae if you have it on a lot. It is used often in marine tanks.

- ✔ **Metal halide** lights produce a very pleasing effect in your aquarium because they have a high red and yellow spectrum and are very bright. Unfortunately, they are very expensive. These are great for heavily planted freshwater tanks because they are made to produce properties similar to natural sunlight.

- ✔ **High-powered mercury vapor lights** can hang over aquariums and are often used to light very deep tanks. Mercury vapor lights are a little short in the green and blue wavelength department and may need supplemental lighting to complete a full spectrum. The cool thing about mercury vapor lights is that they usually retain 90 percent of their original capacity over a period of several years.

- ✔ **Fluorescent lighting** is great for aquariums with live plants. They last a long time, do not emit excessive heat, and have an even spectrum of light. There's a fluorescent light to match almost any system you plan to set up. Even though they continue to burn, fluorescent lights often begin to dim and lose a portion of their power after about six or seven months. This type of bulb brings out the natural colors of your fish and plants.

Whichever lighting you choose, make sure to purchase it from a pet store. Even though a hardware store can sell you a replacement bulb that fits your hood, these bulbs were not intended for that purpose and will not provide good lighting.

Lighting extras

A *power center* enables you to regulate the lighting schedule on your aquarium. You can set the time you want your lights to come on and off and forget about having to remember to do that as you are rushing off to work.

End caps fit over the prong end of your fluorescent aquarium light tube like a sock. They are made of rubber and will protect your lights from getting rusty or damp in the connection area.

Ballast kits allow you to plug lights into sockets that you can clamp onto your reflector using lamp clips.

Sleeves are colored materials that slip over your aquarium bulbs to give a different color effect (such as orange, green, purple, red, or blue) to your water.

Making a hood choice

The best hood/lighting system for you depends a lot on your personal taste. Some hobbyists swear by one certain type of lighting and hood combo, and others swear by another. Here are a few types of lighting systems you can choose from:

Eclipse

The Eclipse hood made by Marineland (www.marineland.com) is probably the coolest setup ever invented. (In fact, everything this company makes rocks.) This system is a hood that contains lighting *and* filtration. Using the Eclipse leaves lots of space on the back of the aquarium, so you can move it closer to the wall as well. You can also put the tank in the middle of the room and give a good 360-degree view as well.

The downside is that you have to remove the hood to gain access to the tank, and don't forget to keep dreaming if you want one to fit a very large aquarium.

Standard full hoods

This is a regular hood that covers the top of your aquarium and has one or more lights in it. There are usually a few small slots you can remove from the back of the hood to allow you to hang things on the tank.

Strip lights

Strip lights can be used to add extra lighting to a tank or to replace hoods. You can buy them to fit across the top of your tank. This is basically the light fixture unit without the rest of the hood.

Fan-cooled hoods

Fan-cooled hoods have built in fans to make sure that you have optimal temperature in your tank while providing proper lighting. The fans help to increase the longevity of the lights as well.

Hanging lighting

You can purchase lights that hang above the tank, which provides one of the best lighting schemes available. These lights are usually halide, and are suspended by wires that are usually included with the lights.

Reflective lighting

You can experiment with hanging lights to achieve *reflected* lighting (lighting that is bounced off another surface such as a wall or ceiling).

The sky is the limit, so have fun creating new lighting schemes. Make sure that whatever you do is safe, secure, and provides your fish and plants with the light they really need.

Hot rodding your aquarium

Hey, we're fish nerds, and naturally we have a few toys. Car nerds get expensive hubcaps and awesome paint jobs, so we get our own little wish lists, too. In fact we wish we had *more* of the equipment on the following list.

Ultraviolet (UV) sterilizers kill parasites and bacteria in your aquarium water. These units contain an ultraviolet lamp, which you need to change two or three times per year. The UV unit sterilizes non-beneficial bacteria and parasites (that are harmful to your fish) so that they cannot reproduce.

They can be expensive, like more than $100. Beware: Looking at an UV light can damage your eyes! Be careful when installing this unit!

Pump timers allow you to hook up several aquarium pumps to the device so that you can control the output of each to create the type of low wave patterns you want.

Carbon block CO2 units/fermentation units release CO2 into your live plant aquarium without using chambers or any type of bottle gas. You can set the unit to release the amount you want. You can also purchase units that use sealed fermentation canisters to create CO2. These units have a buffer that protects them from extreme temperature changes that can effect the production rate.

Short on cash?

Okay, if you're like us and never have any money, you can still set up a halfway decent aquarium system. Probably the least expensive way to get a small system going is to go to a superstore and buy a freshwater aquarium kit. Make sure to check the contents on the box to insure that you have a heater, thermometer, air-line tubing, a filter, light, hood, and pump. Grab a few bags of gravel, a bottle of dechlorinator, fish food, a net, and a few plants on the way out the door, and you're ready to go.

Part II
Fish and How to Care for Them

The 5th Wave   By Rich Tennant

"Honey! I think the angelfish have
outgrown the neon tetras!"

In this part . . .

These five chapters cover the basics of caring for your water-dwelling friends, focusing on what fish need to survive and thrive. Here you learn what makes fish tick, the different parts of a fish, how to choose among different species, what to look for when buying fish, and how to feed and treat them when things go wrong.

Chapter 7

Fish Anatomy

Fish are truly amazing creatures. They have been roaming the earth's waters for almost 450 million years and have adapted themselves over time in order to thrive in their watery environment. A species' body shape, fin length, and other physical characteristics have been specially formed through evolution to meet the needs of different types of habitats. As you find out more about a fish's physical makeup, you increase the odds of becoming a successful fishkeeper with that species.

By becoming familiar with the physical characteristics of aquatic species, you will be able to purchase fish that are healthy, spot problems easier, and recognize disease quicker. Figure 7-1 shows the main parts of a fish.

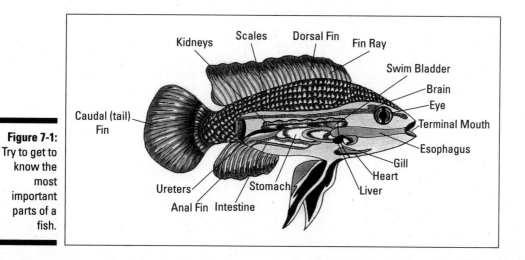

Figure 7-1: Try to get to know the most important parts of a fish.

What Really Makes a Fish Go?

At one time or another, everyone has stood transfixed, watching aquarium fish glide effortlessly through the water and wondering how they navigate through their liquid environment with such ease. What makes a fish swim better than we do? The answer is really quite simple.

Fish have a set of fins (six or seven of them, depending on the species) that they use for locomotion. They also have a cool organ called a *swim bladder* that helps them stay afloat (otherwise they would sink; see the section "The swim bladder" near the end of this chapter for more). Fish have evolved to conquer their watery environment with adaptations that have created the perfect aquatic swimming machine. By contrast, even using rubber fins, humans can achieve only a pale imitation of their aquatic friends.

To understand what makes a fish go, you must first understand each fin's function. Each individual fin has a specific job to do, and the combined effort of all of a fish's fins is what propels her through the water and helps her navigate smoothly. Fin functions are an interaction of muscle power and sheer grace.

The dorsal fin

The dorsal fin is located along the back of the fish between the tail fin and the head. This is the classic fin you see slicing through the water in the movie *Jaws*. If you happen to see a *Jaws*-type fin while swimming in the ocean, you may want to take up beach volleyball for a while. Fortunately for your peace of mind, the dorsal fins on your aquarium fish generally remain underwater.

The dorsal fin provides lateral stability so that your fish can swim in a straight line. Controlled swimming conserves energy. A fish that cannot swim well doesn't live very long because it can't compete for food with its tank-mates. Each fin consists of a series of individual rays (fin segments, some soft and some hard) loosely bound together by a membrane web.

A few aquatic pets, such as some goldfish and knifefish, do not have dorsal fins. They have great difficulty swimming normally because they cannot keep their movement in a straight line. Other species such as rainbowfish have two dorsal fins.

The caudal fin

The caudal fin (tail fin) is responsible for sudden forward movement (bursts of speed) and very fast swimming patterns. Fish also use their caudal fin to slow forward movement and to help make turns. This fin produces the majority of a fish's physical power.

Lengthening the caudal fin of many species (such as the goldfish and betta) for show purposes through artificial selection (breeding for a specific trait) produces a slower-moving fish. Fish with very long caudal fins probably would not survive long in the wild. A 3-inch goldfish with a 6-inch caudal fin dragging the gravel like the train on a wedding dress is bound to have a few swimming problems.

Sadly, many species of fish have been selectively bred to have caudal fins that are so long or unusually shaped, the fish struggle just to stay upright in the water. Fish that have truncated (Chinese fan-shaped) fins can dash quickly even though they normally swim slow and easily. Fast-swimming fish generally have forked fins; rounded fins are found in slower-moving species.

The anal fin

The anal fin is located on the underside of a fish between the pelvic and caudal fins. The sole purpose of this fin is to provide stability — it keeps your fish from rolling over in the water and going belly up. In some species, the anal fin has developed into a double set of fins that are fused together at the base of the fish's body.

In species such as the freshwater guppy, the male's anal fin acts as a sexual organ and is known as a *gonopodium*. This rod-shaped organ inserts sperm into the female's *vent* (female organ) during spawning. Many species of Characins, such as tetras, have small hooks on their anal fins that attach them to their mate during breeding.

The pectoral fins

Pectoral fins provide stability as a fish moves through the water, hovers, and makes slow turns. These paired fins are located near the bottom of the fish, directly beneath the gill openings (one on each side). Pectoral fins are used for navigation and are constantly in motion.

Many species use the pectoral fins to incubate their eggs with water during the brooding period. Many flying fish have adapted their pectoral fins into wings so that they can take short flights through the air. Some species of catfish can "lock" their pectoral fins into a rigid stance when defending themselves from predators.

The pelvic fins

Pelvic fins aid fish in braking, stabilizing their bodies, and changing directions. These fins are located in front of the anal fin on the abdomen of the fish (one on each side). Other uses of the pelvic fins include searching for food, carrying eggs, and fighting. These fins are usually smaller in open water species like the freshwater platy, and larger in some bottom-dwellers.

These fins are often called ventral fins because of their position on the body near the small body-cavity opening on the bottom of the fish.

The adipose fin

A few species of fish such as tetras and some catfish have an extra fin called the adipose fin, located on the back between the dorsal and tailfins. Hobbyists often refer to it as the second dorsal fin. Scientists have not found any physical reason for this fin to exist. At this point, it has no known use. But it looks cool, so why not?

Swimming movement

The special body shape of fish helps increase the overall efficiency of their swimming movement. A fish's body is usually tapered at the head and tail and bulky in the middle (like many of us when we hit midlife). This tapering allows fish to slip through the water without much effort. So, maybe if we can find a way to live in our bathtub, we'll have it made.

Looking carefully at your fish, you may notice that most of them swim with little or no effort, which is surprising because water is much more resistant than air. But water's liquid form supports a body's weight as the body moves. Because your fish's weight is suspended in water, she needs only a small amount of energy to overcome the force of gravity — as opposed to the effort we humans must put out as we move through atmospheric air on dry land.

A fish's muscle force is achieved though energy created by short fibers that run throughout the fish's entire body. These numerous fibers move in sequence and create physical energy in a series of s-shaped curves. This energy is then transferred to the tail to provide locomotion. Finally, the caudal (tail) fin pushes all the water surrounding it backwards, which in turn propels the fish's body in a quick forward motion. This sequence of events allows the fish to move through the water without creating any turbulence — which would slow it down.

Respiration

Just like humans, fish require oxygen for survival. Fish use oxygen that they strip from the water and produce carbon dioxide as a waste product. Any living plants in your aquarium use this carbon dioxide, and eventually expel oxygen back into the water.

The gill method

Unlike land animals, fish don't get their oxygen from air. Instead, fish take their oxygen directly from the water through their gills. Gills are lined with a large number of blood vessels that help retrieve oxygen.

Gills are very similar in structure and form to human lungs, except that they are a whole lot more efficient: Although fish remove up to 85 percent of the oxygen from their aquarium water, humans obtain only about 25 percent of the oxygen in the air they breathe by comparison, so water quality is important! (Of course, if you live in a crowded city, your oxygen consumption may drop to about 2 percent.)

Water enters a fish's mouth and passes across the gills where the oxygen is extracted by the gill filaments. The oxygen-depleted water is then quickly discarded.

Fish with high energy levels who are very active, like the freshwater danio, must constantly keep swimming in order to force water through their gills and obtain oxygen. Species of fish with high energy levels would eventually suffer asphyxiation if kept in a small aquarium that restricted their swimming movement. You don't want to live in a sealed elevator with 20 other people. Neither do your fish.

Make sure that your tank is large enough to provide ample swimming room for your aquatic friends.

When moving fish from one location to another, you must remember that gills are made out of fine tissue that can collapse if removed from water. The gills are structurally supported by the weight of the water itself. So it is very important that you keep your fish in water while moving them, to avoid causing any damage to their gills, bodies, and fins which can be crushed by lack of water support.

The labyrinth organ method

A certain group of fishes (known as the Anabantids), found in Asia and Africa, are able to breathe air directly from the atmosphere, using a specialized organ called the *labyrinth*. The labyrinth, located inside the head behind the gills, has evolved over time to take oxygen directly from the air as a supplement to extracting it from the water.

Anabantids include bettas, gouramis, and paradise fish. In the wild, many of these fish live in dirty, poorly oxygenated waters full of strange-looking creatures. (Not unlike a good day at our public pool.) These fish tend to have wide bodies and enlarged fins.

The physical shape of the labyrinth organ gives rise to its name, which literally means "maze." The labyrinth contains rosette-shaped plates that have thousands of oxygen-absorbing blood vessels, which gather air that is inhaled. The inhaled air is then trapped inside a group of folds (which resembles a sponge) and is eventually absorbed into the main bloodstream.

Anabantids can survive in a smaller aquarium space than that which is normally provided (usually 10 or more gallons) because they can extract oxygen from the air. However, this does not mean that anabantids can or should be kept in very crowded conditions or extremely tiny tanks. Even though they have the ability to breathe "extra" air, these fishes still add as much waste to the water as their tankmates and need proper space and filtration for healthy living.

You will often see betta fish for sale in small jars. The reason many dealers do this is to keep the males separated so that they don't fight. This is not a good practice for the home aquartist to pick up and use. Don't keep labyrinth fish in small bowls or hanging vases for decoration purposes. Give them a good healthy aquarium environment with plenty of room instead.

Anabantids can develop diseases brought on by crowded tanks with bad water conditions, just like other species. Take our word for it, they'll be healthier and happier in a proper aquarium. (Anabantids should be provided with the same high quality filtration, heating, and other proper conditions as is standard with other tropical fish.) They will like you a lot better too.

The Senses

Like humans, fishes have five senses: taste, sight, hearing, touch, and smell. Fish use all these senses to locate food, communicate with one another, attract mates, and avoid bigger and meaner fish. Fish have been known to learn to do without one or more of their senses when they're injured or born with a physical defect. We've seen fish in the worst possible physical condition continue to survive. Think how great they can look and feel if we keep them in the best possible condition!

Sight

Here are some fun facts about fish eyes:

- Most fish have the ability to see in two directions at the same time. This physical phenomenon is known as *monocular vision.*

- Fish can't completely focus both their eyes on a single object at the same time.

- Fish do not have eyelids and sleep with their eyes wide open, resting in a hypnotic state.

- Most fish are nearsighted and see clearly only about a foot away. So, if you stand across the room, smiling and wildly waving both your hands to entertain your fish, don't hold your breath waiting for them to respond.

The lateral line system

Fish have an interesting system known as the *lateral line*, which helps them locate objects in their path and in their surrounding environment that they cannot see normally due to their limited eyesight (see Figure 7-2). This line is incomplete in some species. The blindcave fish use this system to navigate, and killfish use it to help locate insects above the surface of the water.

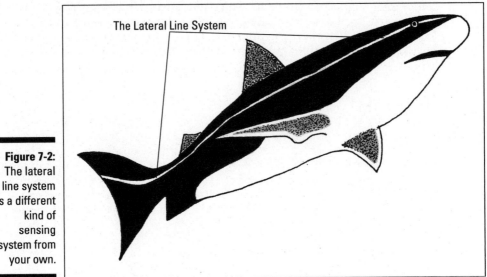

The Lateral Line System

Figure 7-2:
The lateral
line system
is a different
kind of
sensing
system from
your own.

The lateral line is located on both sides of their body and runs from the back of the eye to the base of the tail fin. These lines are composed of small *neuromasts* (receptors) which contain *cilia* (very fine hairs) in fluid-filled canals. These canals detect vibrations in the water, and the vibrations form an "image" inside the fish's brain.

The eyes

A fish's eyes are often large to compensate for the poor lighting conditions that exist under water. Usually the eyes are located on the sides of the head, and some species can rotate them 360 degrees. In certain species that live in areas of total or semi-darkness (such as the blindcave fish), the eyes are absent altogether. Over time, the eyes have been selectively removed through the evolutionary process.

Some fish do have the ability to see a few colors at various depths, but they have great difficulty adjusting to rapid light changes because their iris works slowly. For this reason, fish act "shocked" and may panic when an aquarium light is suddenly turned on or off without warning in a room that is still dark. So if you turn on your aquarium light right after you get up in the morning and then notice that your fish are stuck to the ceiling, you probably frightened them a little bit.

Within the human eye, the shape of the lens is constantly changing in an effort to achieve proper focus. The lens in a fish's eye remains the same shape, but focuses with help from special ocular ligaments that actually move the eye forward and backward in its socket.

Hearing

Fish do not have complex ears like we do because sound travels in water much faster than in air, so by evolution standards this was not needed. Fish ears are composed of a simple inner chamber. Vibrations picked up from the environment are passed over sensory components, which generate sound. Most *ichthyologists* (fish experts) believe that a fish's swim bladder works together with the components of the inner ear to distinguish specific sound patterns.

Smell

Smell plays an important role in detecting food and prey, and in locating a suitable mate. Fish take in smells through their nostrils, which are connected to their olfactory system. This olfactory system is not completely joined with the respiratory system and acts as a separate unit.

Taste

Fish have taste buds on their mouths, lips, and, in special cases, on their fins. The complete range of taste for fish is very short, so they must constantly forage through their environment in hopes that they can "stumble across" the food they need to survive. Catfish have evolved barbels (whiskerlike appendages) that contain taste buds for locating food in cloudy or dark water.

Feeling

The old argument as to whether fish can feel pain or not has been at issue for many years. We would really hate to find out that our fish could feel pain if we did something that caused them harm. The safest bet is to assume always that your fish can feel pain and treat them with respect and great care just like you would any other pet.

Osmosis and the salt to water ratio

Osmosis is a simple process by which a fish maintains the correct salt to water ratio in its body (see Figure 7-3). Through osmosis, water molecules constantly pass through semipermeable membranes in the fish to equalize the amount of salt to water throughout her body. Osmosis is one of the main reasons freshwater fish cannot live in saltwater and vice versa. (As with every other rule, there are a few exceptions to this one.)

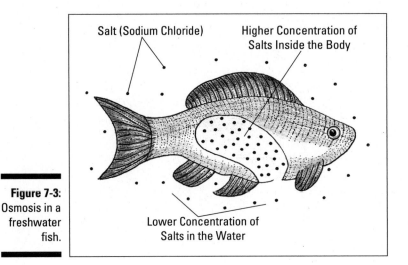

Salt (Sodium Chloride)

Higher Concentration of Salts Inside the Body

Lower Concentration of Salts in the Water

Figure 7-3:
Osmosis in a freshwater fish.

Fish that don't drink water

The salt concentration in the body fluids of freshwater fish is higher than the salt content of the water in which they live. For this reason, water is always being drawn into their cells by osmosis. If fish did not have a means of getting rid of this excess water baggage, they would burst like a balloon that has been filled to a point where it has exceeded its air capacity, or resemble the human body after Thanksgiving dinner.

Water is removed by the kidneys in the form of very dilute urine in freshwater species. Specialized salt absorbing cells located in the gills move salt from the water into the blood. Very small amounts of salt that are present in commercial fish foods also help aquatic species remain in balance. The amount of salt passed into a fish's body is so small that it does not require much energy to get rid of it.

Fish that need to drink water

Just in case you decide to keep marine fish after you have become aquainted with freshwater fishkeeping, you should know that they have the opposite problem when it comes to balancing water and salt in their body's cells. Saltwater fish have a lower salt content in their bodies and must constantly drink water to replace that lost by osmosis to the saltier environment around them. If saltwater fish didn't constantly drink water, they would eventually die from dehydration.

Saltwater fish excrete small amounts of urine. They also rid their bodies of excess salt to maintain their overall osmotic balance.

The difference is this: Freshwater fish have high salt content in their bodies. Water is gained constantly because it comes into their bodies. Excess water is removed through urine to retain salt/water balance. Saltwater fish have low salt content in body. Water is lost constantly because it goes out to the salt-water they live in. These fish drink the saltwater they live in to get the lost water back into their bodies to retain salt/water balance.

Recognizing Traits to Identify Fish

A fish's life, habits, and movement are completely dependent upon its overall body form and size. When you look at the mouth structure and fin design of each species, you can discover many clues to help answer questions about the way a fish survives, eats, and moves through water.

Discovering how a fish's physical form evolved over a long period of time to guarantee its survival in different aquatic environments helps you recognize unfamiliar species and can give you an immediate idea of what their aquarium requirements probably are. Although this is not a scientific rule, it works about 95 percent of the time.

Body shape

The specific shape of a fish's body can tell you about its natural habitat and swimming range. The streamlined body of a zebra danio, for example, allows it to slip smoothly and effortlessly through open water with quick bursts of speed. You won't find danios living in stagnant swamps in the wild.

Other types of fish have different body shapes that help them in their native environments. For example, the tapered shape of a discus lessens water friction and helps the discus conserve its energy as it quickly slips between obstacles (such as tightly packed roots in its native environment) to catch its prey. You find this fish living in areas with sunken tree roots and other types of natural barriers.

Round-shaped aquatic species, such as fancy goldfish, are slow swimmers and tire quite easily. You find these species living in slow-moving waters.

Fish that are flat on their ventral (bottom) side, such as the cory, spend the great majority of their time moving along the substrate bed in your home aquarium.

Taxonomy

Scientists classify fish as such because of their unique traits that separate them from other animals. Mammals such as whales and dolphins are not "fish" because they are warm-blooded and are required to come to the surface in order to breathe. As we know, fish do not need to breathe air because they have the ability to extract oxygen from the water around them.

Scientists classify animals into large groups that have similar physical attributes. This system is called *taxonomy.* Ichthyologists (people who spend their time studying fish) place aquatic species into several categories based on physical traits so that they can, for example, differentiate fish from other aquatic animals.

Scientists classify bony fish as having: a backbone (*vertebrae*), a small skeleton that protects and supports body weight and internal organs, fins, rays made of cartilage or bone, gill respiration, separate sexes, and a brain case. About 90 percent of the world's fish are bony. The common fish you find in your freshwater aquarium are bony fish.

Cold-bloodedness

The fish in your aquarium are *cold-blooded.* All this means is that their body temperature depends on the temperature of the water around them. Metabolic rate also plays a role in body temperature — active fish have a slightly higher body temperature than lethargic fish.

Mouth location

The way a fish's mouth is shaped and the direction it points have quite a lot to do with the manner in which it feeds and the range (bottom, middle, or top) of aquarium water in which it spends most of its time.

Aquatic species such as the hatchet fish have an upturned mouth, indicating that they are top feeders who scoop up flakes and floating food on the water's surface in the aquarium. This upward-turned mouth is also known as a *superior* position.

A turned-down mouth (*inferior* position) is found in many bottom-dwelling species such as catfish. These fish feed along the gravel bed and from flat rock surfaces and plant leaves.

When the mouth faces straight away from the fish's face, this is known as a *terminal* position and is common in species that swim in mid-water, such as goldfish and platys. These species feed by "picking off" food as it sinks.

Scales

Most fish have a body covered by scales that overlap each other like roof shingles. Scales are formed of transparent plates that protect the body from injury. These thin structures also serve to streamline for efficient gliding. A slimy mucus layer covers the tops of the scales to provide smoothness and protect against invading parasites and infection.

Not all fish have scales, however. As usual, there are a few exceptions.

Here are a few types of scales found in bony fishes:

- ✔ **Ctenoid scales** have tiny little teeth on their outer edges.
- ✔ **Cycloid scales** are smooth and round.
- ✔ **Ganoid scales** have a diamond shape and can be found on species such as gars.

Scales grow out from the skin and generally have no color. Scale color comes from pigment cells located in the skin itself.

The swim bladder

Hypothetically, most fish should sink to the bottom of your aquarium because they are slightly heavier than water. Their muscle and skeleton mass is made up of substances not found in great quantities floating around in water. The swim bladder helps fish overcome this problem. The swim bladder is an organ filled with gas that helps fish maintain their vertical position in the water instead of sinking. The organ may be lacking in some bottom dwellers. The walls of the bladder contract and expand regulate the correct amount of gas to stay afloat.

Internal gas adjustments through the use of a specialized duct allow fish to remain suspended with little or no effort. A gas gland introduces gas to the bladder to increase its volume and increase buoyancy when it excretes lactic acid that allows gas in the blood to diffuse into the bladder. To reduce buoyancy, gas is released from the bladder into the bloodstream and then expelled by gills into the water.

When a fish moves to the bottom of an aquarium, its swim bladder automatically compresses, and the fish sinks. To correct this problem, gas must be added to the swim bladder to achieve buoyancy again. When a fish decides to move toward the top of the tank, its upward movement releases gas from its swim bladder. Otherwise, the fish would be forced to expend too much physical energy to move to a deeper depth.

Color and its purpose

Pigment cells (known as *chromatophores*) in the skin are responsible for a fish's color. Different shades of colors in fish warn off predators and attract mates. The social use of this physical attribute has not been lost in the captivity of the home aquarium. Many species of freshwater and brackish fish have adopted new colors that have appeared through selective breeding and use them to their own advantage in mating and aggression displays.

Chapter 8

Finding Your Species

*W*hen you go to purchase your new fish, you need to have a general idea as to which species can survive in your particular type of system. Otherwise, you may end up with a bunch of marine fish floating at the top of your freshwater aquarium. You simply can't mix apples and oranges in aquariums. Save that combination for Sunday's fruit salad.

This chapter gives you a general overview of major fish families and shows you where they fit into each type of aquarium system. This chapter also helps you understand special dietary and social needs of many species. Most of the fish listed in this chapter are excellent choices for beginners. (We give you plenty of warning about those that aren't.)

This chapter presents you with many scientific names. A scientific name is usually based on Greek or Latin, and uses two words. The first word is the *genus* (a group of related species) that the fish fit into. The second word is the *species* (a group of animals that can interbreed) within that genus. The species name is sometimes the same as the person who first described the fish. A named ending in *i* means that a man first described the fish. A name ending in *ae* means that a woman first described the species. Because no one could pronounce half of these strange names, a common name (like guppy) is also given to each fish.

All you need to do is to memorize a few common scientific names so you can look cool around other hobbyists.

Now that you have the scientific information, let's move on to the important stuff.

Freshwater Tropical Fish and Invertebrates

As you already know from the early chapters in this book, the freshwater tropical aquarium system does not require any marine salt (however, some species, such as mollies, enjoy a teaspoon per 5 gallons added) and generally requires some type of heater. This type of system also usually contains live plants and has gravel for substrate.

Anabantids

The anabantids are a group of fish native to African and Asian waters. These fish have a specialized organ called a *labyrinth* that helps them breathe atmospheric air in the low-oxygenated waters of their native environment. This doesn't mean you should keep them in an aquarium that lacks aeration. If you do, your fish will eventually become ill due to poor water conditions.

Anabantids are generally peaceful species that swim in the middle to upper levels of the aquarium tank. They are easy to breed.

Climbing perch (Anabas testudineus)

This amazing fish can live several days without water, and has been known to travel across land in its native environment as it moves from pond to pond. Keep climbing perch in water near 80 degrees F and provide plenty of shelter for them (rock caves and so on). This fish should be kept with its own kind. The climbing perch grows to 10 inches in length, is carnivorous, and swims in all levels of the tank. A climbing perch requires a tank of at least 125 gallons and is a good choice once you have mastered a few of the easier-to-keep species.

Key terms to remember

Knowing the following terms can help you get the most out of this chapter.

Carnivore: Any organism that eats animals as the main portion of its diet.

Herbivore: Any organism that eats plant material as the main portion of its diet.

Omnivore: Any organism that eats both plant and animal material as the main portion of its diet.

Community tank: An aquarium where many different compatible species of fish are kept together.

Betta or Siamese fighting fish (Betta splendens)

WARNING!

The Asian Siamese fighting fish, also known as the betta (Figure 8-1), has been bred for years to develop strains that have long flowing fins and bright colors. Males of this species are aggressive toward each other so you should only have one male per tank. You can keep Siamese fighting fish in a community aquarium as long as the other fish are not fin nippers.

Bettas build bubble nests by blowing air from their mouths in the form of bubbles that cling together in a mass. If you want to spawn them, they should be kept at a temperature of 76–83 degrees F. The betta is omnivorous and swims in all levels of the tank. Bettas enjoy being fed floating foods and freeze-dried bloodworms. Remember that bettas are not a very active fish, so they will not eat as much as more robust varieties.

The betta is a beautiful fish that has a special organ in its head (called the labyrinth organ) which allows it to breathe oxygen from the air at the water's surface. Good tankmates include corys, danios, and angelfish. Other bubble nest builders include some gouramis and paradise fish.

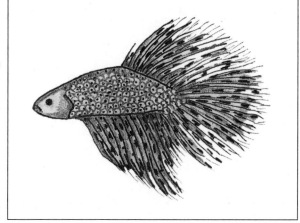

Figure 8-1:
A betta lives on average 2–3 years and grows to about 3 inches in the home aquarium.

Paradise fish (Macropodus opercularis)

The beautifully striped and speckled paradise fish is native to China and South Korea. When frightened, the paradise fish loses its color quickly. Paradise fish build bubble nests for spawning, and prefer a temperature of 75 degrees F. The paradise fish is carnivorous and swims in all levels of the tank, and generally grows to lengths of between 3–4 inches.

The paradise fish is aggressive, and should be kept with other paradise fish in a group and with hardy tankmate species of its own size. Some males constantly fight with each other. Good tankmates include loaches, tiger barbs, danios, gouramis, and red-tailed sharks.

Cyprinodonts and livebearers

The cyprinodont group is also known as *toothcarps* because they have tiny teeth. This group contains both livebearing and egg-laying fish and contains some of the most popular and classic community fish (guppies, platys, and swordtails). Cyprinodonts are friendly, easy to breed, and swim in all levels of the tank.

Killifish

Although most killifish prefer soft, acidic water, a few species can be kept in a community aquarium. The killifish swims in the upper to middle levels of the tank and is carnivorous. Killifish should be kept in schools (three or more fish).

Medaka or rice fish (Oryzias latipes)

This species is native to China, Japan, and South Korea. Keep rice fish in a school (three or more fish) to ensure their survival in a community aquarium. Rice fish prefer a well-planted tank and fertilize their eggs internally (the eggs hatch in 10–12 days.) This species has been known to jump out of a tank, so a tight-fitting hood is a must. The rice fish is carnivorous, requires live food, and swims in the upper level of the tank.

Rice fish enjoy a pH of 7.0 and a temperature of 64 –75 degrees F. They grow to an adult size of about 2 inches. Rice fish enjoy moving water and should therefore be provided with aerated water through use of a filter or airstones.

Striped panchax (Aplocheilus lineatus)

This great community fish is also an aquarium jumper, so make sure your aquarium hood is secure. This egg-laying species uses plants for shelter and to spawn, so provide plenty of plants. The panchax is carnivorous, requires live food, and swims in the upper level of the tank.

Guppy (Poecilia reticulata)

The Central American guppy (Figure 8-2) is an amazing little fish. It has been the staple of many community aquariums since the hobby began. Guppies are now available in a wide variety of colors and fin shapes. Many hobbyists have started out by keeping guppies as aquatic friends. This fish rocks! The guppy is omnivorous and swims in all levels of the tank. Though often inexpensive, do not overlook the beauty of these little fish, because they can provide years of joy as you watch their very active lifestyle and mating rituals.

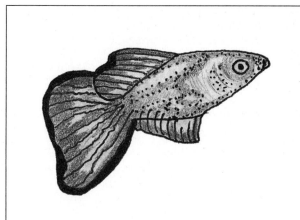

Figure 8-2:
Guppies get along with a wide variety of fish.

The male's anal fin has evolved over time into a specialized organ called a *gonopodium* (a rodlike extension), which it uses to internally fertilize a female's eggs. Guppies are best kept in a well-planted tank in a ratio of one male to every three females.

The guppy should be kept in water that has a temperature of between 78–82 degrees F. Guppies do best with one tablespoon of aquarium salt added for every 5 gallons of water. Guppies do well with flake food and are highly appreciative of frozen brine shrimp as a treat.

Good tankmates can include swordtails, ghost shrimp, glassfish, neon tetras, white clouds, and corys.

Swordtail (Xiphophorus helleri)

The swordtail (native to Mexico, Honduras, and Guatemala) is a brightly colored fish that makes a good addition to any community aquarium.

The males of this species have an elongated caudal fin extension that resembles, not surprisingly, a sword. Male swordtails, like guppies, have a gonopodium (see the preceding "Guppy" section) and prefer heavily planted tanks.

Swordtails are very active and should be kept in water that is slightly hard (has high mineral content such as magnesium, calcium, and sulfates). The water temperature should be kept between 78–82 degrees F. Like other livebearers, the swordtails do well by having one tablespoon of aquarium salt added for every 5 gallons of water in the tank. The swordtail is omnivorous and swims in all levels of the tank.

If you want to breed this fish, you should have a ratio of one male to three females for best results. Having more females helps to ensure that breeding will occur, and will keep the male from harassing one female constantly. Harassment can lead to stress, illness, and death.

Swordtails can reach average lengths of up to 5 inches in captivity and will live 3–5 years in good water conditions.

Sailfin molly (Poecilia latipinna)

The sailfin molly (Figure 8-3) is a beautiful species native to the brackish waters of the United States and Mexico. The male's dorsal fin, when erect, looks like the sail on a ship. Keep mollies in a well-planted tank and provide extra vegetation in their diet.

This species can be aggressive toward smaller fish, but generally makes a great community member. Good tankmates include corys, swordtails, angelfish, tetras such as the red serapae, and platys.

Mollies enjoy slightly salty water, so you can add about one teaspoon of salt for every 5 gallons of water to make them happy. Keep the water between 78–82 degrees. The sailfin molly is omnivorous and swims in all levels of the tank, and generally grows up to lengths of 4 inches during their 3–5-year lifetime.

The one thing we really like about all mollies in general is that they come in such an amazing variety of colors and patterns (marble, patches, metallic, tricolors, and so on). Their round bodies are cool to watch as they make their way through your aquarium.

Make sure that the other species you keep with livebearers can tolerate the extra salt before you add it to their aquarium. If not, mollies can live well without it.

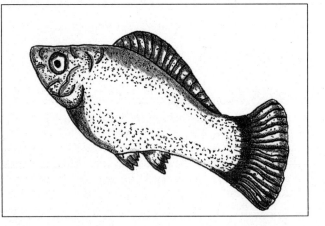

Figure 8-3:
Mollies come in a huge variety of colors and patterns.

Platy (Xiphophorus maculatus)

Platys sport some of the most beautiful colors of all freshwater fish. This hardy species, which is native to Mexico, Honduras, and Guatemala, breeds easily in the community aquarium and is very peaceful. Platys have been developed extensively through commercial breeding and can be found with different fin shapes and in almost every color imaginable. The platy is omnivorous, swims in all levels of the tank, and is easy to breed.

Keep your platys in the same salt conditions as the previously mentioned other livebearers and let them enjoy their water temperature in the 78–82 degree F range as well. Good tankmates include angelfish, mollies, swordtails, corys, larger tetras, and plecostomus. The platy will grow to 3 inches and live several years.

We have to admit that this is our favorite species of fish, simply because of its beauty, cheery round body shape, and amazing colors. The platy also seems very alert to the owner's presence, and we have had many that would swim up to the glass to greet us. You simply can't help but love this amazing little fish which comes in such fascinating varieties as the Mickey Mouse Platy, Marigold Platy, Calico Platy, Painted Platy, Wag Tail Platy, and Sunburst, just to name a few. With fish sporting cool names like that in your aquarium, how can you go wrong?

Catfish

Catfish play an important role in the aquarium system. These species generally feed off the substrate as they gather unwanted debris. Catfish often survive by using their *barbels* (specialized organs used for tasting) to locate the leftovers that fall to the bottom of the tank, but should be provided with a diet of sinking pellets as well. Many species are *nocturnal* (more active at night), so feed them the sinking food formulated especially for them accordingly. Catfish can be aggressive if they are not kept with species their own size, and most are omnivorous.

It is not true that catfish eat fish waste. You have to feed them fish food just like all other kinds of fish.

Bristlenose catfish (Ancistrus temmincki)

The bristlenose catfish is a prehistoric-looking member of the Loricariidae family. Males of this species carry a double row of bristles on their snouts, whereas the females bear only a single row. The bristlenose's mouth is formed into a sucker disk that it uses to feed on algae in its native habitat. This South American catfish is herbivorous, lives in the lower level of the aquarium, and is peaceful.

Glass catfish (Kryptopterus bicirrhis)

The glass catfish is a fascinating animal with a transparent body: You can actually see this fish's backbone and internal organs through its body wall. You can even see the food they have eaten before it is broken down, by looking through their body.

Keep this peaceful Southeast Asian fish in schools (at least three). The glass catfish is carnivorous and swims in the middle and lower sections of the tank. Make sure you have plenty of live plants (such as Java fern) in the tank for this species because they like to hang around them most of the time. Keep their water clean to avoid disease. Glass cats do not do well with many medications, so prevention is the key with this species.

The temperature of the water for glass catfish should be kept between 75–79 degrees F, and soft water with a pH between 6.2–7.0. This fish lives on insects in its native waters; so it should be fed a diet that includes live foods, such as daphnia. Keep this fish in a group with its own kind because it is a schooling fish in the wild and will become very shy and inactive without others of its own type to keep it company. Never keep one alone without other glass catfish.

Glass catfish are good with most non-aggressive community fish such as guppies.

Upside-down catfish (Synodontis species)

True to its unusual name, the upside-down catfish swims with its abdomen pointed upward. This beautiful little fish from tropical Africa changes its body shading according to its swimming position. The peaceful upside-down catfish is carnivorous and swims in all levels of the tank.

This fish does well in temperatures between 72–79 degrees F and have been known to live more than five years. Upside-down catfish grow to lengths of 3–4 inches in the home aquarium, have a forked tail and three sets of barbels, and should be kept in small schools. The dorsal side of the fish is lighter in color, which (used for camouflage) is the complete opposite of most other species that swim in an upright direction. This fish usually has a beautiful mottled body in earth tones.

If you want to keep your upside-down catfish healthy, make sure you have plenty of plants, rocks, and decorations in the tank because they love to search for tasty tidbits along surface areas. Feed this species insect larva and algae discs that they have a great time nibbling at.

Suckermouth catfish (Hypostomus plecostomus)

One of the most famous catfish known to the aquarium hobbyist is the suckermouth. *Hypostomus* is also known as the *pleco*. This fish has a leopard-print pattern of spots and can grow to a length of over one foot, so make sure you have plenty of space for this species to grow. This species can be slightly territorial, so good tankmates can include fish that can hold their own, such as larger cichlids.

Suckermouth catfish do well in temperatures between 69–79 degrees F and is very tolerant of most normal aquarium conditions.

Constantly in search of food, the suckermouth may tear up vegetation if your aquarium is planted as it bashes its way through anything in its path. The suckermouth is herbivorous (it loves to remove algae from your aquarium) and swims in the lower and middle levels of the tank.

If you want smaller versions, you can purchase clown plecos or the bristlenose pleco which only grow to a couple inches in length.

Cory (Corydoras species)

Probably the most popular species of catfish for the home aquarium is the cory (Figure 8-4). Corys come in a wide variety of spotted and striped patterns, are inexpensive, and do a good job cleaning debris (fallen food, dead plant leaves) from the bottom of the tank. The friendly little blackfin cory from South America is one outstanding omnivorous member of this genus that swims in the lower levels. Corys should be kept in schools (at least three) and are easily bred by amateurs. Females are larger and rounder than the males of the species.

They spend most of their time in search of food, so make sure you provide them will sinking pellet foods such as algae wafers. These fish can reach lengths of 2–3 inches on average in a home aquarium and have been known to live as long as ten years.

Keep their water temperature between 72–78 degrees. Good tankmates include livebearers, rasboras, danios, barbs, tetras, gouramis, angelfish, rainbowfish, and other peaceful scavengers such as the pleco.

Figure 8-4:
There are over 50 species of corys that are great for the home aquarium.

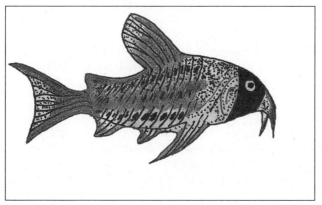

Characins

The characins are one of the most diverse groups of fish, including the small tetras and the big, bad piranha of movie fame. Members of this group are characterized by the bones that link their swim bladder and inner ear. Many characins also have a small adipose fin on their top side between the tail and dorsal fins.

Glowlight tetra (Hemigrammus erythrozonus)

The glowlight tetra of South America is an interesting little fish with a glowing line running from its eye to the base of its tail and a small adipose fin behind the dorsal. When the lights in the tank are dim, you can easily see the beautiful red stripe running down its side.

The peaceful yet very active glowlight tetra prefers soft, acidic water and a well-planted tank that is kept between 75–80 degrees F. It is omnivorous and swims in all levels of the tank. It is normal for their colors to fade if they become too stressed out.

This species is a schooling fish and must be kept with its own kind in groups of five or more in order for it to thrive successfully. This fish will reach lengths of 1–1¼ inches and has been reported to live as long as ten years in good aquarium conditions.

Good tankmates for this fish include other small tetras, small gouramis, danios, angelfish, small catfish, and livebearers.

Bleeding heart tetra (Hyphessobrycon erythrostigma)

The South American bleeding heart tetra earned its name from its physical attributes. This silver-colored fish has a red spot on its side that makes it look as if Clint Eastwood just shot it at high noon. If you loved the movie *E.T.*, you will really enjoy this wonderful little fish.

The bleeding heart needs plenty of swimming room and is easily spooked. This semi-peaceful fish (it may be aggressive toward smaller fish) is omnivorous and swims near the middle level of the tank. The bleeding heart tetra grows to lengths of 2½ inches and should be kept in temperatures between 72–82 degrees F. Make sure you provide plenty of bushy plants for this species.

Like many other tetras, this fish should be kept in a school of its own kind, so that it will feel safe and secure. Bleeding heart tetras will happily eat a wide variety of foods including brine shrimp, bloodworms, frozen foods, and flakes. When you first get these fish home they may have a slightly "washed-out" look (most species will for a few hours to a few days), but they will gain back their beautiful colors after they have settled into their new home.

Neon tetra (Paracheirodon innesi)

The South American neon tetra (Figure 8-5) is one of the most popular and recognizable fish in an aquarium. This peaceful little fish has a blue-green stripe that glitters down the side of its body, and a beautiful red half-stripe below that. The neon is omnivorous, swims at mid level in the tank, needs to be kept in schools (at least six to eight minimum), and is quite difficult to breed in captivity. Males are thinner than the females of the species.

Neons will grow up to an inch and a half in captivity and can live as long as ten years. Keep this fish in water with a temperature between 70–78 degrees F and a well-planted tank. This species does not do well under bright lighting, so make sure to subdue the atmosphere as much as possible.

Unfortunately this fish will be eaten by larger species, so keep it with fish that are peaceful and similar in size such as the cardinal tetra, small community fish, and the glowlight tetra.

Figure 8-5:
Neon tetras can be fed flake food, tubifex worms, and brine shrimp.

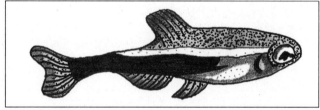

Serpae tetra (Hyphessobrycon serpae)

This fish takes it name from its beautiful color resemblance to a Mexican *serape* (large shawl). The peaceful serpae is a mid-level swimmer and is omnivorous. It is one of the larger tetra species and can be slightly aggressive with smaller fish. It should be kept in a school of six or more of its own species.

Keep their water temperature between 78–80 degrees, as they tend to chill easily. Good tankmates include mollies, swordtails, plecos, and corys. This fish is known to live on average of 5–6 years.

Cardinal tetra (Paracheirodon axelrodi)

The cardinal tetra is similar in appearance to the neon tetra, except that it has a larger area of red coloring on its abdomen. The peaceful cardinal prefers soft, acidic waters (below 6.8 pH) and is omnivorous. This fish swims in all levels of the tank, should be kept in schools (at least six to eight), and should never be housed with any larger, aggressive tankmates.

Cardinal tetras will eat almost any food including flake, live, and frozen.

Rummy-nose tetra (Hemigrammus bleheri)

The rummy-nose tetra is a peaceful fish that should be kept with other small tetras of equal size. Its name comes from the fact that it has a red splotch of color around its nose and eyes.

This species will eat almost any food offered and should be kept in water that is between 72–79 degrees F and softly acidic, with a pH between 6 and 6.8.

Unusual characins

There are many different types of characins. The following sections give examples of some that are quite unusual in physical form. Unusual is cool!

Blindcave fish (Astyanax fasciatus mexicanus)

The blindcave fish has no eyes and navigates in dark, underground caves in the wild using its lateral line (see Chapter 7). The body is pink in color overall with a red gill area. This is an amazing little fish that should not be overlooked as a great asset to any aquarium with compatible species.

This fish grows up to 3 inches in captivity and is an egglayer. A school consisting of five members makes a great addition to the community tank. The blindcave fish is omnivorous and should be kept in waters that are near 72 degrees F with a pH of 7.4. If you are going to keep blindcave fish, make sure you provide them with small caves built out of rocks (or pre-manufactured aquarium caves) so they can feel secure.

Silver hatchetfish (Gasteropelecus sternicla)

The body of the silver hatchetfish body resembles the blade of a large ax. This peaceful South American fish eats live insects and should be kept in schools (of at least three), which will stay near the top of the tank.

This very active species requires excellent water conditions to survive and will not do well in a dirty tank with little oxygen. The water temperature should be kept between 72–79 degrees, with a pH between 6–7. They require an aquarium that has plenty of swimming room and do best if provided with current created by powerheads or other equipment.

Good tankmates include tetras, loaches, livebearers, angelfish, and rasporas. Hatchetfish are good with plants (not eating or tearing them up), so provide them with plenty. Feed them plenty of frozen foods that include insect larvae, as they feed on them in the wild.

The silver hatchetfish can leap from your aquarium to your driveway in a single bound using their winglike pectoral fins, so keep a tight lid on your aquarium to avoid this problem.

Pacu (Colossoma bidens)

Pacus grow quickly in any home aquarium and are related to piranhas. The big difference here is that pacus are mainly vegetarians, whereas piranhas are carnivores. This fish should never be kept in an aquarium that is less than 55 gallons, period. They enjoy a water temperature between 78–82 degrees F.

A pacu looks like a piranha, grows to the size of your mid-sized car, and can eat you out of house and home. This species can grow rapidly and reach adult lengths of 12–30 inches in a home aquarium! These fish have been known to slam against the aquarium glass when panicked, so always provide them with plants or rocks to hide behind.

This fish is suppose to be herbivorous, but don't bet the bank (or your smaller fish) on it. Many hobbyists have seen them attack and swallow smaller fish, so they should be kept with larger species such as oscars, tinfoil barbs, plecos, and knife fish. This species should be fed pellet food that is supplemented with fresh vegetables in small amounts. The pacu swims at mid level.

Red-bellied piranha (Serrasalmus nattereri)

Forget it. Don't even think about it unless you are an *experienced* hobbyist. Too many of these fish have ended up dumped in local rivers by hobbyists who end up disliking their new aggressive pets. These piranhas (Figure 8-6) are a danger to natural species in rivers and should never be put there.

Figure 8-6:
You can forget about owning a piranha until you are very experienced.

Once again, **the piranha is dangerous and often illegal to buy, sell, or own in many states**. It is a large predator! If you temporarily lose your mind and think about buying this fish, seek professional help immediately. They have been known to bite fingers and hands that have been submerged into an aquarium, especially if they have not been fed enough, and this could be tragic, especially if you have young children in the home. Piranha should be left in the hands of experienced aquarists only!

Silver dollar (Mylossoma pluriventre)

This neat fish resembles a silver dollar in form and color. The silver dollar is herbivorous and may destroy aquarium plants if you have them. These fish are generally peaceful, but a few bad apples can become quite aggressive when larger. For best results, keep silver dollars in a school of five to eight in a species tank.

These fish require lots of swimming space, with a water temperature between 78–82 degrees F, and should be kept in tanks larger than 55 gallons because they can grow up to 6 inches in length. Silver dollars are vegetarians by nature and should be fed floating flake food.

Good tankmates for the silver dollar include angelfish, mollies, giant danios, and larger catfish such as the pleco who won't easily be bullied.

Three-lined pencilfish (Nannostomus trifasciatus)

This South American species is probably the world's coolest fish. It looks like a swimming number-two pencil due to the dark band that runs from the nose to the base of the caudal fin. You may not find it in stock at pet stores, but you can usually order it.

The three-lined pencilfish is omnivorous, peaceful, and requires thick vegetation. Add floating plants and dark gravel to diffuse the light so it will feel secure. The temperature should be between 72–81 degrees F with a pH that falls between 6.5–6.9 for best results.

The males become darker as they age than do females and will often battle with other males, although not to usually to the point of injury or death.

Loaches

Loaches are an interesting group of species from Asia and India. Loaches resemble streamlined catfish and, like catfish, are bottom dwellers that use barbels to search for food. These fish can also extract oxygen from the air by gulping it. Most species are nocturnal, so unless you up late at night, you may not see them too often. Loaches are carnivorous, swim in the lower levels of the tank, and are often shy by nature.

Clown loach (Botia macracantha)

The Indonesian clown loach (Figure 8-7) is scaleless (do not add any medications that do not state on the package that they are safe for scaleless fish!), striped like a tiger, and spends most of its time peacefully foraging for food near the bottom of the tank. The clown loach is carnivorous and is best kept in a small school of three to five. Loaches often lay on their sides or backs when resting, so remember that this is normal.

Excellent tankmates include danios, livebearers, small gouramis, corys, and rainbowfish. Try to avoid very slow-moving, mellow tankmates, because the high activity and darting of the loaches can stress out their aquatic companions. This species has been known to live as long as 20 years in the home aquarium (keep this in mind, as older fish can reach lengths of greater than one foot.)

The clown loach tank should be dimly lit and provided with good water current, fine gravel or sand for substrate, and rock caves to match the streams of their natural habitat. They can thrive in waters ranging from 72–85 degrees F. This species will eat almost anything and really enjoys sinking tablet foods, worms, brine shrimp, and tubifex worms as a treat.

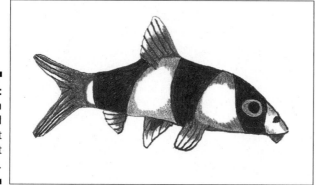

Figure 8-7:
Clown loaches will eat just about anything.

Orange-finned loach (Botia modesta)

The orange-finned loach has a blue-gray body with bright orange fins. Like other loach species, it has small spines on its eyes. This species hides during the day and is very shy. The orange-finned loach swims in the lower levels of the tank, is carnivorous, and makes clicking noises to attract mates.

The water conditions, tank setup, and nutrition for this species are similar to that required for clown loaches.

Zebra loach (Botia striata)

The zebra loach is very nocturnal in nature and becomes very active at night. It is a very pretty fish that sports black and greenish tinted stripes. Tank-mates can include danios, rainbow fish, gouramis, small cichlids, livebearers, and barbs.

The water conditions, tank setup, and nutrition for this species are similar to that required for clown loaches (see earlier in this section).

African cichlids

Cichlids are native to the Americas, Asia, and Africa. Old World Cichlids include species from Lake Malawi, Lake Tanganyika, Lake Victoria, West Africa, India, Sri Lanka, and Madagascar. A few examples of these fish include jewelfish, orange chromides, and mubuna.

Native species like hard alkaline water. Most species (with a few exceptions) tend to be aggressive and are best kept in a species tank with their own kind. Some cichlids require special water conditions — we note them where applicable.

Although many cichlids have a thick body that can grow quite large, a few small varieties are suitable for the home aquarium.

Kribensis (Pelvicachromis pulcher)

The West African kribensis is a generally peaceful, rainbow-colored fish. The kribensis is an omnivorous bottom-dweller. This species can become aggressive during breeding time and should only be kept with other like-size African cichlids and catfish.

It should be fed with vegetable-based African cichlid food, and pairs should be kept in a tank that ranges from 72–82 degrees F in water temperature. Plants and rocks should be provided so that they can feel secure.

Jewel cichlid (Hemichromis bimaculatus)

The jewel cichlid has a pretty golden color with a dark band traversing its body length. It should be fed with vegetable-based African cichlid food and insect larvae and be kept in an aquarium that ranges from 72–82 degrees F in water temperature. Plants and rocks should be provided so that they can feel secure.

Electric yellow cichlid (Labidochromis caeruleus)

This species is marked by its beautiful and bright yellow color and black-marked fins that make it resemble a thin lemon. This species is less aggressive than most cichlids but can be difficult to find.

The tank setup is similar to the *Kribensis,* and it should be fed a diet that consists of both vegetable and meat content such as bloodworms and brine shrimp.

Blue johanni (Melanochromis johanni)

The male of this species has a beautiful, blue-colored body with slightly darker fins and should be fed a diet that consists of vegetable products. The aquarium conditions are similar to the kribensis.

American cichlids

New World cichlids include species from Central America and South America. A few species include oscars, Jack Dempseys, convicts, angelfish, firemouths, and discus.

Keyhole (Aequidens maronii)

The keyhole cichlid is a pale, peaceful fish with a dark band running through its eyes and a black keyhole-shaped spot on it side. This species usually only reaches lengths of 3–5 inches in captivity and should be kept with other non-aggressive fish such as barbs, danios, loaches, catfish, and gouramis.

The keyhole prefers a heavily planted tank and is an omnivorous bottom-dweller.

Angelfish (Pterophyllum scalare)

The angelfish (Figure 8-8) is such a delicate-looking species; you can only wonder how it can possibly be related to other cichlids. Angelfish have long dorsal and anal fins they use for balance. They come in a wide variety of colors and patterns, including marble, white, and striped. Angelfish are one of the most beautiful and inspiring fish on earth. Just having one of these marvelous creatures is enough to suck you into the aquarium hobby for a lifetime.

A deep and long tank is best for this peaceful, carnivorous species, with a water temperature of 78–82 degrees F. Feed them flake food and toss in some brine shrimp for a treat. Angelfish are egglayers and are easily bred in the home aquarium.

Figure 8-8:
Angelfish
make great
community
fish.

Red oscar *(Astronotus ocellatus)*

The red oscar is an Amazonian giant (growing to lengths of over 12 inches in the home aquarium) who may quickly outgrow your tank, so a 70-gallon tank is a minimum requirement for one or two fish. This animal is carnivorous and eats anything it can fit into its large mouth and will eventually need to be fed cichlid pellet food.

One cool thing about an oscar is that you can hand tame it to accept food from you.

Oscars spend most of their time swimming in the middle levels of the tank. You can easily fool your friends into thinking that you are risking life and limb by feeding them.

Oscars enjoy water that is kept between 72–78 degrees and feel secure with a sandy substrate and rocks. Oscars will tear up plants, so if you do use artificial ones, prepare yourself to a daily routine of replanting them. If you put live plants in your oscar tank, say your permanent goodbyes as you are arranging them, because the next time you see them they will probably resemble confetti.

If kept in small groups, oscars tend to bicker with each other, so it is better to keep them in groups of eight or more. Unfortunately keeping this many oscars would require you to borrow a tank from Seaworld, so prepare to keep a single or two who will fight on and off. Tankmates can include knifefish, large plecos, tinfoil barbs, and other large cichlids of the same size.

Oscars can live a very long time. There are reports of them surviving over 25 years in captivity.

Convict (Cichlasoma nigrofasciatum)

If you want to impress your friends with your breeding abilities, the convict cichlid (Figure 8-9) is the fish for you. This hardy cichlid would breed in a puddle of water during an earthquake if given half a chance. Rabbits can't hold a candle to convicts. Both parents care for their young. The convict is aggressive, swims in the middle to lower sections of the aquarium, is carnivorous, and should be kept in a well-planted *species* tank (tanks that only contain fish of the same species).

The convict gets its name from the vertical black and white stripes on its body that resemble the prison uniforms you see in old movies. This fish is constantly alert, quick, and *very* territorial. Pink convicts are another, quite beautiful variety.

Convicts will eat any fish food offered to them. They should be kept in a tank that has plenty of caves for breeding and hiding and has a water temperature of 68–75 degrees F. This species should only be kept with other fish of similar size and bad-boy attitude.

Figure 8-9: Convicts should be kept in their own species tank.

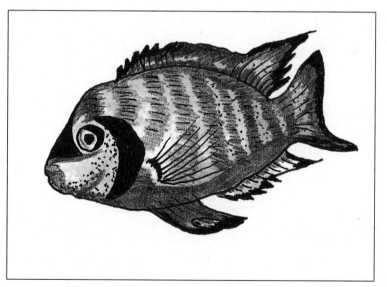

Discus (Symphysodon varieties)

The discus (Figure 8-10) is the king of the cichlids, the Mona Lisa of the fish world. This flat fish, which resembles a plastic throwing disk, has been commercially bred to produce stunning colors. Not only are discus beautiful, they are well behaved as well. Who could ask for more?

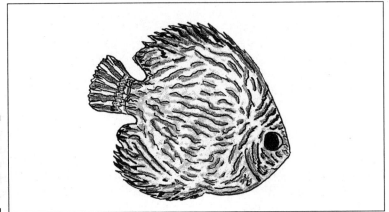

Figure 8-10:
Discus are gorgeous and well mannered.

These fish are carnivorous and should be kept in schools of at least three to five. They can be fed frozen brine shrimp, cichlid flakes, and insect larvae. They will grow to over 5 inches in a home aquarium. Discus live in natural waters that have a temperature between 78–84 degrees F. and a pH of about 4.5–6.0.

Discus water must be soft and acidic. Many hobbyists use RO units to mimic its natural waters and combine this in a mix with tap water. However, you must also add trace elements and minerals (available in liquid form at your pet store) back to the water to make it suitable for your aquarium fish.

Discus can be very expensive, but are very popular and well worth the investment.

Cyprinids

The cyprinids are a diverse family that includes barbs, danios, and rasboras.

Tiger barb (Barbus tetrazona)

The tiger barb (Figure 8-11) is an orange and black striped fish native to Southeast Asia. This fish is omnivorous and swims in the middle and lower sections of the tank. Tiger barb can become quite aggressive and should be kept in a species tank or with fishes of similar size and temperament. Good tankmates could include plecos, livebearers, barbs, rainbowfish, and loaches.

Figure 8-11:
Tiger barbs
are
aggressive
and need a
big tank.

Tiger barbs are territorial, so the larger the tank the better. This species will eat almost anything offered and should be fed a mixture of meaty foods and vegetable-based fish food. The water temperature for this species is 70–74 degrees F. Make sure you have lots of plants and decorations to provide them hiding places when they start to pick on each other.

Cherry barb (Barbus titteya)

Like its name suggests, this species of barb has a light red iridescent color and is shaped somewhat like a diamond. Even the sides of the fish have diamond-shaped markings. Maybe they should have called it the diamond cherry barb.

If provided with a planted tank and a school of its own kind, the cherry barb is generally peaceful and even timid around other species. Tank conditions are similar to the tiger barb.

Green barb (Barbus tetrazona)

The green barb gets its name from its emerald green color. This fish can get slightly aggressive and nip fins. Aquarium conditions and tankmates are similar to the tiger barb.

Zebra danio (Brachydanio rerio)

The South Asian zebra danio is one of the most popular community fish. The little speed demon makes the top of your tank look like the Indianapolis 500. This omnivorous, torpedo-shaped wonder is gold with blue stripes and very hardy. Keep danio in schools of five to seven in a tank with dense foliage where they can lay their eggs. Danios tend to fade away and die without a school, so give them some aquatic buddies.

The zebra danio is often used as a dither fish. A *dither* fish is an active and peaceful species put in a tank with slower moving species, so that the slower moving species become more active like the dither fish. (Whew!)

The zebra danio will eat almost anything the second it hits the water, so make sure your other fish in the same tank are getting their share, too. Danios can live in water temperature between 64–78 degrees and are very tolerant of beginner mistakes.

Giant danio (Danio aequipinnatus)

This is large version of the danio species and is very peaceful community fish. This fish is a jumper and requires lots of swimming space in waters that range from 72–75 degrees F.

Harlequin rasbora (Rasbora heteromorpha)

The omnivorous little harlequin rasbora from Southeast Asia has an unusual marking that makes it stand out in a crowd. The body is gold-green and has a dark blue patch that forms a triangle on each side. This fish only grows to about 2 inches. The rasbora should be kept in schools and swim in all levels of the tank.

Good tankmates include angelfish, tetras, danios, catfish, community livebearers, and gouramis. This fish prefers a well-planted tank with waters in the 73–77 degree F range and a pH of 6.0–6.5.

Oddballs

Here are a few other tropical fish considered oddballs as far as physical characteristics are concerned. However, despite their unusual appearance, they can be real showstoppers in your home aquarium once you have become an experienced freshwater fishkeeper. They can impress and amaze your friends as well.

Elephant fish or elephant nose (Gnathonemus petersi)

The African elephant fish is a peaceful, carnivorous species with an extended jaw that resembles an elephant's trunk. The egglaying elephant fish can emit electrical impulses (it has poor vision and uses them to navigate) and should be kept by itself in an aquarium. It is nocturnal, so you won't see much action during the daytime.

This fish enjoys subdued lighting and a well-planted tank. The elephant nose will thrive well on tubifex worms, bloodworms, and mosquito larvae.

Clown knifefish (Notopterus chitala)

The carnivorous knifefish resembles the curved blade of a Japanese sword and grows greater than 10 inches in length. This fish is nocturnal and should be kept by itself or with larger fish such as oscars. This species lives in the lower levels of the tank and moves by undulating its body They have been known to live over seven years in captivity.

The knifefish tank should be 55 gallons or larger, include dim lighting, 75–78 degree F waters, a tight-fitting lid (they are jumpers), plenty of rocks (make sure there are no sharp edges because this species does not have scales), and driftwood for hiding places. This species should be fed a diet of frozen and fresh brine shrimp, bloodworms, and plankton. They really like the live food best and should only be fed once every night after the lights have been turned off.

Leaf fish (Monocirrhus polyacanthus)

The carnivorous South American leaf fish has a blotched skin pattern that makes it look like a decaying leaf floating through the water. The leaf fish floats head down and snags its prey as it floats by. This fish is cool looking and grows up to 4 inches.

Keep it with fish of its own size or in a species tank because it is a predator. Generally this fish will refuse any food that is not alive, so be prepared to buy small feeder fish. The leaf fish lives in all levels of the tank and should be kept in water that is 72–77 degrees F, with a pH of 6–6.5.

Freshwater tropical invertebrates

There are many invertebrates you can buy for your aquarium. *Invertebrates* are not fish because they lack a backbone.

Ghost shrimp (Paleomonetes species)

Ghost shrimp are small (only 2 inches at maturity), have segmented bodies, and are almost transparent except for a colored spot on their tails. This peaceful and delicate creature with ten sets of legs makes an interesting aquatic pet.

This species needs to be kept with passive fish that will not tear it limb from limb. Many hobbyists set up a 10-gallon aquarium just for their ghost shrimp so that they don't have to worry about predators. The reverse is also true: many hobbyists use them as feeders for other fish.

Ghost shrimp will eat almost anything in the aquarium using their tiny claws to scoop it in. They will consume waste, algae, and almost any live, frozen, or manufactured food. They are true scavengers.

Freshwater Clams (Corbicual species)

Freshwater clams are from Asia and only grow to about 2 inches in the home aquarium. This invertebrate has banded brown and black colors and spends most of its time *filter feeding*. This type of feeding helps to keep your aquarium clean and reduce nitrates as it removes floating particles and uneaten food that is suspended in the water.

Freshwater clams can live in water temperatures ranging from 68–85 degrees and are peaceful.

Singapore flower shrimp (Atyopsis moluccensis)

This beautiful red shrimp is native to Asia and reaches lengths of almost 4 inches in the home aquarium. This invertebrate is able to quickly change colors depending on it surrounding environment.

Singapore shrimp should be kept in aquariums of over 10 gallons and happily feed on aquarium debris by filtering it with special appendages shaped like fans that are attached to their legs.

Ramshorn snail (Marisa cornuarietis)

This peaceful cool gold or cream-colored snail has a shell that looks like a ram's horn. It can live in water temperatures ranging from 70–85 degrees F and only grows to about 2 inches.

The interesting thing about this snail is that they require air to breathe. They accomplish this using a siphon that sticks out of the water, like an escaped convict using a reed to breath underwater in an old prison break movie. For that reason you need to leave a couple of inches of open airspace on the top of the aquarium water.

The ramshorn snail is great for cleaning up debris in the aquarium.

Freshwater Coldwater Fish and Invertebrates

Freshwater creatures that live in coldwater tanks do not require heating, because they generally live at lower temperatures than do tropical ones. The rest of the coldwater aquarium equipment is the same as for tropicals. However, if you keep fish in an outdoor pond during the freezing winter months, you may have to move them into a warmer area such as a holding tank in your garage until the frigid weather passes. Goldfish secrete a lot of waste, so good filtration is a must.

Although many fish such as the guppy can live in cooler waters, we will focus on other non-tropical varieties. In today's market, for example, many beautiful varieties of goldfish will fascinate and amaze you. These are not your garden-variety feeder goldfish found at carnivals!

Koi

Koi (*Cyprinus carpio*) is a highly colored omnivorous pond fish that is related to goldfish (Figure 8-12). Because of its large size at maturity (up to 3 feet in length), it is unsuitable for an indoor aquarium. The torpedo-shaped koi requires a good filtration system and many plants, which it uses for food and shade. Champion varieties can be very expensive, but have outstanding color and beauty.

Koi do not do well in acidic water, so their pH needs to be kept between 7.0–9.0. They must be kept in ponds that allow them to remain cool throughout the year.

Figure 8-12:
Koi get too big for an aquarium, but are great for ponds.

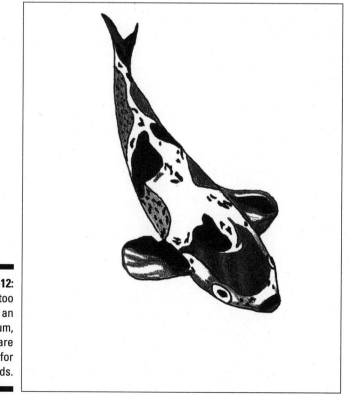

Goldfish

Goldfish are one of the oldest aquarium fish known. These fish were specifically bred from carp for their beauty and have no known natural varieties. All goldfish variations are grouped into the same species, *Carassius auratus*. There are four main types of goldfish:

- ✔ **Egg goldfish:** Egg goldfish have no dorsal fin, are egg shaped, and have double tails.

- ✔ **Wen goldfish:** The Wen goldfish have a fancy style tail and a dorsal fin.

- ✔ **Dragon-eye goldfish:** Dragon-eye goldfish have eyes that protrude in the form of telescoping or bubbles.

- ✔ **Common goldfish:** These fish are similar in appearance to the carp from which they were bred, but have more color variations.

Fancy goldfish have been bred for many physical characteristics including bubble eyes, split tales, long fins, and unusual head coverings (*growth*). These species can be kept in either a coldwater aquarium or a pond. Either way, these omnivorous fish need a good filtration system and plenty of foliage.

Black moor goldfish (Carassius auratus)

The black moor is a cool-looking goldfish that really isn't gold at all. It is black. The body is slightly hunched, and the caudal fin fans downward like a lace veil draped over the top of a glass. Like many goldfish, Black Moors tend to wobble as they swim, which is quite amusing to watch, and have protruding, velvety black eyes.

Because they belong to the carp family, goldfish are very hardy. Black moors should be kept in tanks of 20 gallons or larger that is outfitted with either artificial or thick-leafed coldwater plant species. Goldfish tend to dig around in the gravel and will destroy dainty plants. Toss some smooth river rocks into the goldfish tank and watch them flip them all over the place. Keep the water temperature between 65–70 degrees.

Due to their physical makeup, goldfish should have their protein intake limited to no more than 25–30 percent of their nutritional intake. The best thing to feed them is manufactured goldfish food.

Good tankmates for almost all goldfish species include scavenging catfish, such as the pleco, and other goldfish.

Lionhead (Carassius auratus)

Lionheads resemble a lion in color, have a head growth like a lion's mane, and have thick bodies These are slow-moving fish (because they have no dorsal fin) that need very good water conditions in order to avoid disease. Aquarium conditions are similar to those of the black moor. This fish comes in many colors including orange, white, blue, and black and calico mixtures.

The lionhead can growth to lengths of 10 inches and like other large goldfish requires a lot of tank space to remain healthy and happy.

Bubble-eye goldfish (Carassius auratus)

The peaceful bubble-eye is one of the most amazing looking goldfish around. Like the lionhead, it has no dorsal fin and wiggles to swim. As the name suggests, this fish has huge fluid-filled bubble sacks beneath each eye. As the fish gets older, the sacs grow larger and can become very heavy to the point of slowing down their motion and keeping them near the bottom of the tank.

Because they spend a lot of their time near the substrate, make sure that all gravel, rocks, and other aquarium decorations have smooth edges that won't damage their delicate eye sacks. This species also has to be kept with other non-aggressive goldfish. The aquarium should be as large as possible so that it has plenty of room to swim around without risking damaging its eyes on things in the aquarium.

It is best to feed your bubble-eye goldfish sinking pellets so that they can easily get their fair share of nutrition. Keep their water slightly warmer in the 70–75 degree F range.

Telescope-eye goldfish or dragon-eye goldfish (Carassius auratus)

This species of goldfish has round eyes that protrude outward more and more as the first few months of development pass by. These eyes resemble those of fictional dragons. The fish was first developed in the 16th century. This gentle goldfish has been known to live up to 25 years in captivity.

This goldfish should be kept in water between 65–75 degrees F and should be kept in as large a tank as possible.

Coldwater invertebrates

As you have learned, some invertebrates live in tropical tanks. There is also one fairly common species that enjoys living in coldwater aquariums.

Understanding setups

When your aquarium setup is complete, make sure that you match your fish to it. Using this chapter as a rough guide gives you a good head start. When in doubt about an unfamiliar species, check with your local fish shop owner because some friendly fish have been known to go bad and vice versa. It is better to be prepared with knowledge than face instant disaster.

So much of the road that leads to becoming an expert fishkeeper is dependent upon practical experience as well as knowledge. Sometimes when trying to choose compatible species, you have to experiment a little to see what works best for you and your individual setup. The size of your tank, the number of fish it contains, and the types of decorations in it can all have an affect on how well your tankmates get along.

Florida blue crayfish (Procambaris alleni)

The Florida Blue Crayfish is a beautiful combination of blue and gray that can live in temperatures as low as 50 degrees F. These are best kept in a species tank so they don't have to worry about being eaten, and you don't have to worry about them eating other inhabitants. Crayfish are vulnerable when molting.

Crayfish are good climbers, so make sure you aquarium has a good lid.

Captive-Bred Species

People tend to think that oceans, rivers, and lakes are an endless realm overflowing with aquatic animal life. But as an ecologically concerned fishkeeper, you must remember that only a small percentage of the world's waters contain the fish that you put into your aquarium. Each year, fish populations decline due to overfishing, the curio trade, and other human interventions, such as pollution and introduction of non-native fish into areas that are altered by their presence. Be it freshwater, brackish, or marine, the problem exists and is worth mentioning.

Often fish dealers offer both captive-bred species (fish or other aquatic animals that have been raised in hatcheries for the aquarium trade) and animals that have been caught in the wild. By purchasing captive-bred fish, you can help slow down the elimination of wild species. Most freshwater fish are now commercially bred to one extent or another and are usually less expensive than those caught in the wild.

The bulk of the problem occurs in the marine side of the hobby. Few marine fish are bred commercially because they can be quite difficult to spawn. In the last few years, marine fish hatcheries have made great progress in reproducing many species of clownfish, wrasses, and other types of saltwater fish. At the present time, captive-bred marine species can be a little more expensive than those caught in the wild, but in the long run it is well worth the extra money to help save our natural aquatic resources. Remember this if you go on to keep a marine tank.

The collection of live coral has also hit an all-time high in recent years. Many areas are now prohibiting collection of live coral because the world's reefs are beginning to disappear due to repeated harvesting for curio shops and the marine aquarium trade.

Many marine fish are caught by people using illegal practices and products such as cyanide, which also destroys large portions of any coral reef that it comes in contact with. Purchasing wild animals only encourages wholesalers to continue removing fish and invertebrates from their native habitat.

So if you have a choice, always purchase captive-bred species (ask your dealer if his stock is captive bred). That way your grandchildren won't have to have an aquarium with plastic fish suspended in it.

Buying Fish on the Web

Now you have a few good ideas about some interesting and amazing species of fish and invertebrates for your freshwater aquarium. Remember that the species listed in this chapter are only a drop in the bucket when you look at the total number of fish available. It would take volumes to list every species.

Some species are easier to obtain than others are. You should patronize your local shop whenever possible, but don't forget that you can use the World Wide Web to find many fish at reasonable prices. These Internet companies are good about shipping their stock on time, and in good condition, so don't worry about getting what you paid for. Just make sure you check their shipping costs (which vary from company to company) so that you can add them into the total cost for your purchase.

Following are a few suggestions for purchasing fish on the net to get you started.

AquariumFish.Net

www.aquariumfish.net

This site always seems to have excellent fish that are in good condition. We have ordered fish from this site and have always received healthy fish on time. Another cool thing about this site is that even though it may not stock a certain type of fish, it still gives you good information on that species. The site is therefore a good source of information about fish species. The prices are very reasonable as well.

Fish2u.com

www.fish2u.com

Okay, this site has an *amazing* selection of fish and plants. We have ordered a lot from this place, which probably has the best stock we have ever seen in an Internet company. It has good customer service and seems to stand behind product. Add this place to your favorites.

Marine Depot Live

www.marinedepotlive.com

If you decide later on to go into the marine side of the hobby, this site has a great selection of fish and invertebrates to choose from. It also sells equipment if you need that, too. The stuff is top of the line, and his marine fish and invertebrates rule.

The giant gourami is a bubble-nest builder and is the largest of all gourami species.

Koi grow very large and are great fish for coldwater ponds.

The cardinal tetra is one of the most popular aquarium fish due to its beautiful coloration and peaceful nature.

The bones and internal organs of the glass catfish can easily be seen inside its transparent body.

Ghost shrimp are fresh-water invertebrates, not fish.

Orandas have a distinctive hood-shaped growth on their head that is also known as a "wen."

Danios are great fish for beginning hobbyists because they are very active and easy to see.

This bubble-eye actually has poor vision.

Siamese algae eaters help to keep algae in an aquarium under control by dining on it continuously.

The beautiful kuhli loach is a peaceful fish that does well in a community aquarium with other small, non-aggressive species.

When properly acclimated, sailfin mollies have been kept successfully in freshwater, brackish, and marine aquariums.

A pencilfish has horizontal stripes that make it resemble a standard school pencil.

Swordtails are colorful, hardy fish that are easy to breed.

The Mickey Mouse platy was named due to black markings near the tail that resemble Mickey Mouse ears.

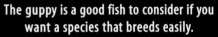

The guppy is a good fish to consider if you want a species that breeds easily.

The angelfish is one of the few non-aggressive cichlid species.

Oscars are very friendly, and many hobbyists compare them to other household pets.

The serape tetra is an egglayer that can live more than ten years in captivity.

Pearl gouramis are generally timid fish that should be kept with other peaceful species.

Swordtails are good jumpers, so make sure you have a tight-fitting lid on your aquarium. This is a tux swordtail.

Balloon mollies may be very big eaters, but their temperament is peaceful.

The redtail shark is not a true shark; it is actually a cyprinid.

A plecostomus can attach itself to aquarium walls, rocks, plants, and other decorations using its mouth like a suction cup.

Comet goldfish have a metallic shiny appearance and were first bred in China over a thousand years ago.

Goldfish like this black moor will eat all types of live and dried foods.

Platys are colorful, friendly fish that are perfect for a community tank.

A community tank is a great place to keep several different varieties of fish who can live in harmony.

Chapter 9

Purchasing Your Fish

· ·

· ·

*O*ne of the best ways to start out as a beginning hobbyist is to develop a good relationship with a local tropical fish dealer. A quality vendor can help you make informed decisions on the type of aquarium best suited for you, the proper equipment for your new tank, and the best aquatic species for your system. A good vendor can also locate hard-to-find products (such as a filter or lid for an irregularly shaped tank) and can help you with water testing on a regular basis.

Of course, you can do many things as an informed hobbyist to help you start off your fishkeeping adventure with success. Choosing healthy pets from a good local vendor is the best way to start off right, and this chapter can help.

Choosing a Quality Dealer

The aquarium hobby is generally a lifelong addiction. (We ourselves are candidates for Aquariums Anonymous.) It is really difficult to lay this fascinating hobby aside once you take the plunge. In the years to come, you will need to purchase fish, replace worn equipment, and keep stocked up on chemicals and proper food.

During the course of your hobby, you also need expert advice on fishkeeping skills once in a while, and someone to keep you informed on the newest trends in equipment and other aquarium-related paraphernalia. No matter what your skill level in fishkeeping, there is always something new to learn. This is why you need to find a good retailer who specializes in the aquarium aspect of the pet industry.

A knowledgeable aquarium fish dealer, especially one that is conveniently located in your neighborhood, can help you anytime you have a problem or emergency with your aquatic pets. Building a personal relationship with this type of merchant also helps you stay informed on aquarium-related issues. For these reasons and more, it is important to make contact with an informed and trustworthy vendor. (Besides, if you get to know a dealer well, you may be able to snag a few freebies as well.)

The search for a fish store

When you want to buy a house, you don't just purchase the first one you see, do you? No, you look around a bit first. The same principal applies to your aquarium hobby. Look for the best and don't settle for less. There's nothing wrong with checking the gossip in your neighborhood to determine whether the local dealers have a good reputation among other businesses and their customers. Friends, aquarium clubs, and family members are a great place to start asking questions. If your family is like ours, you'll not only hear all you need to know about local aquarium shops, you'll pick up a few juicy extra tidbits at the same time.

In today's consumer-conscious environment, you cannot afford to end up with mediocre service because you were afraid to investigate the references or character of a particular dealer. You can obtain valuable information through this age-old method.

The best strategy is to visit as many local dealers and aquarium shops as your time and budget allow. These fun little investigative trips provide you with a solid foundation on which you can compare dealers' overall quality of service, livestock selection and condition, friendliness, willingness to help, and prices on fish and equipment. (Of course, if you are visiting New York City, this could mean renting an RV for a couple of months until you have seen all the retailers in the area.)

In choosing a tropical fish dealer, take into consideration a few important factors (covered in the next sections) before you pledge your loyalty to one particular shop. In fact, we find it best to frequent at least *two* fish shops minimum. It's kind of like having an ace in the hole (or up your sleeve) at a poker game: If one shop goes out of business, or has an internal problem that affects your ability to get good equipment or livestock, you're still covered.

After you compare all your local fish shops, choose the two retailers you think can satisfy all your aquarium requirements.

The importance of great service

When deciding on the two best local dealers, see whether the employees are friendly and offer good advice. Do the clerks make every attempt to help you out when you come in, or do they just stand around shooting the breeze?

Do the shop's workers take a personal interest in your aquarium? Are they willing to go out of their way to make sure that you find exactly what you need? Are there adequate personnel to provide good service to you even during the peak hours of the day? If you have to blitz and tackle a clerk to make him talk, then you need to find another place to shop. A reputable and caring owner who takes pride in her business and in providing customer satisfaction makes sure that her shop is well staffed with knowledgeable and caring employees.

Employees who stand around and do nothing generally do not have an interest in their employer's business, and probably don't have an interest in making sure that you get the stuff for your aquarium, either. (Hopefully you won't see those clerks the next time you visit.)

The store's appearance

When you go to an aquarium shop (even if you're checking out a new one that just opened up in the neighborhood), carefully inspect all the display tanks for obvious signs of dealer dedication or apathy. If the place looks like the owner couldn't care less about how the tanks look, he probably cares just as little about the rest of his business, including the fish. A visual inspection can tell you quite a bit about a shop's habits. As you look around the shop, check for clues that distinguish a good dealer from an uncaring one.

The tanks

Quality retailers understand that the overall condition of their shop makes a big difference as far as customers' first impressions are concerned.

The physical condition of the tanks is a good indication of how well the fish are taken care of on a daily basis. Ask yourself these questions:

- Are the tanks free of excess algae or do they resemble the Florida swamps?

- Are the proper mixtures of compatible species displayed in the tanks or does it appear that a bunch of fish have been thrown in together to save space?

✔ Is the tank water clear or murky?

✔ Do the tanks look like they have been properly vacuumed lately?

✔ Is the front of the glass clean or does it still bare smudges and finger-prints from the grade school class who visited the shop the week before? Someone who won't even take a couple minutes to clean the front glass doesn't care very much about presentation or the impression the shop makes on its customers, and usually does not care about the health of their fish, or their customers' best interests either.

✔ Are the shelves full of merchandise, neatly stocked, and organized, or is everything just tossed together on one shelf?

The fish

A good quality retailer has good quality fish. No exceptions. If a dedicated dealer is not happy with his suppliers, he quickly looks for another who can provide high-quality fish. While you are browsing through a store, see whether the dealer's fish are swimming boldly (out away from the decorations) in the open spaces of the aquarium, or hiding in the corners. Fish that hide in corners usually have health problems after you bring them home. If the fish in the shop look like they just swam through a waste dump, find another pet store.

Here are some things to look for when examining fish:

✔ Do the fish look generally healthy?

✔ Are the fish's fins erect?

✔ Does the body display proper color?

✔ Does the fish have a good shape, and is the body correctly formed for the particular species?

✔ Do all of the merchant's fish appear to be in good health, or just a few?

✔ Has the dealer shown honesty by turning the lights off or putting a sign on sick tanks to indicate diseased fish — or is the store just selling fish in bad condition?

The equipment

There are times when your equipment will wear out or fail, and you need to replace it. Make sure that the dealers you choose have an adequate supply of equipment and parts. Nothing is more frustrating than having to run from store to store to find a simple piece of equipment such as a net, pump, or filter. Make sure that your dealer has a wide selection on hand. If not, make sure the shop can order needed supplies and get them in within a reasonable amount of time.

Chemicals and food

Does the shop have a good supply of chemicals, medicine, and foods available? You may not have time to wait for a dealer to order medications if your fish are really ill — it's much better to have it available when an emergency arises. Check to see if the store carries a wide selection of frozen foods as well as food for fish with special or unique dietary needs.

Dealer Practices: the Good, the Bad, and the Ugly

We classify dealers into good dealers (Do Bees), bad dealers (Don't Bees), and ugly dealers (Wanna Bees). We have seen all types during our years in the aquarium hobby. All we can do is give you a little personal advice as to what to look for when you are trying to determine who is the good guy and who is the bad guy. We cannot stress this enough, because if you do not have a good place to purchase fish and aquarium equipment, you may become frustrated with fighting a continual uphill battle to maintain successful aquariums.

Do Bee dealers

A Do Bee dealer helps you find success. Some of the signs of a good retailer are

- Friendly, helpful, knowledgeable staff members who answer your questions willingly, go out of their way to help, and who are familiar with aquarium equipment, the different types of aquarium systems, and individual species of fish.

- A large selection of aquarium equipment, food, medication, and fish on hand — they carry more than one or two brands.

- Free services, such as water testing.

- Some type of guarantee on the fish they sell and the commitment to stand behind the equipment that they sell. A really good Do Bee offers free repair service on basic equipment that they have sold to you.

- A willingness to tell you where you can get a certain species or piece of equipment if they cannot get it themselves. This includes offering competitors' phone numbers.

- Autopsies of dead fish to help determine the cause of the disease (if the dealer has qualified staff) and medication advice to help prevent the need for an autopsy.

✔ A genuine interest in you and your aquariums.

✔ Clean tanks and shops.

Don't Bee dealers

Don't Bee dealers own aquarium shops you want to avoid. They are really quite easy to spot when you recognize the symptoms of their "I have no business being in the tropical fish trade because I don't really care about my job, or I am just in it for the money" disease. Avoid these dealers at all costs!

You can recognize Don't Bees by the following characteristics:

✔ They're willing to tell you to take a hike if you question the quality of their service or livestock.

✔ They let you stand around without offering to help you find what you are looking for.

✔ They spend a lot of time answering phone calls and leave you waiting for service until they finish yacking.

✔ They try to give you a snow job if you ask them a question they don't have an answer for.

✔ They try to sell you a bunch of junk you don't need because they believe that you don't know any better.

✔ They sell fish they know are diseased just to get rid of them.

✔ They use the same net to capture fish in all their tanks without sterilizing it between uses.

✔ They have dirty aquariums and a filthy shop.

✔ They sell you fish that are not compatible just to make a few extra bucks (which they obviously they don't spend on the upkeep of the shop).

✔ They refuse to go out of their way to order any special equipment or fish for you.

✔ They don't keep regular store hours and show up whenever they happen to feel like it.

✔ They are extremely rough with the fish when bagging them up for transport.

Wanna Bee dealers

A Wanna Bee dealer is the owner of a pet shop that appears overnight and disappears within a few months because she didn't have the proper finances to keep it afloat long enough to establish itself. These dealers sell you poor quality fish and equipment at inexpensive prices to get some money coming in and then simply fall off the face of the earth. If a new shop opens up and you are unsure as to whether you should purchase fish from the new owners, simply wait a few months to see if it stays open. During this time, keep your ear out for information from other customers concerning the quality of the shop.

Developing a Good Relationship with Your Fish Dealer

After you make your final decision and pledge your loyalty to a couple of dealers, try to become acquainted with as many of the employees in the shop as possible. Go out of your way to meet the owner or store manager, who can likely help you with any serious problems you may have.

A great majority of dealers are very enthusiastic when given the opportunity to work with regular customers. After the initial conversation, your aquarium, ideas, or wishes may become as familiar to them as their own personal tanks. Many merchants beam proudly at a customer's first successful aquarium setup (after all, the merchant helped create it). A caring vendor also mourns with you at the loss of your favorite fish. A vendor who can't remember your name after you have been buying from their shop for months probably should be avoided.

Making the effort required to solidify a personal relationship with your local dealer puts you in good position to receive quality advice and the highest degree of comprehensive service available. When a merchant is familiar with you, the type of systems you own, your special interests, and other personal aquarium specifications, he has a better opportunity to help you become a successful hobbyist.

Selecting Healthy Fish

Now, whether you find a good dealer or not, you still need to take responsibility for choosing the healthiest fish possible. Starting off with diseased fish is the quickest way we know to lose interest in the hobby. You always take a risk when you purchase a live animal because unseen problems may manifest later on, but you can improve the odds of success by starting off with the healthiest fish possible.

Don't buy the first fish off the boat

Avoid buying any new arrivals your dealer recently received. If the fish are still in a packing crate, that should give you a clue. You should see a large number of bags containing fish floating in the aquariums on the days the store receives new shipments. Most dealers receive new fish on one or two specific days each week. Ask your dealer which days these are. A good dealer doesn't allow customers to purchase fish until she's had sufficient time to *quarantine* them. This quarantine period reduces the fish's stress from shipping and allows the shop's personnel to treat any disease that shows up in the first few days after arrival.

If you happen to see some fish that really catch your eye while they are still in the bags, ask the dealer to hold them for you until a reasonable quarantine period has expired. Most dealers willingly agree to do that. Helpful merchants who take the time to grant such simple requests to provide customer satisfaction are definitely worth patronizing in the future. Stop for a moment and ask yourself one simple question: If I owned this fish shop, would I do this for my customer? If the answer is yes, then you should expect your dealer to do the same thing.

Don't be Doctor Doolittle

Never allow anyone, including your dealer, to talk you into buying a sick or ailing fish in the honorable but mistaken belief that you can quickly nurse it back to vibrant health. This is one of the biggest mistakes a beginning hobbyist can make. We have purchased fish that we wanted to save from destruction, but were not novices at the time. We saved these fish with round-the-clock care, but a lot of experience is usually required to get the job done. (The ones we did save, however, quickly became our favorite pets.)

Playing Florence Nightingale for aquatic pets only works when you have the proper knowledge and equipment to pull it off. Diseased fish can cause water problems and infect your other fish as well. Don't buy any fish from tanks that the dealer is currently medicating, because diseases can spread to your other fish.

If you notice dead fish floating in a healthy-looking tank, avoid buying any of the livestock from that same aquarium. Do not purchase a fish with an unusually humped back (unless normal for the species) — as this generally indicates old age. A good dealer never allows a customer to purchase old, dying, or diseased fish, but instead tells you that certain fish are being medicated and are not for sale until the condition clears up.

Just because a fish has been medicated does not mean that it is completely well again. Let your eye be the best judge; carefully inspect any fish for signs of disease, such as torn or clamped fins, white spots or growths, or irregularly shaped bodies.

Start simply

If you are new to the hobby, never buy hard-to-maintain and feed species of fish such as piranhas, pacus, or oscars.. Fish that have special dietary requirements may be too much to handle in the beginning when you are still trying to get the hang of how your equipment works. Wait until you are completely familiar with your system before trying your luck with the harder-to-maintain species of tropical fish.

Go with what you know

Do not buy fish that are completely unfamiliar. Just because you are browsing the store and happen to a see a cool-looking fish doesn't mean you should take it home. Some species can be very difficult to feed and require strict water conditions to survive. Leave them in the hands of the pros to avoid heartache. Fish marked as "hardy" (guppies, platys, and swordfish, for example) are easier to keep for beginners. If you do want to try a more difficult to keep species, make sure you do your research (via Internet sites dedicated to particular species and talking to experienced hobbyists and pet store personnel who keep that type of fish) before buying so that you know exactly what that fish will require to flourish.

Look for signs of good health

You can look at several physical characteristics to determine whether your fish are in good health. There is never a guarantee of complete success, but if you follow these rules, you increase your chances of getting a healthy specimen. Look for the following:

- ✔ Body color is rich, not faded or dull. The color should be complete and not missing in any areas (unless it is typical for the species).
- ✔ There are no open sores, visible ulcers, boils, or obvious skin problems, such as peeling scales or blemishes.

✔ Fins are long and flowing, or short and erect. The fish should not have any ragged, torn, or missing fins.

✔ Scales are flat and smooth, not protruding away from the body.

✔ The stomach is well rounded, not sunken or concave.

✔ Girth of the entire body is of normal size, not bloated or emaciated.

✔ Visible excreta (fish waste) should be dark in color, not pale.

✔ All the fins on the fish's body should not be collapsed or completely clamped shut.

✔ Eyes are clear, not cloudy or popping out of the sockets.

✔ No visible parasites, such as ich or velvet.

Know your fish's behavior

A few behavioral characteristics (how the fish acts) are worth taking a look at. Healthy fish should

✔ Swim in a horizontal motion, not with its head up or down.

✔ Swim with complete ease, not continually fight to stay afloat.

✔ Swim throughout the aquarium, not lurk in the corners or hiding behind decorations.

✔ Breathe normally, not gulp for air or hang around the top of the tank with its mouth gasping the top of the water.

Getting the Right Fish

To be a successful hobbyist, you need to understand your purchases. What we mean by that is that you need to know which fish are best for you. By now, you know how to spot a healthy fish, but there's more to it than that. You also need to pick fish that are compatible and won't tear each other to bits and turn your aquarium into a war zone. Making a shopping list and understanding a fish's ultimate size are two ways that you can avoid disaster. Here are a couple good charts to get you started:

✔ www.liveaquaria.com/general/fwcompatibility_chart.cfm

✔ www.ratemyfishtank.com/freshwater_compatibility_tool.php

When you go to purchase your fish, take paper and pen with you and write down the names of all the fish that appeal to you. By writing down the names of the fish, you don't have to remember names (scientific names and even common names can be a little confusing at times) and can go back and find certain tanks quite easily. This can be a real advantage if the shop has several hundred display tanks. When you finish your list, locate your dealer and check to see whether all the species you chose are compatible with each other, don't have unique dietary needs, and don't have special aquarium requirements.

Keep an eye out for other compatibility issues. For example, if you buy a convict cichlid and a guppy, you will probably find the convict alone and well fed in the morning.

Quick reminders:

✔ Many shops have little stickers or labels to tell you which species are compatible and which are not. But not all fish stores offer the customer this courtesy.

✔ Leave difficult species in the expert hands of experienced hobbyists who know how to take care of them properly. Start simple so you won't be disappointed.

✔ A reputable dealer can answer all your questions about aquarium requirements and compatibility as well as offer pertinent suggestions of his own as to which species may be more successful for a beginner.

✔ Have an idea about what type of fish you want to keep before you go, so that you are not talked into getting something you don't want.

✔ Don't be afraid to order fish and supplies from Web sites if you can't find what you need locally. Good Web sites offer great deals, a great selection, and good service.

✔ Make sure you get and keep receipts for everything you purchase just in case you need to return equipment or you are sold sick fish.

How did this fish get so big so fast?

The problem with many of the fish you see in pet stores is that they may be still in their juvenile stage of growth and have not yet reached mature adulthood. For example, we were at the pet shop the other day and saw a 2-inch pacu. It was so cute! But this fish can grow to lengths of 10 inches or more, leaving smaller tankmates to end up as Sunday buffet.

If you have any doubts, consult your local dealer. Larger fish are great for some hobbyists, but they do tend to limit your aquarium space and your choices of other tankmates. Here is a list of *average* sizes for many fish in home aquariums:

Platy 1.25"

Tiger barb 1.0"

Black moor 3.0"

Swordtails 2.0"

Dwarf gourami 1.5"

Cory 1.0–2.0"

Pleco 2.0–12.0"

Red serape tetra .05–1.0"

Neon tetra .05"

Black molly 1.25"

Yellow rainbowfish 2.0"

Pacu 5.0–35.0"

Chapter 10

Diet and Nutrition for Your Wet Pets

*J*ust like their human counterparts, your aquatic pets need proper nutrition so that they can remain active and healthy and live long lives. A proper diet can be found by using most manufactured fish foods, but you can also increase your fish's good health by providing a variety of fresh vegetables and other products.

Basic Nutrition

Unfortunately, you can't feed your fish the cheeseburger, fries, and apple pie that keeps many kids happy, so you have to supply other types of food to meet their dietary needs. Fortunately, you can combine many good nutrition sources to form a proper diet for your fish. Aquarium food can be quite varied and includes brine shrimp, dry flake, fresh shrimp, algae, daphnia, pellets, algae wafers, tubifex worms, and beef heart — to name just a few choices. These foods are all good sources of nutrition, but only if they are distributed in proper amounts. Tossing an entire beef heart into the tank for your guppy's breakfast doesn't cut it.

When purchasing any type of aquarium food, the most important rule is to select the finest quality your finances can handle. Aquarium foods are not really that expensive when you look at the total amount of food you get for the price, so why not purchase the best? Top-quality commercial foods are enriched with vitamins and minerals and help keep your fish in optimal health. Low-grade food promotes poor health and disease.

Feeding your fish can be a really relaxing activity and also provides an excellent opportunity for you to check them for any signs of illness. What's more entertaining than observing a bunch of animals pigging out? Watching your aquatic pets interact socially (pushing each other out of the way, stealing food from each other, hoarding the choicest items, turning their noses up at others) can be very educational. If you're like us, you probably see the same thing at your own dinner table. At least you don't have to cook for your fish.

What your fish need

What you feed your fish should contain the following components:

- **Carbohydrates:** These provide energy for your fish and also help them resist disease.

- **Proteins:** These help your fish build strong muscle and tissue. Fish obtain proteins through a diet that includes meat, fish, insects, and manufactured foods. Proteins are an important factor in promoting physical growth, so it is important to remember that younger fish need a little more than full-grown adults.

- **Vitamins:** These are vital to your fish's good health. A balanced diet that combines live and processed foods easily supplies the necessary vitamins. A balanced diet includes vitamin A (egg, greens, crustaceans), vitamin B (fish, greens, algae, and beef), vitamin C (algae), vitamin D (worms, algae, shrimp), vitamin E (egg, algae), vitamin H (egg, liver), and vitamin K (liver, greens).

Experienced hobbyists realize that feeding their aquatic pets can be an art in itself (especially if you own an overgrown piranha). With so many different natural and prepared foods to choose from, not only in fish shops but on the Internet as well, beginning hobbyists can easily get confused about nutritional issues. Just remember that no one product can satisfy every fish in your aquarium. Variety is always good. But as this chapter shows you, learning to feed your fish properly is not as hard as it first seems. A little experience and practice can make all the difference in the world.

Overfeeding

You want to make sure that your tropical fish receive all the nutrition they need. However, it is easy to make mistakes until you get the hang of a new feeding routine. Many new hobbyists tend to overfeed their fish. Overfeeding can lead to obesity and other health problems. If your fish resemble overinflated tires, cut back on the grub. Too much food in an aquarium tank can also build up and foul the water or increase the risk of disease.

Excess food around the edge of the substrate is one sign of overfeeding. This wasted food accumulates on the bottom of the tank, turns muddy brown, and begins to spoil. Spoiled food can cause health problems for your fish if they happen to eat it. If excess food piles up, decrease the amount you feed and try putting the food in a different area of the aquarium.

Remember that your fish's stomach is no larger than its eye. So, if you dump a half a can of fish food into the tank, you had better hope your fish has an eye the size of a dinner plate; otherwise, you're in for a few problems. Excess food breaking down on the substrate surface can cause an overabundance of harmful ammonia. If you do happen to overfeed, remove the excess with a standard aquarium vacuum.

Underfeeding

Because so much emphasis is placed on overfeeding and its polluting effects, many hobbyists don't feed their fish enough. Well, the point is, don't over-feed or underfeed. Feed the correct amount.

Just-right feeding

The general rule is to feed only what your fish can eat in a period of three to five minutes per feeding. Now, this does not mean that you have to stand around with a starter's whistle and stopwatch at every meal. Just check to make sure that your fish polish off all the food within five minutes. Another option is to purchase a plastic feeding ring that keeps most dry foods confined to a small area on top of the water. A feeding ring can keep most of the food from quickly falling to the bottom of the tank.

If at all possible, feed adult fish three small meals per day instead of just dumping a bunch of food in at one time. Juvenile fish and fry need be fed more often to insure that they grow properly, so give them a couple of extra light feedings each day.

It's best to feed your fish at different times of the day, usually morning, afternoon, and night. Because many nocturnal fish feed only at night, make sure they receive their fair share.

It's not a bad idea to make your fish fast one day a week. Going 24 hours without food keeps a fish's dietary tract in good physical condition.

Vacations and automatic feeders

When you go on vacation, try to find a trustworthy person to feed your fish while you're away. A relative or mature neighborhood kid is usually a good choice. To make sure that they feed your fish properly, place individual servings in plastic bags so that your substitute knows exactly what to put into each tank. This may sound like a hassle, but it's better than returning home to find your prize goldfish, the size of a basketball, beached on a mountain of uneaten food.

Another option is to purchase an automatic feeder from your local fish shop. These units automatically dispense a certain amount of food (you can choose the amount) at daily intervals that you preset. Models can be purchased that hang on the aquarium rim, whereas others are free standing. Dispensers run on either batteries or AC power, and some models offer both options. Automatic feeders are a great way to feed your aquatic pets the proper amount of food regularly.

Never add a bunch of extra food to the tank before going on vacation. Your fish won't eat the extra food before it starts rotting, and by the time you get home you may have a serious water problem.

What Type of Eater Do You Have?

One reason many aquarium species face starvation and poor health is because hobbyists who are unfamiliar with a particular species fail to provide the proper nutrition for individual needs. If you take the time to do a little research into a fish's natural habitat and feeding patterns, you gain a better understanding of their individual dietary requirements.

For example, danios need to be fed often because they have high metabolism rates. Their high activity level burns off food quickly. If you have a very clean system, there may not be adequate amounts of natural foods, such as algae, to provide the fish with something to tide them over until their next scheduled feeding. Give danios an extra feeding every day. Here are a few examples of how some species eat (remember, this may vary slightly depending on the age and temperament of your fish):

- **Heavy eaters:** tiger barb, swordtail, oscar, convict cichlid
- **Medium eaters:** guppy, gouramis, angelfish, cory
- **Light eaters:** balloon mollies, bubble eye goldfish, betta, pencilfish

Never feed your fish cat food, dog food, or other types of animal feeds. Non-fish manufactured pet food is difficult for your fish to digest properly, and it doesn't provide the essential amino acids and nutrients they really need.

Just like people, fish can be good eaters or bad eaters. The following hints will help persuade those fish that don't want to jump on the scheduled feeding bandwagon.

When they stop eating

There are times when your fish simply stop eating. After you panic, stop and ask yourself this question: What caused this sudden lack of appetite? Here are some possible answers:

- ✔ **Incorrect food:** When your fish stop eating, the first thing to do is to make sure that you're giving them the correct food for their species. For example, large goldfish need pellet foods that float. If you are only feeding them algae discs, they will not thrive. On the other hand, bottom-feeding catfish would appreciate the same disc. Top feeders like danios do best on floating and flake foods. If you're feeding them the wrong thing, switch to the proper food immediately. If the problem persists, read on for other causes.

- ✔ **Crowded conditions:** Overcrowding causes stress and encourages excessive competition for food. Normal eaters may become shy or frightened and not get their share of the food.

- ✔ **Disease:** Fish stop eating regularly as they start to drop off physically.

- ✔ **Poor water conditions:** Polluted water and other bad aquarium conditions can have a major effect on your fish's normal feeding habits. Also check the temperature and pH and nitrate levels (see Chapter 14 for more information on this subject) if your fish suddenly stop feeding.

- ✔ **Temperature or weather changes:** Hotter weather may mean a decrease in oxygen in the aquarium's water. If this is a problem, add an extra air-stone (to split the air into smaller bubbles) or install a power head (which you can purchase at your local pet shop) on your undergravel filter. You will find more information on aquarium equipment in Chapter 6.

So remember, the fact that your fish are not eating may not be caused by improper feeding conditions. You need to take other factors into consideration as well.

Some fish refuse to eat just because they're picky. There may be no other reason than that. Try different types of food until you find one they are happy with.

Carnivores

Feed *carnivores* (meat eaters, such as piranha) small amounts of meat and insects to help balance their flake or pellet diet. Carnivores need a good filtration system because they excrete a high amount of waste generated by the meaty foods.

Vegetarians

Many freshwater fish need vegetable matter in their diet to flourish and achieve proper growth. For example, most species of freshwater catfish and cichlids enjoy vegetables. You can purchase vegetable fish food at your local aquarium shop. Specific types of vegetable foods such as algae wafers are manufactured to meet the needs of these types of fish.

If you feel creative, you can try preparing a vegetable supplement at home. You can boil lettuce and spinach leaves until they are soft and then put them on a special feeding clip (available at your local fish store), which holds them at the top of the tank. This clip is similar in design to a clothespin but wider. Chopped up small pieces of potato, fresh peas, and zucchini are also a welcome treat for almost any type of fish if they are slightly cooked to soften them.

If you give your fish fresh vegetables in this manner, make sure you remove all the uneaten food at the end of each day. Fresh vegetables decay and foul the water when left in the tank too long.

Fish that eat anything that falls into the tank

There are sociable (and gluttonous) fish that continually try to mooch food by imitating a starving animal. (Nothing new there, our teenagers have that routine down to a science.) These fish also try to eat anything that falls into the tank, including pet food, sandwiches, toys, and your hand. Overfeeding these fish can quickly become a problem, because they snag most of the food before the other fish even realize that it's chow time.

If you have a tank hog grabbing all the food, try feeding less food more frequently, and spread the food to different parts of the tank.

Types of Food

You have many types of foods to choose from in an aquarium shop. Most fish eat just about anything. Most fish can survive on any type of aquarium food, but that *doesn't* mean they will live up to their full potential if they are fed improperly. By combining different types of food, you can give your fish a head start on good health.

In the artificial environment of an aquarium, *you* need to provide the proteins, fats, vitamins, and carbohydrates that are a part of fish's natural diet. If you don't, your fish won't reach their full growth potential. Lack of proper nutrition also makes them more susceptible to disease. Most foods supply the essentials, but combining different products (such as flakes, cooked veggies, and fresh strips of fish) can ensure your success.

Comparing prepackaged and frozen foods

Fish food manufacturers offer a wide variety of well-balanced foods that are easy to use and store.

Prepackaged dry foods generally contain most of the nutrients your fish need to survive. You can purchase dry food in many forms, including flakes that float on top of the water, disks that sink to the substrate for bottom-feeders, and large pellets for koi and other types of pond fish. There are large-grained foods for big fish, and small foods for tiny fish. You can drop tablet foods to the bottom of the tank or stick them to the aquarium glass (using the afore-mentioned food clip) at different levels to help ensure that the fish at all the different feeding levels get their fair share. Pretty neat, huh?

Flake foods are a good staple that can satisfy most of your fish. Your can purchase flakes to meet the need of your particular species. For example, some cichlid flakes contain high amounts of fat and protein for quick growth; goldfish flakes often contain garlic, which inhibits parasites, and the extra vegetables that are a natural part of the goldfish diet. Flakes generally float on or near the water surface and sink as they become saturated.

The moisture level in manufactured flakes should be less than 4 percent of the total product, because many nutrients dissipate quickly in aquarium water.

Floating pellets are made for surface feeders; bottom feeders, such as pond fish, can gobble up sinking pellets. Granular foods sink quickly and are generally used to feed bottom-dwelling species.

Frozen foods are usually mixes of live food, such as brine shrimp, silversides, bloodworms, daphnia, meat, or vegetables. You can purchase this type of food in a variety of forms, such as sheets and cubes.

Little frozen cubes are a great way to keep an accurate account of exactly how much you are feeding at every meal. You must keep frozen foods from thawing before you need them because once they melt, they cannot be refrozen without a major loss of nutrients. Also, melted brine makes your house smell like a shrimp boat. Before feeding, take the frozen food and thaw it in a small cup of dechlorinated water (tap water with dechlorinator added) or bottled water. Dispersing the food in water allows the food to move throughout the entire tank so that aggressive feeders don't get a chance to eat it all before the rest of their tankmates get any.

Freeze-dried foods

Freeze-dried foods contain preserved small crustaceans, shrimp, larvae, and worms. This is one type of food that fish seem to love or hate, so just keep a little bit around for a treat or emergencies.

Spirulina

Spirulina is a natural micro-algae that is rich in proteins, helps enhance color, and promote a healthy mucus layer on your fish's skin. Adding spirulina to all your fish's diets gives them healthier fins and increases their resistance to skin infections. You can usually purchase spirulina in both flake and frozen form. Spirulina has a soft cell wall and can be digested quite easily. It contains fatty acids that are important in proper development of the body's organs, and is also rich in A and B vitamins, iron, and calcium.

Research shows that most of a fish's color comes from the food it eats. Spirulina contains a high percentage of carotenoid pigments that give your fish outstanding color.

If you want the best of both worlds, you can purchase spirulina-enriched brine shrimp. These are shrimp that have been fed on dry spirulina powder.

Live food — the stuff they really love and want

Very few aquarium shops carry live food, making it very difficult to find. Your best bet for locating live food and the supplies to culture them is on the Internet. Live food includes:

- ✔ Fortified brine shrimp
- ✔ Bloodworms
- ✔ Silversides
- ✔ Feeder guppies
- ✔ Feeder goldfish

To get you started, here are a few places on the Net that sell live fish foods:

- ✔ www.wormman.com/cat_fish.cfm
- ✔ http://aquaticfoods.com/Feedergoldfish.html
- ✔ www.livefoodcultures.com/babybrineshrimp.html

Feeder guppies and goldfish are usually to feed large carnivores such as pacu and Jack Dempseys.

Some people balk at feeding their aquatic pets live fish, and you should do what feels right for you. It may help to remember that live feeding just means going along with the natural pecking order in nature's food chain. Feeder guppies and goldfish are raised in large hatcheries specifically for food purposes — if no one bought them, they wouldn't have existed at all.

Certain live foods should not be introduced into your aquarium because they may attack smaller fishes or fry. These predators include leeches, hydras, beetles, and dragonfly larvae.

Brine shrimp

Brine shrimp (*Artemia franciscana*) are tiny saltwater crustaceans that are appreciated by most fish (see Figure 10-1). Brine shrimp are available frozen, though a few pet shops carry live brine.

If you want to raise your own live food, you can buy a kit at your local pet store and hatch brine shrimp from dried eggs. These shrimp are usually fed to marine fish, but freshwater fish appreciate them as a treat.

Figure 10-1:
Brine shrimp look different and are smaller than the kind you get in restaurants.

The only problem with hatching your own brine shrimp is the awful smell. Try raising them in a garage or basement — otherwise, your family and neighbors may move away without leaving a forwarding address.

One other important point about brine shrimp: Even though your aquatic pets are in a captive environment, they still enjoy hunting live food. Survival is an important instinct that cannot be removed by the presence of four glass walls or by birth in a hatchery. Providing live foods keeps your fish more healthy and active, too. Think about it: If you had to chase down your own pig to snag a few pork chops for Saturday's barbecue, you'd probably work up a little bit of an appetite.

But along with the good comes the bad, as the old saying goes. Live foods have a higher risk of transmitting disease into the tank than manufactured products do. Live brine shrimp at your local fish shop are pretty safe; however, if you go out to a river or pond to collect live food, you run the risk of introducing disease.

Infusoria

Infusoria (paramecium and amoeba) are small animal protozoans that make an excellent food for small, newborn fry. Infusoria are very tiny and form a cloud when added to your aquarium water. Infusoria can be cultured at home by soaking vegetable matter (such as a piece of lettuce) in a clear jar of water placed in direct sunlight for at least a week. Check for infusoria when it becomes cloudy by shining flashlight into the jar. The infusoria will appear as small dust-like particles.

Rotifers

Rotifers are small invertebrates raised on farms. You can find the addresses of these farms in most aquarium magazines, or try the Web sites mentioned earlier in this chapter.

Tubifex, bloodworms, mosquito larvae, and earthworms (yuck!)

We know these worms sound gross, but your fish will love them! You can purchase freeze-dried tubifex and bloodworms in cubes or shredded form to use as a treat periodically. They can cause digestive problems, so don't feed them to your fish regularly. Mosquito larvae provide good health and coloring for show fish, but can be difficult to find. Fish readily accept earthworms, but clean the worms thoroughly with water and chop them up before serving.

Feeding Fry

Young *fry* (baby fish) require a different type of diet than adults because their digestion systems have not yet matured. The good news is that you can feed many fry special foods available at your local fish shop. The bad news is that young fry need to be fed constantly, so swing by the pharmacy on the way home and grab some drops for your sleep-deprived eyes.

Microworms

Microworms (*Anguillula silusiae*) are non-parasitic worms that float freely in water. These worms reproduce in a matter of days.

You can easily culture microworms at home, and they make a good starter food for young fry because of their tiny size. All you need to do is mix a little oatmeal, yeast, and water in a bowl until it forms a paste. Add a small amount of microworms to the paste from an existing culture (which you can purchase on the Internet) and allow it to stand at room temperature for a couple of days. When worms appear on the sides of the bowl, transfer them to the fry tank.

Liquid, powdered, and growth foods

You can purchase manufactured liquid fry food that comes in a tube that resembles toothpaste. Use this product sparingly because it can foul the water.

Powdered food is used to feed newborn fish. The powder is too small to be used as feed for adult fish, and will end up fouling your tank if not used for baby fry.

Fish food manufacturers make a wide variety of foods to match the growth stages of your young fish. Hikari makes a wonderful line of baby fish foods which are made to fit the growth stages of fish.

Read the labels carefully to choose the correct product for the age of your developing fry if purchasing from a pet store.

Chapter 11

Diseases and Treatments

- -

In This Chapter

▶ Learning about stress

▶ Spotting problems ahead of time

▶ Treating common diseases

▶ Preventing disease

▶ Using quarantine and hospital tanks

- -

*I*f you want your fish to live long and healthy lives, then you need to make sure that they remain as disease free as possible. Many factors, including stress, bacteria, fungus, parasites, chemicals, and poor water conditions, can cause disease. By monitoring your water conditions daily and checking your fish for signs of disease, you can stay ahead of the game and keep your aquatic pets in prime condition.

An Ounce of Prevention . . .

. . . is worth a pound of cure, right? Preventing disease is generally the best way to battle physical problems. Sounds simple doesn't it? It is. You can provide optimal living conditions for your tropical fish simply by following a few simple maintenance routines.

Keeping abreast of the water and equipment conditions in your aquarium, which takes only a few moments a day, gives you a safety margin to quickly correct any problems that show up. The schedule suggested here gives you a few pointers on watching for signs of disease and other problems such as equipment malfunction.

Daily measures

Maintaining the following daily routine is not as difficult as it sounds. It takes only a few minutes a day, and after a week or so, it will become second nature — just like grabbing a midnight snack while your spouse is asleep.

Check the equipment

It is very important to make sure that all mechanical equipment is functioning properly each and every day. Are the filter systems putting out the optimal flow that the manufacturer suggests? Is the water flowing smoothly, or is it running too slow? If the water seems to have slowed down to the point where it resembles a still life painting, check to see whether the filter and tubes are clogged and make sure that the motor is not wearing down (water flow is slow or the filter is making noise).

Many filter motors can be rebuilt with parts supplied by the manufacturing company that produced the product. If the filter pads are clogged or extremely dirty, replace them or rinse them gently under water until they're clean. The only real disadvantage to replacing or washing filters is losing the biological bacteria that lives on the pads.

Are the air pumps in your aquarium in prime working condition? Carefully inspect them to make sure that they are running properly and not overheating. If the pumps are not putting out enough air to run the extra equipment and decorations efficiently (you'll know when the little plastic diver turns blue and keels over), you can usually rebuild them by replacing worn diaphragms with parts you special order at your local fish shop. If your local dealer cannot find the parts for you, take a couple of aspirin, then call the manufacturer or check out its Web site to find the parts you need. If the pump is very old and no parts are available, it's probably time to purchase a new one.

Check the water temperature

Monitoring water temperature is another important part of your daily routine. Any fluctuation in temperature more than two degrees from the norm can quickly lead to serious health problems. If the temperature is not within correct range (your fish are either floating around in the center of an ice cube or have melted into a blob), check to make sure that your heater is not stuck in the on or off position.

Always measure the water temperature at the same time each day to get the most accurate readings. Replace any faulty heaters immediately and install a heater that contains an internal regulator if your finances allow. An internal regulator lets the heater turn itself on and off automatically to maintain a set temperature.

One common cause of overheated aquarium water is excess natural or artificial lighting. Check the amount of natural sunlight the tank receives every day. If too much natural light is causing the temperature to rise during peak sunlight hours, then you need to move the tank, block out the light with a thicker or darker background, or cover the windows with heavy drapes or shades.

The duration and intensity of artificial lighting can be a problem as well. If a light is constantly overheating your tank, switch to a lower wattage bulb or leave the light off longer. Otherwise, your pets may end up looking like floating fish sticks.

Check the fish

After you get up in the morning and choke down a few dozen cups of coffee, make a quick inventory of all the fish in your aquarium. If any fish are dead, remove them from the tank and take them to the bathroom for the final flush.

Rotting fish can cause serious biological problems and upset the tank's balance.

If any fish seem to be sick or diseased, immediately transfer them to your hospital tank (we explain setting up a hospital tank at the end of this chapter) and begin treatment. If you check the health of your fish daily, you can take care of problems before they get out of control.

Check the overall health of your fish very carefully. Take a close look at their physical condition. Are they swimming normally, or consistently lurking in the corners of the tank? Are their eyes bright and alert, or clouded over? Are their fins erect, or clamped shut and drooping? Do they have a straight spine, or do they look like Quasimodo? Do their bodies have normal, well-rounded proportions, or are their stomachs swollen or sunken? If you can visually identify physical problems, you need to check the aquarium's water and equipment.

Weekly measures

Weekly routines are just like daily maintenance. Choose one day per week to carry out the following tasks.

Check the water

Change at least 15 percent of the water in your aquariums every week. Many large new filter systems and chemicals claim that you never need to change any water ever again if you purchase and use that product. Nevertheless, water changes are a good way to keep the water stable.

Cure-all equipment and medications pose a real danger to your fish. When you stray down untried paths instead of using the standard, proven road that you know leads you where you want to be, you run a serious risk of losing your fish.

The water in a fish's natural environment is constantly replaced by seasonal rains, tidal flow, and run-off. But in aquariums, the same water remains in the tank between water changes. Take a moment and pretend that the water in your aquarium is your only drinking supply for the entire day. Would you be comfortable drinking it? Remember, your aquatic pets have to live in it 24 hours a day.

Carefully check your pH and nitrate levels with a test kit each week to make sure that they remain within the range required by your species of fish. If they are not correct, you can slowly change your pH by water changes or chemicals if your tap pH does not match your species (pH should be kept within 2.0 of the required pH).

If chemical tests indicate that your nitrate levels are too high, the best way to fix the problem is to change 20 percent of the water daily until the nitrate levels return to normal. Don't forget to check your aquarium conditions, so that you can identify and correct whatever is causing your nitrate levels to soar higher than the national debt. A few causes of high nitrates include poor filtration, overcrowding, lack of water changes, and chronic overfeeding.

While you are doing your weekly maintenance routine, take time to siphon off any accumulated debris on the substrate's surface area by using a simple gravel cleaner or aquarium vacuum (see Chapter 6). Remove any dead vegetation such as decaying plant leaves from the tank. This type of living debris can quickly cause a large fluctuation in the water's nitrate levels. If you need to use searchlights to locate the gravel in your tank, then the water needs to be cleaned.

Make the fish fast

Ideally, your aquatic pets should *fast* (that is, not be given any food for 24 hours) at least one day per week. We know this may seem difficult and harsh at first, but avoid the temptation to give them treats such as cinnamon rolls and donuts because you feel sorry for them. Fasting often happens in the wild and it helps clean out your fish's digestive systems and guards against constipation problems. Remember to fast your fish on the same day each week, so they don't go too long between feedings.

Give medications

Take a close look at all the medications you use for common illnesses such as ich and fungus and make sure you have all the standard treatments (see later in this chapter for more). Is there enough dechlorinator (which removes chlorine from your tap water) in your home to make daily water changes if they become necessary? Have you sterilized your hospital tank since its last use? Is it ready? Being prepared can make all the difference between saving your wet pets and losing them.

Monthly measures

Monthly chores are much easier to remember if you mark them down on a calendar. Or you can simply tack a reminder note up on the fridge.

Replace all filter mediums that contain carbon. Carbon loses its effectiveness after a period of time. If your filter isn't carbon-based, gently rinse it under water to remove debris. Don't use hot water for this task, as excessive heat can destroy the entire beneficial bacteria colony living on the filter.

Clean all algae from the glass so that your fish won't think they've gone blind.

Common Ailments and Cures

The list of common tropical fish illnesses in this section gives you general guidelines for identifying and treating various diseases (Figure 11-1). Keep in mind that several common medications and salt treatments may be detrimental to live plants, some species of catfish, and other delicate or sensitive tropical fish. It is always best to treat sick fish in a hospital tank, away from the main population.

How stress leads to disease

In your home aquarium, your fish live in an enclosed ecosystem that is very different from and slightly imbalanced compared to the natural stability of their native environment. The majority of health problems tropical fish experience are the direct result of stress, which is often caused by being moved around and by poor environmental conditions when they are placed in a home aquarium.

Your fish are capable of carrying all types of diseases that generally are not a threat to their everyday health. These diseases usually remain dormant until your aquatic pets are weakened by fluctuating environmental factors such as unstable temperature and pH, dirty water, and poor diet. When environmental stability problems occur, your fish's latent disease can manifest quickly and cause health problems. Sick fish can be a real bummer, but this chapter helps you overcome most fishy health problems.

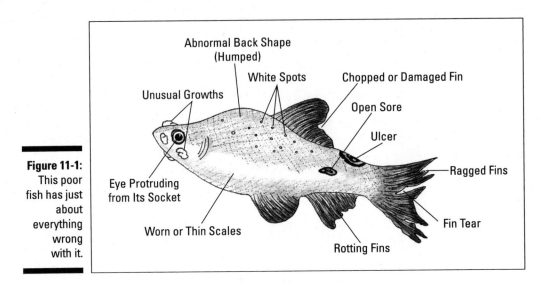

Figure 11-1:
This poor
fish has just
about
everything
wrong
with it.

Abnormal Back Shape
(Humped)

White Spots

Chopped or Damaged Fin

Unusual Growths

Open Sore

Ulcer

Eye Protruding
from Its Socket

Ragged Fins

Worn or Thin Scales

Fin Tear

Rotting Fins

Common bacteria infection

Symptoms: Blood spots; open sores; ulcers; frayed fins.

Cause: *Aeromonas.*

Treatment: Antibiotics.

Constipation

Symptoms: Reduced appetite; little or no feces; swollen stomach; inactivity.
(If your fish haven't left the gravel for over a month, they may be constipated.)

Cause: Incorrect nutrition; overfeeding.

Treatment: Add 1 teaspoon of magnesium sulfate for every 2 gallons of water.
Fast your constipated fish for several days. Improve your fish's diet by feeding live foods frequently.

Dropsy

Symptoms: Swollen body; protruding scales; fish looks like a pincushion.

Cause: Organ failure from cancer and old age, or poor water conditions.

Treatment: Antibacterial given through medicated food. Improvement of water quality through water changes also provides a little relief to afflicted fish. Complete recovery from dropsy is rare.

Fin rot

Symptoms: Reddened or inflamed rays; torn, choppy, ragged, or disintegrated fins. Your fish may look like it just swam through an electrical fan.

Cause: Fin rot is a highly contagious bacterial infection that, in its advanced stages, can completely erode the fins and tail all the way down to the body. Bad water quality and fin injuries are usually the main causes of this disease. Fin rot is frequently followed up with a secondary fungal infection.

Treatment: Spot treat infected areas with gentian violet and use *proprietary medication* (a treatment that is labled for one particular disease, such as fungus cure, ich cure, and so on). Add 1 tablespoon of aquarium or marine salt for each 5 gallons of water. Remove activated carbon from all filters during the medication period. Frequent water changes are necessary to help improve water conditions.

Fish louse

Symptoms: Disk-shaped parasites attach to the skin. Ulcers often develop close to the area of parasitic attachment. Bacteria or fungus problems may follow after.

Cause: Crustacean parasite. After feeding on the skin, the adult parasite leaves its host and lays gelatinlike capsules full of eggs on the substrate and aquarium decorations. Often the eggs don't hatch until the aquarium temperature rises, and may stay in the tank for extended periods of time.

Treatment: Remove all parasites from the afflicted fish using a small pair of tweezers. Dab any wounds using a cotton swab dipped in commercial

Mercurochrome. Remove water from the main tank and sterilize all decorations and substrate. In other words, start over.

Freshwater velvet

Symptoms: A golden-velvet or grayish-white coating on the body or fins. If your fish has velvet, it looks like it has been sprinkled with gold dust. This disease is very common among certain species such as bettas.

Cause: *Piscinoodinium* parasite. The adult parasites attach themselves to the skin of tropical fish and then fall off after seven days or so. These parasites immediately drop into the substrate and begin to multiply. The new parasites are then released into the water and move around until they re-infect the fish in your aquarium. If the parasites cannot find a living host within a period of two to three days, they die.

Treatment: Proprietary malachite green remedy. Add 1 tablespoon of aquarium salt for each 5 gallons of water.

Freshwater ich

Symptoms: The sudden appearance of small white spots, which look like little grains of table salt, on the body and fins. Fish infected with this disease continually scratch themselves on gravel and decorations during the advanced stages. (If your fish look like they are making love to the rocks in the tank, they probably have ich.)

Cause: *Ichthyopthirius* parasite. Adult parasites fall off of the host and multiply in the substrate. Soon after, new parasites search for another living host.

Treatment: Proprietary ich remedy (formalin or malachite green). Even if you remove the infected fish to a quarantine tank, you must still treat the aquarium water in the main tank with medication to kill off any remaining free-swimming parasites.

Fungus

Symptoms: White growths on the body or fins that are fluffy in appearance and make your fish look like a cotton puff or marshmallow.

Cause: Fungus often attacks regions where the mucus or slime coating on the fish has worn off due to damage by injury or parasites. Once the slime coat is damaged, the fish is more susceptible to all types of other disease.

Treatment: Spot treat with gentian violet, methylene blue, or use aquarium fungicide in extreme cases.

Gill parasites

Symptoms: Redness in the gill areas; labored respiration; scratching; excessive mucus coat; glazed eyes; inflamed gills; loss of motor control (your fish resemble slam dancers).

Cause: Flukes (*Dactylogyrus*).

Treatment: Sterazin or other proprietary treatment. Formalin baths can be effective as well.

Hole in the head

Symptoms: Pus-filled holes on the head, near the lateral line or the base of the tail. This disease is most common among cichlids.

Cause: *Hexamita* parasite.

Treatment: Flagyl. Recent findings show that Vitamin A and C supplements are effective in treating this disease (aquatic vitamins, not Flintstones Chewables).

Intestinal parasites

Symptoms: Worms sticking out through the vent; emaciation of the body.

Cause: Several different varieties of intestinal worms.

Treatment: Standard fungus cure or in advanced cases, veterinarian-prescribed anthelminthic added to the daily diet. Add 1 tablespoon of aquarium salt for each 5 gallons of water to help your fish with normal body fluid functions. Remove any activated carbon during treatment. Change 15 percent of the water daily to keep environmental conditions optimal.

Large skin parasites

Symptoms: Scratching; visible parasites.

Cause: Fish lice (*argulus*) and anchorworms (*Lernaea*).

Treatment: Remove large parasites with tweezers. Apply an antiseptic solution to the injured site.

Mouth fungus

Symptoms: White cottonlike growths around the mouth area (your fish looks like Santa Claus having a bad hair day) or patchy white skin in the same region. In advanced stages, the jawbones begin to deteriorate badly.

Cause: Usually *flexibacter,* which follows after other infections have begun.

Treatment: Proprietary fungus treatment or methylene blue in the early stages. If this treatment is not effective and the fungus is out of control, consult your veterinarian about antibiotics immediately.

Pop-eye

Symptoms: Eyes inflamed and protruding from their sockets to the point where they almost "pop" out of the head. Often the fish's eyes develop a cloudy, whitish haze. Inflamed eye sockets are also common with this disease.

Cause: Parasites or poor water conditions.

Treatment: There are no known commercially packaged medications to treat or cure this disease. The only thing you can do to help is to improve the aquarium's water conditions with frequent changes. It may also be beneficial to add 1 tablespoon of aquarium salt per 5 gallons of water to help with osmoregulation (the control of the levels of water and mineral salts in the blood).

Check and adjust all water conditions (pH, ammonia, nitrites, and nitrates) with test kits to make sure that they remain within proper ranges.

Septicemia

Symptoms: Redness at the base of the fins followed by blood streaks that appear on the fins and body. Other symptoms include hemorrhage, loss of appetite, and listlessness. This disease usually follows fin rot or skin infections. Septicemia often results in major heart damage and blood vessel problems. These complications can in turn lead to fluid leakage in the abdomen, which in some cases causes dropsy.

Cause: *Pseudomonas* or *streptococcus* bacteria inflames body tissues made susceptible by a skin infection.

Treatment: Antibacterial Furan2 or Triple Sulfa. Change the water every 24 to 36 hours.

Skin flukes

Symptoms: Inflamed skin; excessive mucus coating (your fish looks like it was baptized in Vaseline); scratching.

Cause: *Gyrodactylus.*

Treatment: Proprietary medication with labeling recommending for skin flukes.

Slimy skin disease

Symptoms: Gray-colored slime on the body or fins; scratching; frayed fins; excessive mucus coat; shimmying like a politician during questioning.

Cause: *Costia, trichodina, cyclochaeta,* or *chilodonella* parasites.

Treatment: Proprietary remedy of malachite green and frequent water changes. Short-term (five-minute) formalin and salt baths can be effective. Check and correct any poor water conditions.

Swim bladder disease

Symptoms: Abnormal or irregular swimming patterns (your fish do the doggie paddle upside down) and complete loss of physical balance.

Cause: Bacterial infection; physical injury to the swim bladder from fighting; breeding: netting; transportation from the dealer; poor water quality.

Treatment: Treat with an antibiotic in a clean, shallow tank. (The water should be about 2 inches higher than the dorsal fin on the fish.) Carry out water changes as frequently as once a day if possible.

Tuberculosis (TB)

Symptoms: Fin deterioration; a paling of body color; clamped fins (fins are closed up or folded together); excessive weight loss; ulcers; and pop-eye.

Cause: A highly contagious bacterial disease caused by poor filtration or overcrowding in the aquarium.

Many medical personnel believe that this disease can be transferred to humans through contact with the infected areas on the fish.

Treatment: At this time, there is no known effective treatment of tuberculosis, and in our opinion it is not worth risking your own health, or the health of your family, to try treating infected fish. Use strict care when handling these infected fish! Use plastic gloves when removing any fish infected with tuberculosis. Any tropical fish that has this disease should be euthanized immediately. Do not leave the TB-infected fish in the main aquarium because other tankmates will probably eat it and may develop the disease shortly thereafter.

Frequent Causes of Disease

There are many causes of disease that are not related to parasites and infection, such as carbon dioxide poisoning, poor water quality, metal poisoning, chemical poison, improper diet, overfeeding, and fright. These important physical and social conditions should be monitored frequently.

Carbon dioxide poisoning

Symptoms: Listlessness; increased or rapid respiration — your fish may hang near the top of the water.

Cause: Lack of oxygen; too much carbon dioxide in the water.

Treatment: Add more aeration to improve gas exchange at the water surface; cut down on plant fertilization; check and correct any poor water conditions; and carry out frequent water changes.

Poor water quality

Symptoms: The first sign is that your tropical fish are gasping for air at the water surface of the tank and are generally inactive. Clamped or closed fins, overall bad health, and poor coloration are a few more symptoms of incorrect water quality.

Cause: Poor water quality due to infrequent water changes, poor filtration, and overuse of standard chemicals.

Treatment: Make daily water changes until any high ammonia, nitrite, or nitrate levels return to lower readings. Make sure the aquarium has enough aeration and add an extra airstone or bubble disk if necessary. Make sure the pH of the water is within the proper range (a couple degrees of what is normal for the species).

Metal poisoning

Symptoms: Erratic behavior; paleness.

Cause: Metal objects coming into contact with the aquarium water.

Treatment: A complete water change. To avoid accidentally poisoning your tropical fish, never allow any metal to come in contact with the aquarium water. Metal hoods and metal equipment clips are two common sources of poisoning. To keep this equipment from poisoning your fish, use plastic clips and make sure that the glass cover on your aquarium fits properly so that no water comes into direct contact with the hood and light fixture.

Chemical poisoning

Symptoms: Erratic behavior; gasping for air; fish lying on their sides; paleness; clamped fins; refusal to eat.

Cause: Other common sources of water poisoning in aquariums are cleaning, cosmetic, and insect-control products. Never use insecticides, hair sprays, or mist cleaners near your aquarium. Small drops of these airborne products can easily fall through the small equipment holes in the top of your tank and poison your fish. If you have to use one of these products near your aquarium, tightly cover your tank ahead of time with plastic sheets or large towels to protect your fish.

Treatment: Complete water and filter change.

Improper diet

Symptoms: General poor health; paleness of color; inactivity.

Cause: You. Poor nutrition.

Treatment: An unbalanced diet doesn't contain all the vitamins and minerals important to your fish's health. Begin feeding a wide variety of commercially packaged flakes, small servings of fresh lettuce, peas, and other green vegetables, and live foods (see Chapter 10 for more information on what foods are good for which species).

Overfeeding

Symptoms: Lethargic fish; excessive weight gain; and constipation.

Cause: Overfeeding your tropical fish on a regular basis.

Treatment: Fast your fish for two days. Improve poor or fouled water conditions caused by uneaten, rotting food before it leads to more disease problems. If your fish are beginning to resemble the Goodyear blimp and are bobbing up and down in the water like corks, start measuring each serving of food so that you don't feed them too much at one time (see Chapter 10 for more).

Frightened fish

Symptoms: Your fish dash for cover when the aquarium lights are first turned on; constant physical injures from collisions with decorations.

Cause: Sudden changes in lighting, quick human movements, people rapping on the glass, and pets trying to get into the tank.

Treatment: Gradually increase room lighting by opening drapes and turning on lamps before you switch on the aquarium lights.

Home Remedy: Salt Bath

Here's a good home remedy that you can try to avoid giving your fish large doses of medications. This method works really well and can save you a lot of money.

A salt bath as a method of treating freshwater fish has been around since the aquarium hobby first began. Salt baths have proved effective over time to help cure problems such as fungus infestations, ich, and several other types of parasites such as gill flukes. Basically what happens is the parasites are submerged in the salt solution along with your fish and begin to take on water until they burst and fall off.

We have used this home-remedy method for more than 20 years and have found that it has a very high rate of success in treating different types of diseases. (Don't try this in your home bathtub with your own sores, or you may end up peeling yourself off the ceiling — you've heard of salt in an open wound? Not good for nonfish.)

A salt bath is really very simple. All you have to do is add one teaspoon of table salt for each 5 gallons of water in your hospital tank. Continue adding 1 teaspoon of salt twice a day for the first five or six days. If the infected fish is not completely well by the sixth day, continue to add one teaspoon of salt for another three days.

We're not talking about adding salt to your main tank. When you hear that people have salt in their main freshwater tank, it is because they are keeping species such as the Molly which actually thrive better with a bit of salinity to their water. Don't confuse this concept with standard salt bath in a hospital tank.

The Sherlock Holmes Method

Everyone wants to do a little bit of detective work at least once in their lifetime. If you're like us, you couldn't find more than one pair of matching socks in the dryer if your life depended on it. Fortunately, looking for clues that indicate the presence of a tropical fish disease is much easier to do the laundry. To get started, all you need to do is find one of those cool-looking hats, a pipe, a long coat, and follow the clues we give you in this section.

We cannot overemphasize the importance of checking the overall health of your fish very carefully every day. Shimmying, abnormal loss of appetite, weight loss, paling or darkening of colors, increased or labored respiration, and miniature For Sale signs on the aquarium's porcelain castles are a few of the warning signs that disease or environmental conditions are causing them discomfort.

Other tell-tale clues to look for include: a bloated look, obvious visible damage to your fish's eyes, fins, or scale areas, and abnormal spots on the body. If your fish is hanging around the heater, continually scratching on tank decorations or substrate, or is normally active but is suddenly moving slowly, it may have a serious problem.

If you notice any of these problems, don't panic. Take the time to make careful observations on the efficiency of the equipment, condition of the water, and other disease-related factors. After you compile all the information you can, you're in a better position to make a sound judgment on the proper course of action. If you're unsure about what to do for a diseased fish, contact your local vet or fish dealer. The people there can give you good advice and help you with your fishy problems.

Using Quarantine and Hospital Tanks

A *hospital tank* helps you treat sick fish and is simply a small aquarium that acts as a hospital ward. You remove diseased fish from the main tank and place them in the hospital tank for chemical or other types of treatment. It's as simple as that. A *quarantine tank* is used to hold fish for a week that you have just brought home from dealer, so that you have time to see if any illness develops before you put them in your main tank. Both tanks are very important.

Purpose and advantages of quarantining

All tropical fish go through a tremendous amount of stress being transported to your home aquarium. Think about it — if someone snagged you with a giant pair of panty hose and then stuck you in a large plastic bag, wouldn't you have a little bit of a problem with that?

Fish are really not that much different from us when it comes to mental stress. A quarantine tank can be the perfect way to provide your new tropical fish with a suitable recovery area — it gives them time to regain their strength before moving into their brand-new home. This recovery period also gives you time to see whether any latent diseases or physical problems manifest themselves.

Quarantine time

The very first thing that you need to do when you bring your new acquisitions home (unless they are *starter fish,* the very first fish in a new aquarium) is to place them in a quarantine tank for one week. You don't quarantine starter fish because you need them to begin the nitrogen cycle. While your fish are in quarantine, check them daily for signs of disease and make sure they are eating normally.

Writing it all down

A journal can help you keep track of your fish's quarantine and health record. You can check these records for information on previous treatments. Keep a separate page for each fish and include the fish's name, date of purchase, size, health record, length of quarantine, and any other information you feel may be important in future medical treatments. To look like a real pro, write something important looking like "Scientific Information" on the journal's cover. Your friends will be impressed.

The tank

We think a 10- or 20-gallon tank is good for quarantining unless you plan on buying some very large fish. All the equipment you need to get your quarantine tank going is a good-quality power filter and a submersible heater. Make your new fish feel secure by adding some gravel and a few artificial plants. The last thing you need is for your new pets to go into a bare tank where they can easily be frightened.

Don't forget that a quarantine tank needs to be cycled just like your regular tank. A starter fish or two helps begin the biological cycle. When you go down to your local dealer to purchase starter fish for the main tank, pick up a couple of extras for the quarantine tank at the same time. The water conditions (pH, temperature) in your quarantine tank should be similar to those in your permanent aquarium. This prevents fish being stressed further when you move them to the main aquarium.

Remember, it is much better to be patient and wait until your new fish complete their quarantine cycle than it is to place them immediately into a main tank where they can spread disease that could have been caught and treated. In the long run, treating disease can cost you quite a bit more money than setting up a simple and inexpensive quarantine tank.

Setting Up a Hospital Tank

Unfortunately, there is no 911 number for your aquatic pets should they become ill. So you need a hospital tank to help treat them when they become diseased. Hospital tanks are similar to quarantine tanks. The only difference is, hospital tanks are used to treat ill fish, whereas quarantine tanks are used to hold new acquisitions for observance. It is much more practical to treat diseased fish in a separate hospital tank because many common medications affect different species in different ways. For example, a malachite green formula used to cure ich in most species has the potential to destroy any tetras in your aquarium.

Treating diseased fish in a hospital tank also lowers the risk of the disease spreading. Many antibiotic treatments destroy essential bacteria and cut down on the efficiency of a tank's biological filtration system, leading to even more health problems and new diseases. Using a hospital tank prevents these problems.

It really doesn't take much money to set up a hospital tank if you purchase a small aquarium (5- or 10-gallon) and a simple sponge filter to provide a good base for beneficial biological bacteria. Filtration systems that contain carbon don't work very well in a hospital tank because the carbon often absorbs the medication. The frequent water changes you need to do when treating sick fish are much easier to handle in a small aquarium. A good submersible heater with an internal rheostat lets you monitor water temperature as needed. Diseases such as ich can be treated more quickly if you raise the standard temperature by a few degrees.

Remember that overly bright lighting reduces the effectiveness of many medications. Try to use a lower wattage bulb for your hospital tank setup. Add a few extra airstones to the hospital tank to increase the oxygen supply because many medications tend to reduce the oxygen supply in the aquarium.

Understanding Medications

There are a large number of medications on the market, and many of them can be used to treat a variety of diseases, so deciding which one you should actually use can be very confusing. More often than not, the final choice of medication rests with you. Each case is unique, and many aquarists prefer one medication over another.

In time, you'll discover which medications work best on certain diseases and different species of fish. Until you reach that point, try to keep a wide variety of medications around so that your friends and family think that you have everything under control. The following list gives you an idea of how to use common medications, and the pros and cons of each drug:

- **Salt:** Common table salt or marine salt is generally used to treat ich and other parasitic diseases in freshwater fish. The normal dosage is one tablespoon per gallon of water in the aquarium. Salt is very inexpensive, but you can't use it in tanks containing certain species, such as catfish.

- **Methylene blue:** You often use this liquid to treat diseases such as ich, fungus, and velvet. You achieve the correct dose by adding enough methylene blue so that the water is difficult to see through, usually about five drops per gallon. The bluish cast in the water disappears with proper filtration, but stains decorations and gravel, and cannot be used with many species of living plants. Methylene blue is hard to get out of clothes and stains everything it touches.

- **Malachite green:** Use this wonderful medication to treat velvet, fungus, and ich. It is very effective in battling disease, but cannot be used in tanks that contain fry (newborn fish) or certain species of fish such as tetras. Malachite green can be very toxic if used in large doses.

- **Formalin:** This is a bath-type treatment only and should not be used in the main display tank. This is a great remedy for parasites, but it doesn't work well on internal infections and can be very toxic.

- **Penicillin:** Penicillin treats bacterial infections and is non-toxic. The main disadvantages of this drug are the expense and the difficulty of obtaining it.

- ✔ **Tetracycline:** This antibiotic is great for bacterial infections and is non-toxic. The only problem with this medication is that it can turn the water yellow and cause unsightly foam to collect on the water surface.

- ✔ **Acriflavine:** Acriflavine treats ich and fungus, but may turn the water green.

Part III
Water, Chemicals, and Plants

The 5th Wave   By Rich Tennant

"Oh no, we don't use any chemicals in the aquarium, just imported sparkling water with a twist of lemon and a mint leaf garnish."

In this part . . .

We show you how to keep your aquarium system healthy. We concentrate on the chemical aspects of the aquarium, which involve maintaining water quality and thus a healthy environment for your freshwater pets. We also discuss the benefits of those natural and beautiful components of balance in your system called underwater plants.

Chapter 12

All Water Is Not Created Equal

Adding the correct type of water to your aquarium is very important to the long-term health of your fish. Water can be obtained from many sources, but only a few of these sources provide the correct requirements for your aquatic pets. Understanding the correct water parameters for your tank and choosing reliable water sources can help you become a successful hobbyist right off the bat.

For example, Maddy's college biology professor made her class look at pond water through a microscope. She could barely believe her eyes. There must have been 800 billion creatures crawling in it. Remember that almost any natural source of water has some type of living organism in it. In the wild, fish are not confined to a small amount of water, so the threat of illness is small. You need to find alternative sources of water if you want your fish to be healthy and happy.

Depending on where you live, your water supply from the city or from a well can vary greatly. Some water sources have more metal content and debris than others. One farm Maddy lived on had water that was so thick in iron it had the appearance of a melted down automobile. Never assume that your main water source is automatically safe for your fish because it can contain contaminates such as rust.

Comparing Different Water Types

You can get water from a variety of sources. Here we talk about the pros and cons of tap water, rainwater, bottled water, natural lake/pond/river water, and well water.

Tap water

In order to protect the human population from being killed off by drinking water, water companies add chemicals such as chlorine or chloramine (ammonia bonded to chlorine) to wipe out small organisms that could make us all sick. This treated tap water may be safe for humans, but it can be deadly to your aquatic pets.

You have to get rid of the chlorine from any water source that you use to fill your aquariums. Chlorine kills all types of fish and invertebrates.

Dechlorinating with dechlorinator

You have a few options for removing chlorine and chloramines from tap water to make it perfectly safe to use in your aquarium. One option (and if you're like us, you'll opt for this method because it's the easiest) is to go down to your local fish store and purchase a bottle of *dechlorinator*, a product which instantly removes chlorine and the chlorine in chloramines from your water. After adding dechlorinator, you can safely put your new starter fish in the aquarium water.

The best time to add dechlorinator is after your tank is filled and all equipment is up and running. You need to dechlorinate all the water you add to your aquarium — even the water you put in to replenish water lost to evaporation.

Dechlorinating the old-fashioned way

Your tanks are low, and you're out of dechlorinator because your local fish store has run out. If you want to be a practical hobbyist, you can simply dechlorinate water the old-fashioned way. (Don't panic; this method doesn't involve a lot of work.) Take a few plastic jugs (gallon milk containers work great) and rinse them thoroughly with clear water. Glass jars work fine, but they can break, so plastic is really your best bet for safety. Make sure you allow the water to run from the tap for a few seconds before rinsing to eliminate any water that has sat stagnant in the piping. Water can pick up trace amounts of metal if it sits unmoving in household pipes.

Never use soap or other chemicals to clean out containers for aquarium water! The soap leaves a residue that can be deadly to your fish.

After rinsing, fill the plastic containers with tap water, allow them to sit with the lids off for 48 hours, and voilá, chlorine-free water!

You can add an airstone (a small stone that splits an air supply from your pump into smaller bubbles) to each jug to cut your waiting time in half (to 24 hours). See Chapter 6 for more on airstones. Attach the airstone to a spare aquarium pump by tubing. If you keep three or four jugs like this sitting around, you always have a supply of safe water. Simply use a gang valve (again, Chapter 6) so that you can use one pump to power several airstones at once. When company is on the way, grab a jug and start filling your tanks.

Floating dust particles, paint sprays, and so on can get into these water jugs. Keep the jugs in an area that doesn't have a lot of air-borne debris. Placing a small cloth over the top of each jug can help keep out unwanted particles.

Guarding against metals

It's not just chlorine you have to worry about. Depending on your area, your tap water may also contain metal deposits, such as copper. Too much metal can be deadly for your fish. To be safe, buy water treatments from your pet dealer that safely remove the metals from water.

As mentioned previously, let the water from your tap run down the sink for a minute before you start filling containers with water for your aquariums, just as you did when you rinsed them. This precaution allows water that's been in constant contact with metal sink pipes (and is slightly contaminated as a result) to flow through.

Rainwater

A few hobbyists collect rainwater for use in their aquariums. If you have an extremely large tank, this is not a very practical method. The process is really more trouble than it is worth, unless you have a lot of spare time, small tanks, energy on your hands, or live in a region of the country that receives a tremendous amount of annual rainfall. If you live in the desert southwest, your fish will probably die from old age before you collect enough water to top off your tank, and it may not always rain when you need it to.

Another problem with rainwater is that it may contain contaminants from factory emissions, smog, and other pollutants. To be honest, you may end up spending twice as much for chemicals to treat your rainwater than if you had just used your trusty old kitchen faucet.

If you decide to gather rainwater to help condition your fish for breeding, make sure that you use non-metallic containers for collection. In fact, never use metallic containers to collect water for any aquarium. Also keep in mind that rainwater tends to be very soft (low in dissolved minerals) and may not be suitable for hard-water fish. Hard-water fish (such as red-tailed sharks, blindcave fish, and oscars, whose water has a high mineral content in the wild) that are forced to live in soft water conditions cannot spawn properly or maintain good health.

You should always check the water parameters (specific water requirements) for your particular aquatic species before using rainwater.

Never collect rainwater from metal gutters. Over time, gutters rust and become filled with debris such as leaves, dirt, paper, and pieces of roofing shingle. No matter how often you clean your gutters, you are risking metallic and natural contamination by using metal gutters to funnel water for an aquarium supply.

If you're bent on collecting rainwater, one solution is to use an open container with a large plastic funnel inserted into the top of the collection jug. Just make sure you don't use the funnel for adding oil to your car or other household duties between rainwater collections.

The advantages of bottled water (not Perrier)

Okay, when we mention bottled water, we're talking about the kind you get in a machine outside of your local grocery store or the gallon jugs that you can purchase inside. Put it this way: If the water is really expensive, it's the wrong kind; if it's inexpensive, it's the right kind. Don't spend a fortune on expensive bottled water when the least expensive will do just fine.

You can very likely use bottled water in your aquarium without adding any chemicals to it. But to be safe, we always add dechlorinator to our water no matter where it came from. Spending a few pennies on dechlorinator is a much better route to take than losing a bunch of expensive fish.

Well water (don't count on it)

As we mentioned earlier, Maddy once lived on a farm. A deep well, located somewhere out on the back 40, furnished the farm's entire water supply. The water from this well was truly one of life's great mysteries — all the filters and chemicals in the world couldn't change the composition of this amazing liquid.

The water was guaranteed to turn every color of the rainbow within a period of five minutes during a shower, and Maddy's body took on those glorious copper colors when she stepped out. Instead of buying an expensive Halloween costume, trick-or-treaters saved money by coming over to the house for a shower.

The point of this reminiscence is that well water is generally not a good source to use for filling your aquariums because too many bad things can get into it, including sulfur, lead, and mud. Well water is usually lacking in good oxygen content and is high in dissolved nitrogen and carbon dioxide instead.

If you insist on using it anyway, take a small sample down to your local water company and ask them to test it for you. Water companies are pretty good about testing your water for little or no money, even if it is from your own well. Most standard aquarium and home water test kits are not made to accurately test the chemicals, metals, and other odd items that can be found in well water. If you get a dirty look from the water department clerk because your sample destroyed her expensive equipment, you can forget the bad idea of using well water altogether and use bottled water or treated water from a friend's city water supply (dechlorinate it before using).

If your well water is free of metals and does test acceptable for human consumption, make sure you follow up with an aquarium test kit to check for tropical fish perimeters such as pH and nitrites. They may have to be adjusted using aquarium chemicals before you use it for your aquatic pets.

Collecting Water from Bodies of Water (Why You Want to Forget This Bad Idea)

If you're planning to set up a freshwater aquarium, someone has probably suggested that you can be a real naturalist and go down to your local river or pond to snag the water for it. You may be thinking that this isn't a half-bad idea — you can keep your fish closer to their natural environment. However, after your dream of a cameo on National Geographic fades a bit, you can go ahead and forget this idea entirely.

Why? Because most of the freshwater fish you purchase from the pet shop are raised in a hatchery and have never been near any river or pond. These fish are raised in standard aquarium water conditions. When you collect water from a pond or river, you take a great risk of introducing disease into your tank.

If you don't want to worry about the shelf life of your test kits, purchase individual kits like those offered by Aquarium Pharmaceuticals (www.genkikoi-supply.com/aquarium_pharmaceutical_test_kits.html). These kits have long shelf lives and have the advantage of allowing you to replace one part of the kit when needed without replacing the entire thing.

Adding Water to Your Aquarium

When you're ready to add your carefully treated water to your aquarium, pour it slowly so that you don't disturb the substrate or any of the decorations already in the tank. One trick is to place a small dinner plate or saucer on the substrate and pour the water directly onto the plate, which acts as a barrier to keep your substrate from being spread all over the tank into tiny anthill-like mounds. Another strategy is to slowly pour the new water down the inside of the glass.

If you have a very large aquarium to fill, you may want to consider purchasing a new garden hose and an adapter that will allow you to hook it up to your kitchen or bathroom faucet. This setup will allow you to fill your aquarium quickly. An even better solution to filling a large tank is to purchase a Python. A Python (see Chapter 6) works on the same principle as the garden hose, except it has all the attachments needed and allows you to easily control and reverse the flow of water with a simple switch for water changes that you will be doing on a weekly basis.

Home Sweet Home

Your fish's water environment is comparable to the air in your own home. The water is what keeps your fish alive and must be one of the most important factors to take into consideration. Take time to make sure that the water that you are going to use is perfect for your aquatic pets. It never pays to rush or take huge shortcuts.

Here are a few rules to help you maximize your tropical fish's health and happiness:

✔ Make sure the water you use is as free of debris, chemicals, and metals as possible by conducting water tests on well or city supplies, or by using bottled water.

- ✔ Dechlorinate either with dechlorinator or by using the jug method described earlier in this chapter.

- ✔ If you are going to collect water, make sure you use a clean, non-metallic container and funnel system.

- ✔ Make sure the water perimeters in your aquarium match the perimeters in the water at your dealer where your aquatic pets are coming from.

- ✔ When carrying out water changes, make sure that your replacement water is of equal temperature and pH. to the water in your tank.

- ✔ Monitor your water conditions with a home test kit each week.

Good water quality will keep your tropical fish healthy and happy for years to come.

Chapter 13

Those Crazy Chemicals

Have you ever been at the aquarium store and noticed shelf after shelf of mysterious-looking chemicals? Ever wonder whether you need a wizard's license or some type of magical scroll to decipher and use them properly? Well, you really don't need to worry too much, because the chemicals are actually fairly easy to understand and will become second nature as you progress through the hobby.

A very wide variety of chemicals for your aquarium is available, so it is understandable that it can seem a bit confusing at first. But once you read this chapter and learn the basics of some of the most popular and useful aquatic chemicals on the market, you will be able to look at chemicals in a whole new way.

Right now we take a closer look at a few of these chemical products made for use in home aquariums and explain their purpose. Because there is such a multitude of aquarium chemicals out there, it is impossible to cover them all here. (We doubt we could cover them all in an entire book!) But by the time you finish reading this chapter, you will be on the road to becoming a real chemical wizard.

Understanding Chemical Use

Just as there are guidelines to follow for using the chemicals you find around your home (especially in the laundry room and kitchen), there are rules for using aquarium chemicals as well. After all, you wouldn't even think of mixing ammonia and chlorine to help whiten your laundry unless you wanted to spend five days in an oxygen tent, right? Well, your fish don't cope well with excessive mixtures and overuse of chemicals either.

Chemicals are chemicals. We cannot stress this point enough! *Any* chemical can be dangerous if it is mixed with the wrong substance. Although this is not a common hazard with aquarium chemicals, certain mixtures and overdoses can be lethal to your fish. Before you use any type of chemical, read the bottle very carefully.

Overdosing — adding too many chemicals at one time, or even adding too many chemicals over a long period of time — can affect the water conditions (pH and so on) in your aquarium. Dumping bottle after bottle of treatments into your tank also makes your fish look like they're swimming around in a swamp, and we guarantee that they'll end up hating you for it. The point is that you shouldn't just dump 15 bottles of chemicals into your aquarium hoping one of them will work. (If you have to step carefully while walking across your fish's room to avoid crushing discarded chemical bottles, you're probably overdosing.)

When should you use chemicals?

When you treat diseases, use chemicals as a last resort. Try one of the many more natural ways available (weekly water changes and keeping an eye on temperature and pH) to help your fish avoid illness (see Chapter 11). If you're just starting an aquarium, you can use chemicals a little more frequently because you need to dechlorinate your water and condition it. But you still don't want to over do it. Too much of anything is usually bad in some way or other.

Following instructions to the letter

Always follow all the manufacturer's instructions on the label! Don't skip any steps and follow through on the entire recommended treatment or usage time!

If you don't understand the instructions or the ingredients on a chemical's label (sometimes they seem to be written in some weird alien dialect), don't hesitate to contact the product's manufacturer and have someone there help clear up your questions. You will often find a 1-800 number right there on the label. If you're in a hurry, ask your local dealer for help.

Chemicals You Need to Start Your Aquarium

When you first set up a brand new aquarium, certain chemicals can help you out a great deal. You can purchase most of the chemicals mentioned in this section at your local pet shop, and the other ones you can most likely find at the supermarket or even around your own house.

Glass cleaner

You can use a household glass cleaner to clean the outside of your aquarium and its frame. Standard window cleaning products such as Windex work very well. Make sure you cover the top of the tank with a towel so that mist from the cleaner does not get inside the tank. Cleaners that have a citrus base seem to work the best. They leave the glass clean and streak free and also help to keep fingerprints from reappearing on the glass. (This is especially useful when you have small children in the house.)

Never use a household glass cleaner on the *inside* of your tank! Glass cleaner residue can kill your fish very quickly. The only thing that should be used to clean out the inside of an aquarium is fresh water. Never use soaps or any other types of chemicals on the inside glass.

Dechlorinator

When you first add water to your aquarium, you have to remove the chlorine from it first. Chlorine will kill your fish. *Dechlorinator* usually comes in liquid form and removes harmful chlorine instantly. With most brands, you need to add only a few drops per gallon to do the job (read the label carefully, of course). Basically, the main purpose of dechlorinator is to make the aquarium water safe for your fish without your having to wait for the chlorine to dissipate naturally (which usually takes 24–48 hours).

Water conditioner

Water conditioners often combine a dechlorinator with other chemicals that instantly detoxify the heavy metals in tap water. You can use a water conditioner when you are setting up a new aquarium, changing water, or adding water. Many sources of water (old wells and the like) may contain harmful metals that a water conditioner can detoxify. Even if your water "tests safe," you never know when its properties may change, so a water conditioner is always a good bet.

Cycling chemicals

We know it can be really hard to wait around for an aquarium to complete the nitrogen cycle (see Chapter 14). Depending on the type of system you have — freshwater, saltwater, or brackish — and the overall size of your tank, the entire nitrogen cycle can take weeks or even months to complete. *Cycling chemicals* have been around for a long, long time. During the nitrogen cycle, beneficial bacteria convert harmful ammonia (produced by fish waste) into less toxic nitrites. Following this conversion, another kind of beneficial bacteria convert the nitrites into even less harmful nitrates. The nitrates are only harmful to your fish after they begin to build up in large quantities. The nitrates can be removed from your aquarium water though water changes.

Some cycling products can start your nitrogen cycle and speed it up as well. The appealing idea behind this particular product is really very simple. The faster your tank cycles, the faster you can add more new fish to your aquarium. And the sooner you have fish in your aquarium, the sooner your neighbors will envy you.

If these natural bacteria products speed up the cycling time and give your starter fish that extra edge, why not use them? The only danger that we can see is that of looking at cycling chemicals as a cure-all for a tank you overstocked. These products are an aid to the nitrogen cycle, not a substitute for it!

Put it this way: If you set up a 55-gallon freshwater aquarium and toss in a couple of tablespoons of cycling formula in an attempt to offset the 75 goldfish you started your tank with, you are in for some serious problems. These products have a specific purpose, and should not be pushed to the limit.

Bacteria in a bottle

Some products speed up your aquarium's cycling time because they contain massive amounts of various beneficial bacteria held in a dormant state. After you add the bacteria formula to your aquarium water, the bacteria become completely regenerated and rapidly consume ammonia and nitrites. These different types of micro-organisms combine to create a powerful nitrifying team. Most of these products are nonpathogenic, meaning they won't harm any plants or fish in your aquarium. It is impossible to overdose your tank with bacteria in a bottle. One good example of this type of product is NitroBac Freshwater Bio-Starter (www.azgardens.com/aquarium_ chemicals.php).

Bacteria on a medium

You can purchase a good home for this bacteria product that comes as a rapid-action biological filter medium. This type of medium is called *precolonized* (meaning it already has the bacteria attached) with a multitude of nitrifying bacteria which, in some cases, can cut your cycling time in half. The medium prevents clogging and helps maintain good water circulation in your filtration unit. A bacterial medium is designed to have a maximum surface area to encourage the largest supply of beneficial bacteria.

Water clarifier

A water clarifier (such as Aquarium Pharmaceuticals's Accu-Clear Water Clarifier) removes excess cloudiness in your aquarium caused by bacterial *blooms* (growth spurts) that have gotten out of control. Blooms are usually a result of excess nutrients (nitrates and phosphates) or excessive lighting.

Chemicals You Need to Maintain Your Aquarium

Here are some other useful chemicals that can come in handy once you have started up your aquarium system.

Waste eliminator

Products such as Hagen Nutrafin Waste Control Organic Waste Eliminator rapidly reduces organic waste in aquariums and cleans filters, gravel, and the interior surfaces of the tank.

Prevention and control treatments

Several chemical treatments protect the *slime coat* (a natural coating that helps to protect it against disease) on your fish's body. These products (Stress Coat is a good example) also help relieve stress and deter the onset of disease. Slime coat products are important for your fish, especially ones that have just been transported or netted. Your fish's natural slime coat can easily be worn off and leave bare patches that are open to attack by various diseases.

Snail control products destroy snails in your freshwater aquarium and help you keep them from coming back. Most snails are brought into the aquarium system on live plants. Snails are very sneaky and crafty (kind of like our kids) and have the ability to slip by even the most experienced eye. Snails can multiply faster than your household bills and can ruin the appearance of an aquarium as they get out of control. Nip them in the bud. Once your aquarium is overrun with snails, they are almost impossible to get rid of and they often carry diseases that can damage your fish's health.

Aquarium salt

Aquarium salt adds electrolytes (sodium) and helps your fish breathe better by increasing their gill function when they are diseased.

pH regulators

pH regulators increase or decrease the pH of your aquarium water. You want to increase or decrease pH depending on which way you need to go (see Chapter 14 for more on pH) to achieve the proper pH for your particular species.

Cichlid buffers

A *cichlid buffer* is a mixture of trace elements, sulfates, sodium, calcium, magnesium, potassium, and carbonates that provide natural water chemistry for rift lake fishes. (See Chapter 8 for more on cichlids.)

Chemicals You Need for Your Plants

For all you hobbyists out there with green thumbs, we present several chemicals you can use to help your living aquarium plants thrive to their full potential. (Don't try them on plastic plants, because they may turn funny colors or something.)

The living plants in your aquarium system have special needs that you need to meet. Your plants deserve the very best, just like your fish do.

Creating your own rainforest

If you have plants in your aquarium that come from the Amazon region (Amazon swords, for example), you can purchase chemicals to help create a rainforest condition in your tank. Products such as Instant Amazon increase lush plant growth (without nitrates or phosphates), discourage algae and parasite growth, detoxify ammonia and nitrites, and help your plants create beneficial oxygen for your fish. They also give your plants a better chance of obtaining nutrients from the aquarium water and enhance biological filtration.

Amazon products (products that create water conditions similar to that found in the Amazon region) provide essential macro-nutrients (proteins, carbohydrates, and fiber) without stimulating algae and give your aquarium water the natural look of "peat" (yellow-tinted water that is native to Amazon fishes). You can use these products for soft-water fish such as discus, angelfish, neons, barbs, and gouramis to create a yellow color to the water, simulating their natural environment. This type of product often contains trace elements, vitamins, bark, and wood.

Keeping a clear head

In order for your fish to keep a clear head, you have to do the same. If you get carried away and turn your aquarium water into a chemical nightmare, your fish are going to start acting funny, suffer health problems, and face the possibility of death from toxicity. Make sure you check that your water conditions are correct for your system (temperature, salinity, pH, and nitrate levels) before you add medications. It is also important to make sure pumps and heaters are running properly, and filter pads are clean.

The golden rule of chemicals states that an aquarist should always attempt to remedy aquarium water problems naturally before adding chemicals. Think about it. Why add something that is not needed? Proper aquarium maintenance helps keep your water in good condition so that you don't have to add chemicals to correct problems. Carrying out consistent water changes once a week now will help ward off serious problems in the future.

Remember, many chemicals claim to cure just about any problem under the sun. Always take each product's claims with a grain of salt until you check them out yourself!

Plant grow

This product enhances intracellular reactions in plants and provides them with better coloration and improved growth.

Root Tabs

Root Tabs supply aquarium plants with magnesium, potassium, iron, and sulfur. These tabs help new aquatic plants get a good start in your aquarium and keep already established plants flourishing.

Algae control

Algae-control products such as Algone (www.algone.com/algone_ information.asp) reduce and prevent algae blooms by coloring the aquarium water blue. This coloring process absorbs/blocks sunlight, which the green algae need for survival.

Chemicals Your Fish Need for Medication

No matter what you do, disease is going to strike. Even the most experienced fishkeepers must deal with aquatic health problems from time to time. The following list gives you a few examples of products you can use to fight back when all other methods have failed (Chapter 11 has more on diseases and keeping your fish healthy):

- ✔ **Formalin** is used to treat fish that have contracted external parasites. A formalin bath helps alleviate problems such as skin flukes.
- ✔ **Antibiotics** treat bacterial infections, fungus, ulcers, gill disease, popeye, and dropsy.
- ✔ **Malachite green** is often used in the treatment of ich (Ichthyophthirius multifilius).
- ✔ **Paragon** treats inflamed gills, anchor worms, copepods, open sores, hemorrhaging, and hole-in-the-head disease.

Medications can be very confusing. Many manufacturers combine medications to treat a variety of illnesses. The label of most medication bottles lists the types of illness the product treats. These label listings help you wade through the confusion and choose the right product for the job.

Chapter 14

The Nitrogen Cycle and Water Testing

*W*ater quality is an important element in maintaining a successful aquarium system, so it is important that you learn a few basics about water chemistry such as the nitrogen cycle, pH, and hardness. Excellent water conditions in your aquarium will allow your pets to live long and healthy lives. Poor water conditions can leave your fish in poor health or cause their demise. Fortunately, monitoring and maintaining proper water conditions for each species can be easily done with a few simple test kits.

Take the time to monitor your water conditions on a weekly basis so that you can correct any problems with ease. Your fish have to live in their aquarium water 24 hours a day. Make sure that you provide them with the best conditions possible.

Eliminating Fish Waste

Your fish are gonna look great swimming around in your new tank. The water and the decorations are going to look sparkling clean and will impress everyone. But it won't stay that way without proper biological filtration and cycling, because your fish have to settle themselves with Mother Nature each and every day. Depending on the total number of fish in your tank, that can quickly add up to a whole lot of waste being excreted. This waste takes the form of *ammonia,* a dangerous chemical that in high amounts can be lethal to your fish, and CO2. Don't worry; for every aquarium problem there is always a solution.

To solve the waste problem, your fish and you join forces to provide proper *biological filtration* (utilizing living bacteria that constantly remove waste) and *cycling* (building up bacteria at the beginning to convert ammonia to nitrites and then to less harmful nitrates.) The CO2 is removed by plants in the aquarium through photosynthesis and by air from airstones and filters running in the tank.

Now for the good news: There is no problem getting these certain bacteria, which are present in the water to start with, to help take care of excess buildups. Now, we know that the word bacteria is usually associated with bad and scary things such as infections, but in an aquarium system, bacteria actually act as the good guys and save the day.

To understand all the weird and wonderful processes taking place in the water of your aquarium system, then, you need to know about ammonia, bacteria, cycling, and the other aspects of the *nitrogen cycle*. These ideas may seem a little complicated at first (only because they are!), but the tips and explanations in this chapter can help you cut a clear pathway through the darkness that plagues the topic of water conditions.

A new system is not as biologically stable as an old one (conditioned aquarium), but in time, of course, a new system becomes old and stable.

Conditioning Your Tank

You need to *condition* (also known as accomplishing the nitrification process, start-up cycle, and biological cycle) your new aquarium to provide your fish with the best possible chance for good health and survival. Conditioning sets up a bacterial colony to get rid of the nasty waste products your fish excrete. You have to be patient during this conditioning cycle because it does take time.

Rushing headlong through this vital conditioning process will undoubtedly lead to quite a bit of heartache as you lose your fish to a condition known as *new tank syndrome* (see the section "Preventing new tank syndrome," later in this chapter).

The main danger in any new aquarium is the rapid build-up of ammonia in the water through excretion and the decay of nitrogen products such as fish food and waste. As your aquarium begins to age, beneficial bacteria begin breaking down the ammonia so that the levels do not become too high. Bacteria are always present in your tank, but not enough in the beginning to take care of the problem.

Generally, conditioning takes about four to six weeks, but the time needed depends on the temperature of the water, the type and number of filtration units, the size of your system, and the number of livestock (starter fish) doing the backstroke around your tank.

Starting the Nitrogen Cycle

The nitrogen cycle plays a very important role in your aquarium system (Figure 14-1). During the first part of the nitrogen cycle, as we have mentioned, beneficial bacteria called *nitrosomonas* convert lethal ammonia to less toxic nitrites. During the second part of the cycle, another beneficial bacteria (*nitrobacter*) convert nitrites to less harmful nitrates. Nitrates are harmful at high levels but can be removed though frequent water changes.

About two weeks after you add starter fish to your aquarium, the ammonia build-up in your tank begins to peak. (You won't really have any ammonia in your aquarium until after you add your fish and they start excreting waste, or leaving food uneaten.) You're probably wondering what to do with the ammonia, right? Well, just sit back, because your friendly neighborhood bacteria take care of everything.

During the weeks of the conditioning period, several types of bacteria multiply rapidly in order to remove toxic chemicals from the water. As the number of bacteria increases, they render larger amounts of waste product less toxic by converting them to less harmful substances in the nitrogen cycle.

Encouraging nitrosamonas (good bacteria number one)

When uneaten food and fish waste is broken down, it is turned into either ionized ammonium (NH_4+, a pH lower than 7.0 will cause more ammonium) or non-ionized ammonia (NH_3, a pH higher than 7.0 will cause more ammonia.) The ammonium is not harmful to your aquarium, but the ammonia is a whole other story and needs to be taken care of.

As mentioned previously, during the first phase of the nitrogen cycle, the nitrosomonas bacteria in the aquarium water increase to detoxify and remove the ammonia from your aquarium. The by-product of this process is harmful nitrites. High levels of nitrites can still seriously kill or harm your fish, but they're not as bad as ammonia. Nitrosomonas bacteria require a good oxygen supply (which can be provided though filtration and airstones) in order to multiply and grow correctly.

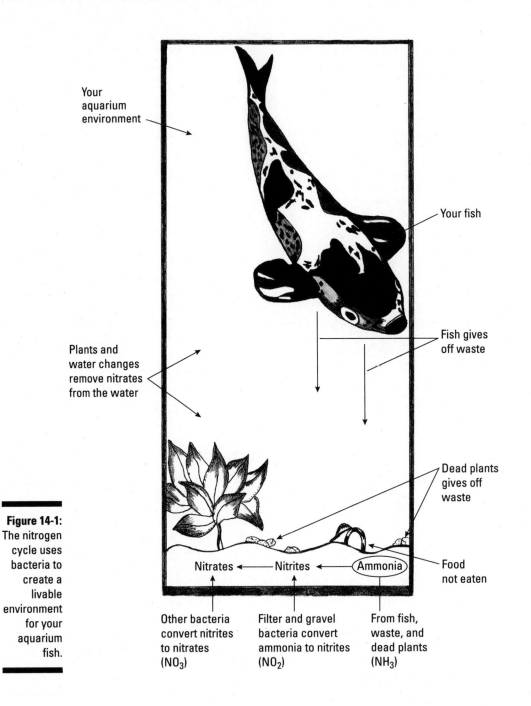

Your aquarium environment

Your fish

Fish gives off waste

Plants and water changes remove nitrates from the water

Dead plants gives off waste

Figure 14-1:
The nitrogen cycle uses bacteria to create a livable environment for your aquarium fish.

Nitrates ← Nitrites ← Ammonia

Food not eaten

Other bacteria convert nitrites to nitrates (NO$_3$)

Filter and gravel bacteria convert ammonia to nitrites (NO$_2$)

From fish, waste, and dead plants (NH$_3$)

Promoting nitrobacter (good bacteria number two)

In a short time, the nitrites produced by the nitrosomonas bacteria begin increasing toward toxic levels. When nitrite levels begin to climb, a second type of bacteria known as nitrobacter converts them to less deadly nitrates.

So far, the ammonia produced by waste has been converted to nitrites, and then to nitrates. Now what happens? Nitrate levels continue to increase slowly over time, but you can maintain them at proper levels through frequent water changes. If you don't change your water, the nitrates build up to the point where they are just as toxic as the ammonia you got rid of.

During the conditioning period, you need to monitor pH, ammonia, nitrite, and nitrate levels using standard test kits (available at aquarium shops) so you can see how the cycle is progressing. Notice that the pH level decreases a little during the conditioning process. This is normal.

Don't use chemicals and medications during the conditioning process, because they can potentially damage proper bacterial growth and, in turn, interfere with the nitrogen cycle.

Speeding things up a bit

You can start up the nitrogen cycle by adding one or more of the following things to your tank:

- **Starter fish:** Adding one or two fish is a good way to provide a minimum amount of waste to your tank so that essential bacteria can multiply at a normal rate. Using a couple of guppies or hardy danios to start the maturation process is one of the best ways to begin your nitrogen cycle.

- **Mature gravel:** Gravel from a mature (and disease-free) aquarium already has a large bacteria population on its surface and acts as an excellent starter culture. Add a few pinches of food each day so that you can test for nitrate production with a test kit.

- **Food:** Adding a small amount of food to the tank each day can help begin the nitrogen cycle. The only problem with this method is that it is very unreliable and can lead to water fouling if food is not added in the correct amounts. The correct amount would be a few pinches twice a day to start the ammonia production as the uneaten food begins to break down.

  ✔ **Commercial additives:** You can purchase additives such as freeze-dried bacteria at your local pet store to help speed up the nitrogen cycle. We never had much luck with the older products. However, many new products, such as *pre-colonized mediums* (you add them to your filter box or canister) can significantly increase cycling time.

The best way to begin the aquarium maturation cycle, in our opinion, is to add a small amount of mature gravel and a few starter fish.

Despite the fact that your starter fish begin the process of proper bacterial growth, it takes time to build up a well-established biological colony. Don't add too many fish right away because they can overload the biological filtration system and result in new tank syndrome (see next section).

Instead, simply wait a couple of weeks after the tank is cycled, then add a few small fish each week to the aquarium. This gradual increase in livestock keeps ammonia levels within an acceptable range for the bacteria present to do their job correctly.

Frequent, small water changes (replace 5 percent of the water per day) help lower any excess waste build-up.

During the cycling period, you may notice cloudiness in the water. Don't worry; it isn't a sign that all has gone wrong. The cloudiness is a beneficial bacterial bloom and is perfectly normal. If your aquarium has adequate filtration, the water should become clear again within a few days.

Preventing new tank syndrome

As time passes, waste builds up in your tank and needs to be eliminated. After a month or two, the significant amount of bacteria living in the substrate bed and filters (or any surface they can attach themselves to) take care of any fishy waste products.

New tank syndrome occurs when ammonia or nitrite is not properly converted to less harmful nitrates. *Overstocking* (putting too many fish in your aquarium) when you first set up your tank usually causes new tank syndrome.

New tank syndrome is a silent killer, often striking without warning. It causes extreme physical ailments or even death. Your fish may look a little out of joint one day and be dead the next. You must learn to recognize the symptoms of this problem: Fish suffering from new tank syndrome often lose some of their coloring, hide in corners with clamped fins, and lie near the bottom of the aquarium.

If you notice any of these unusual behaviors, immediately test the ammonia and nitrite levels and carry out water changes as needed to reduce excess waste products.

Testing Ammonia, Nitrites, Nitrates, and pH

To *maintain* healthy water conditions at the beginning of the cycle and throughout the life of your aquarium system, you need to continue to test your water's ammonia, nitrite, and nitrate levels frequently. Keeping these levels where they should be helps your fish stay much healthier overall.

Changing the water frequently

One of the best (and oldest) methods of keeping your ammonia and nitrate levels down is to change the water frequently. Water changes help remove unwanted waste, and at the same time replace depleted trace elements. Besides, if you change your aquarium water frequently (yes, that means more than once a year!) your fish will love you for it.

Research shows that fish that live in aquariums where the water is changed often, display better coloration, live longer and healthier lives, and fight off disease with superhuman (we mean *superfishy*) strength. Water changes also help your filtration system function better.

You may wonder how much water you should change. We prefer to change about 15 percent of the water in our tanks every week. We know that this may sound like a chore, but it really isn't. You can get a special kind of hose, called a Python, to help you out. You can also do it the old-fashioned way, using a bucket.

Do not do lift heavy buckets of water if you have any health problems. Get someone to do it for you. One of your neighbors probably owes you a favor anyway.

A Python connects to the tap on your sink. You can use it to remove the water you want to change from your tank so that it drains directly into the sink. You can then reverse the flow and add water (that is the same temperature as the tank) in smaller amounts to a bucket placed near the tank. Simply add dechlorinator to the bucket water and then add it to your tank.

If you don't keep changing the water in your aquariums every week, your nitrate level may rise to the point where it becomes lethal. There is really no practical way to get rid of excess nitrate levels without water changes. Sometimes some of the oldest methods are still the best.

As your aquarium system matures, the pH level drops due to acid build-up. Water changes help eliminate this problem as well.

Maintaining proper pH levels

The pH of your aquarium is simply a logarithmic scale that tells how alkaline or acidic your aquarium water is. The pH scale goes from 0 (highly acidic) to 14.0 (highly alkaline) with a value of 7.0 being considered neutral.

When you set up you new aquarium, you need a pH test kit, available at almost any pet store. Don't be afraid; they're really quite simple to use. Special test kits for freshwater aquariums test pH in the lower to neutral range to the higher ranges. Don't bother trying to use a home water testing kit as they are expensive, hard to find, and are not made to test aquarium conditions.

One type of aquarium water testing kit consists of a simple color card, plastic measuring tube, and chemicals that either lower or raise the pH. Usually, you fill the measuring tube with water from your aquarium and add a few drops of *regent* (a water color-changing chemical supplied with the test kit). Then you compare the resulting color to the color on the provided kit chart, which indicates the pH value of your aquarium water. This system is difficult if you have color vision problems like we do.

Some aquarium water testing kits have strips of litmus paper that, when you dip them into your aquarium, change color to indicate the pH level. With others, you read your pH level read electronically by inserting probes attached to a machine into the water.

The type of test kit you choose depends on how much mad money you have to blow when you find yourself picking up supplies. We like the probe type testers because they are the easiest to read due to their digital output. They can be a bit pricey, though. Buying a simple, inexpensive test kit is fine if you cannot afford the higher-priced equipment.

Check the pH level of your aquarium water when you first set up your tank and at least once a week after the nitrogen cycle is complete. Many species of fish prefer to live in slightly alkaline; others like to hang out in acidic waters; and some like to remain in between (neutral). So the pH level you need for your particular system depends on what species of fish you have.

The pH values in a freshwater system can fluctuate very rapidly. Even the smallest change in pH level can really stress out your fish and make them much more susceptible to various diseases. So keep an eye on the situation.

A pH of 5 is ten times more acidic than a pH of 6. So don't let the little numbers fool you — they can change your water chemistry drastically.

When you purchase your fish, make sure that your various species' pH requirements are compatible. Chapter 8 lists some general pH guidelines for a number of popular freshwater species. If you are unsure, check with your local pet dealer to find out the pH of any species you are purchasing from him.

Recall that ammonia is more toxic in a system with a higher pH.

If there are any fish in your aquarium, change the pH level gradually. Changes of more than one range value per day (for example, from 6.5 to 7.5) can shock your fish and result in their death.

Acidity

If, after testing, you find that the pH level of your aquarium water is too low (that is, too acidic), you can raise it by adding sodium bicarbonate (also known as baking soda) from the test kit or through water changes which also remove organic build-up. This organic build-up reduces pH. If your test kit does not have the chemicals, you can purchase them at your local pet store.

Alkalinity

If you find that the pH level of your water is too high (meaning too alkaline), you can lower it by adding the sodium biphosphate from the test kit, or by adding de-mineralized water. Remember that pH-lowering chemicals are phosphate based and can encourage algae growth.

Testing Hardness (dH)

The degree of hardness (measured by a term called *degrees of hardness,* or dH) in water refers to the amount of dissolved mineral salts (mostly magnesium and calcium) in your water. The more minerals that are present, the harder the water. You don't have to worry about your water's degree of hardness unless you live in an area where the water is very hard (150+) or very soft (0–4). You can test for hardness by using a simple hardness test kit available at your local fish store.

Some fish like to live in slightly hard water, and others don't. If you have one in *very* hard water that is supposed to live in soft water, it can lead to illness and death.

One way to dilute hardness is to add rain or distilled water to your tank. Another way is to boil the water and let it cool before adding it to your tank. Both methods lower the pH levels. Extreme hardness is found in alkaline (high pH) waters. *Reverse osmosis* units soften aquarium water, but these units tend to be expensive and use a lot of tap water in order to produce a small amount of mineral-free water.

You can also use a water softener or add peat moss to your filter (boil the peat first to remove any unwanted organisms). Hardness can be easily increased by adding sodium bicarbonate in small amounts at a time (about a teaspoon per 55 gallons) and then monitoring the change.

During the conditioning period, closely monitor pH, ammonia, nitrite, and nitrate levels using standard test kits. Take daily readings. The pH level goes down as a normal part of the conditioning process. You can raise it again through frequent water changes if you live in an area with harder water (hard water and high alkaline levels go together). Allowing the pH to decrease over a long period of time during the conditioning process keeps helpful bacteria from multiplying to its full potential. When nitrite and nitrate levels begin to overstep their limits, daily water changes help alleviate that problem.

Do not use an excess amount of chemicals or medications during the conditioning period because they can potentially damage bacterial growth.

When the conditioning process is complete, you can begin adding a few fish every week to allow the bacteria bed to increase at a normal rate. If you make the mistake of immediately overstocking your aquarium, ammonia levels (ammonia spikes) will gradually build up. To correct this situation, reduce the number of fish in the tank or add more filtration.

There you have it, the basics of aquarium water. With test kits you can always be on top of the situation and provide your fish with water to match their needs.

Chapter 15

Putting It All Together

*I*f you are reading this chapter, you have probably purchased most of the equipment for your new aquarium. If you haven't, take a look at the first eight chapters of this book, which cover equipment, substrate, and tanks. But we're sure many of you are wondering in what order all those hoses, funny-looking pieces of tubing, and gadgets all fit into your system. That's what this chapter is for.

You are probably crossing your fingers in hopes that we talk about the type of system that you want to set up. Never fear! We're going to show you how to set up a freshwater tropical system, a coldwater system, and an indoor pond system. You can't beat that with a stick!

The setups covered in this chapter are our own personal choices for a beginning hobbyist. You can find many other types of equipment, substrates, and so on that can be put on these systems, but we want to lead you though the simple steps of putting together a minimal setup that will work fine and not cost you mega bucks. Later on, you can add more equipment if you choose to do so. Part of the excitement of the hobby is learning and trying new things, and we would not want to take that opportunity away from you by giving you system setups that are set in stone. Begin with the basics, do your research, and then let your imagination lead you from there.

Don't forget to read the directions on every piece of equipment that you purchase. There are a lot of good tips and advice that the manufacturers have printed out for your convenience. Take advantage of that. These instructions usually come with pictures and other good information about replacing broken parts, so don't be afraid to take a few minutes to scan the enclosed materials. If the piece of equipment has parts, do a dry run to make sure they all fit together before you place them in your aquarium.

Setting Up Your Tropical Freshwater System

What follows are the basic steps to set up a tropical aquarium. For this example, we will be using an undergravel filter, a background, a power filter, and live plants.

1. **Find a good location.**

   Choose a place that has a solid floor and is away from windows, doors, and high-traffic areas. Make sure you have adequate electrical outlets and a handy water supply.

2. **Set up the stand.**

   Place the stand so that it is stable (that is, it doesn't rock). You can use a carpenter's level to accomplish this goal. Lay the level along the length of the stand to make sure that it is completely level. If not, use hardwood shims (available at hardware stores) to level the stand by placing them one at a time under the legs.

   Make sure you leave room behind the stand for hanging equipment and leave enough room for yourself to do cleaning and maintenance.

3. **Clean out your tank.**

   Clean out your aquarium with clear water and a soft sponge. Do not use soap or other chemicals! Make sure you dry the outside of the glass with paper towels to avoid streaks that may be hard to reach after the system is completely set up.

4. **Place the aquarium on the stand.**

   Make sure that the tank fits properly on the stand. Do not allow any of the tank's bottom edges to hang over. If you want, you can place a thin sheet of Styrofoam underneath the tank to cushion it and even out minor changes in level.

5. **Add a background.**

   If you want to add a background, now would be the time to tape it onto the back of the tank so that you don't have to work it around the equipment and cords later.

   Another option is to paint the back glass on the *outside* with a roller. This is a great way to hide any cords or other objects that you don't want to show behind the tank. Apply two coats of paint and make sure that it is completely dry before you continue. Take care not to splash any paint into the interior of the tank as it can be toxic. You can cover the top of the tank with a towel while painting. We like to use an ocean blue paint for the back of our tanks, as it allows the fish to show their true colors and helps reflect lighting. Midnight blue and black look great, too.

6. Install an undergravel filter.

Now is the time to put in your undergravel filter, before the substrate is laid down.

Lay the perforated plastic plates on the bottom of the tank. Put the plastic uplift tubes in place over the large holes in the plate. Put an airstone connected to air-line tubing down inside of the plastic uplift tubes. Most undergravel caps have a hole that the air-line tubing passes through. Place the caps on top of the uplift tubes. Connect the air-line hosing to an air pump. Do not plug in the pump yet!

7. Wash and add your substrate.

Wash gravel with clear water. You can use a colander to rinse the gravel. Set the colander over a bucket and rinse the gravel under water until the overflow is clean. This will remove dirt, dust, and excess dye.

Put two inches of gravel over the undergravel filter plate. Slope the gravel so that it is about one half an inch higher in the rear.

8. Add a powerfilter.

On this system we are going to add a powerfilter (see Chapter 6) to make the total filtration system complete. Place the filter on the tank by hanging it on the outside of the rear glass. The intake tube should hang inside of the aquarium. Rinse the filter pads under clear water and place them in the slots inside the filter. Do not plug the unit in yet!

9. Fill the tank up ⅔ of the way with water.

This allows you to arrange the gravel if it has moved during filling and provide leeway to add decorations later without spilling water out of the tank.

Pour the water into the aquarium by letting it splash on top of a small plate that is resting underwater on top of the gravel. This will make sure that the water does not move the gravel and decorations all around while you are filling the tank. Make sure the water is the correct temperature for your species.

10. Install the heater.

Install a submersible heater at an angle along the rear piece of glass. If you are using a non-submersible heater, attach it onto the rim of the tank.

Do not plug in the heater yet!

11. **Put the thermometer on the tank.**

    Hang a hanging thermometer on the rim of the tank or stick a floating thermometer in one corner of the tank. If you have a stick-on thermometer, stick it on to the outside of the glass. We like to place these on the side of the tank in one corner so that they do take away from the front view.

12. **Add decorations.**

    Add rocks, driftwood, and other decorations.

13. **Fill the aquarium.**

    Add water until the aquarium water is at the same level as the bottom edge of the aquarium frame that wraps around the top of the glass.

14. **Add dechlorinator to the water.**

    Follow the instructions on the product for the correct amount.

15. **Plug in all the equipment and set the heater to the correct temperature for the fish and plants you are going to purchase.**

    Add water from the tank to the powerfilter to prime it if necessary.

16. **Check the pH.**

    Use a test kit to test the pH of the water. If it is okay continue on. If not adjust it until it is correct.

17. **Put the hood on top of the tank.**

18. **Add lighting if you have strip lighting separate from a hood or top glass.**

    Place the light on top of the tank and plug it in.

19. **Let the aquarium run for 24–48 hours.**

20. **Do a pH and temperature check and then adjust as needed.**

21. **Add live plants.**

    Bury plant roots in the gravel. Place taller plants in the back and shorter plants up front. You may have to take a little water out of the tank so that it doesn't flow over while you are planting.

22. **Put in your starter fish.**

    Just a few small ones! Don't go overboard!

There you have it in a nutshell. Remember that you must monitor your water conditions *daily* (using test kits you buy at aquariums shops) to keep an eye on ammonia, nitrite, and nitrate levels until the tank has finished cycling. You can start to slowly add more fish after the chemical levels stabilize and check the conditions once a week thereafter. Be patient during this process!

Setting Up Your Coldwater System

Sure, tropicals are great, but there is a lot of beauty to be found in coldwater species as well. What follows are the basic steps to set up a coldwater aquarium. For this example we will be using a bio-wheel and artificial plants

1. **Find a good location.**

   Choose a place that has a solid floor and is away from windows, doors, and high traffic areas. Make sure that you have adequate electrical outlets and a handy water supply.

2. **Set up the stand.**

   Place the stand so that it is stable (that is, it doesn't rock). You can use a carpenter's level to accomplish this goal. Lay the level along the length of the stand to make sure that it is completely level. If not, use hardwood shims (available at hardware stores) to level the stand by placing them one at a time under the legs.

   Make sure you leave room behind the stand for hanging equipment and leave enough room for yourself to do cleaning and maintenance.

3. **Clean out your tank.**

   Clean out your aquarium with clear water and a soft sponge. Do not use soap or other chemicals! Make sure you dry the outside of the glass with paper towels to avoid streaks that may be hard to reach after the system is completely set up.

4. **Place the aquarium on the stand.**

   Make sure that the tank fits properly on the stand. Do not allow any of the tank's bottom edges to hang over. If you want, you can place a thin sheet of Styrofoam underneath the tank to cushion it and even out minor changes in level.

5. **Add a background.**

   If you want to add a background, now would be the time to tape it onto the back of the tank so that you don't have to work it around the equipment and cords later.

   Another option is to paint the back glass on the *outside* with a roller. This is a great way to hide any cords or other objects that you don't want to show behind the tank. Apply two coats of paint and make sure that it is completely dry before you continue. Take care not to splash any paint into the interior of the tank as it can be toxic. We like to use an ocean blue paint for the back of my tanks, as it allows the fish to show their true colors and helps reflect lighting.

6. **Wash and add your substrate.**

   Wash gravel with clear water. You can use a colander to rinse the gravel. Set the colander over a bucket and rinse the gravel under water until the overflow is clean. This will remove dirt, dust, and excess dye.

   Slope two inches of gravel so that it is about one half an inch higher in the rear.

7. **Add a bio-wheel filter.**

   Place the filter on the tank by hanging it on the outside of the rear glass. The intake tube should hang inside of the aquarium. Rinse the filter pads under clear water and place them in the slots inside the filter. Place the bio-wheels in their marked slots. Do not plug the unit in yet!

8. **Fill the tank up ⅔ of the way with water.**

   This will allow you to arrange the gravel if it has moved during filling and provide enough water to add decorations later.

   Pour the water into the aquarium by letting it splash on top of a small plate that is resting underwater on top of the gravel. This will make sure that the water does not move the gravel and decorations all around while you are filling the tank.

9. **Add decorations.**

   Add rocks, driftwood, plastic plants, and other decorations.

10. **Fill the aquarium.**

    Add water until the aquarium water is at the same level as the bottom edge of the aquarium frame that wraps around the top of the glass.

11. **Add declorinator to the water.**

    This is not always needed with two-day wait time on fish, but it never hurts to add it anyway.

12. **Plug in all the equipment.**

13. **Add water to the bio-wheel unit if it is not self-starting to start it.**

14. **Check the pH and adjust as needed.**

15. **Put the hood and lights on the tank.**

16. **Let the tank run for 24–48 hours and retest pH. Adjust as needed.**

17. **Put in your starter coldwater fish.**

Setting Up Your Simple Indoor Goldfish Pond

A good place for this pond would be on an enclosed patio or in a finished basement. For this setup, we will be using a half whiskey barrel with a submersible pond filter:

1. **Place your half whiskey barrel in a level area that is free from windows and drafts.**

2. **Add the pond liner.**

   If it is pre-fit barrel liner, just set it in place. If you have to make your own, use a flexible liner and fit it into the barrel, allowing the excess to hang over the edges.

3. **Fill the barrel with water, leaving about six inches at the top.**

4. **Add several inches of gravel or smooth river stones to the bottom and set your pond filter down into the barrel after attaching it to your pump.**

5. **Add dechlorinator and then trim off the excess liner.**

   You can tack the end of the liner six inches below the rim on the outside using a staple gun.

6. **Place your pond plants in the pond.**

   Add a few floaters to start with. For stand-up plants, you can use overturned clean flowerpots as a base to raise the level of your plants.

7. **Plug in your pump and add a top.**

   There are several ways to add a top to the barrel, but our favorite way is to have a lumberyard cut a heavy board in the shape of a circle with a large donut hole in the middle. Simply set the board on top and you'll have a little rim around the opening to place decorations and small rocks. This also covers the overhanging liner.

8. **Let the pond run for 24–48 hours then add your starter goldfish.**

One Last Thing

Don't forget that there are many different variations you use on equipment for your aquarium or small indoor pond. Make sure to follow the manufacturer's instructions on all equipment as you go along. If you still have problems, your local fish store will be happy to help.

Be bold and experiment with different combinations of equipment. Take time to research your fish and plants and add them slowly over time (a couple a month) so that your system remains stable. Remember not to overstock.

Chapter 16

Live Plants for Freshwater Aquariums

*L*ive plants are one of the most overlooked but truly wonderful aspects of the aquarium hobby.

Plants come in a wide variety of sizes, shapes, colors, and densities. Living plants offer a unique and natural beauty that cannot be achieved with artificial substitutes. All you need to enjoy live aquatic plants are proper water conditions, good lighting, and a little patience. Take time to bring your fish a step closer to their natural environment with live plants, and they will love you for it!

Live plants are a lot of fun, look cool, and help boost your image as a serious hobbyist. What better reasons can you think of to keep them in your aquarium? Actually, there are a lot of other good reasons to keep live plants, as you will learn in this chapter. Unfortunately, many small fish shops don't carry live plants, and even if they do, they may have limited stock. If your local dealer does not have the plants you are looking for, ask about special orders. Many aquatic shops have access to live plants but only order them on demand because of limited tank space.

The Internet can save you, too! You can find an entire aquatic forest just by cruising the cyber highway for an hour or so. Here are a couple Web sites to get you started:

✔ www.aquariumplants.com

✔ www.freshwateraquariumplants.com

If you don't have a computer, borrow your neighbor's for a while (tell her you're doing international biological research).

What Live Plants Do for Your Aquarium

You can use live plants to enhance the natural look of your freshwater aquarium, and they can be very beneficial and beautiful at the same time. Plants can produce a calming affect (both for you and your fish) and help maintain a natural, biological balance in your aquarium. Don't get us wrong. Many hobbyists aquascape their aquariums with artificial plants and are perfectly happy with the outcome. Then again, many hobbyists use plastic plants because they don't have the knowledge to maintain live aquatic plants successfully, or don't have the time to care for them.

Certain species of fish destroy any live plants you may put into your tank, so in certain situations artificial plants are much more beneficial than the real McCoy. Artificial plants are only slightly less costly than live plants, so don't let cost alone affect your decision. If you really want live plants but are on a limited budget, just start out with a few and add them when you are able to grab a bit of aquatic "mad money." (See Chapter 17 for a lot more on plant species.)

If you do choose to use artificial plants, try not to get too carried away in the color department. Plastic plants are manufactured in every color under the sun. If your tank ends up with shocking pink plants on one side, black in the front, and red and green striped ones in the back, your fish may think they've crash-landed at Woodstock. They may die from sheer fright or become color-blind (okay, just kidding). Even though they pose no real physical danger, loudly colored plants can keep your fish from spawning on a continual basis and may cause them to hide in the corners of your aquarium.

A well-planted aquarium:

✔ Offers good shelter for pregnant females who want to escape from aggressive mates

✔ Supplies shade and cooler temperatures during the warmer months

✔ Helps protect small and shy fish from bullying tankmates

✔ Provides a safe refuge for all your delicate and long-finned fish that may otherwise end up on the aquatic lunch menu

✔ Inhibits algae growth by providing resource competition. Plants use the excess nutrients in the water to thrive. These are the same nutrients that algae need to survive. Plants help "starve" algae production by keeping them from having enough nutrients to flourish.

Live plants can condition the water in your tank by removing carbon dioxide and sulfur substances and by harboring bacteria to remove other wastes. The biological filtration (provided by the bacteria) in an aquarium breaks down existing ammonia into less harmful substances that live plants use for food. Plants can use these nitrites and nitrates to gather life-giving nitrogen. By utilizing light during photosynthesis, plants also create food for themselves within their own cells and release oxygen, which is very beneficial to your fish, during the process (Figure 16-1). When you turn off your aquarium lights, plants start absorbing oxygen. They then release carbon dioxide in a process similar to your fish's respiration process.

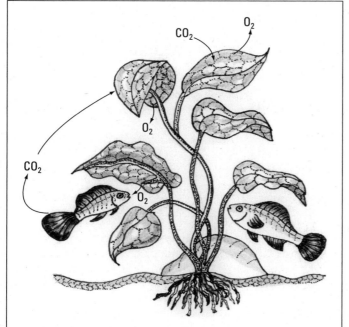

Figure 16-1: During daylight hours, plants absorb carbon dioxide and expel oxygen.

Living plants can also be a food source for fish that prefer a high amount of vegetation in their diet (of course you'll have to continually replace plants as they get munched). Your fish's color is much more intense in a naturally planted tank. And because plants provide security, your aquatic pets also act much more confident in a planted tank. (They won't have to spend the entire day trying to dig an escape tunnel.)

Plant Types

You can find three basic types of plants in an aquarium shop: aquatic, marginal, and terrestrial. Unfortunately, many dealers sell terrestrial (grow-in-the-earth) plants as aquatic plants. Each type of plant is unique in its requirements for survival and growth, so you need to know exactly which species you can accommodate before you purchase any plants. Make sure each plant type is labeled correctly before you take it home! (Chapter 17 gives you good examples of live aquatic plants that you can enjoy in your home aquarium without having to worry about them too much.)

Aquatic plants can be entirely submerged beneath the water line of your tank and still survive. These plants die when they are removed from the water. Sagittaria (*Sagittaria natans*) and pygmy sword (*Echinodorus quadricostatus*) are two good examples of aquatic plants.

Marginal plants spend only part of their time submerged beneath the water. These types of plants flower and seed out of water during the dry periods of the year. Examples of marginal plants include cryptocoryne (*Cryptocoryne balansae*). Marginal plants require special handling and should be left in the hands of expert hobbyists.

Terrestrial plants live on land and do not survive very long if they're completely submerged. We do not recommend them for use in the home aquarium.

Let's proceed to the more common kinds of aquatic plants, the ones that are used most in home aquariums.

Floating plants

Floating plants do not anchor themselves and drift around the top of your aquarium. Floating plants can grow very quickly, so you need to thin them out — or prune them — when they become too thick and bushy. If you don't, they may block out the light that enters your aquarium from the hood. The resulting loss of light can lower the temperature of your aquarium water, which has a devastating effect on the health of your fish and plants. Floating plants reproduce easily by sprouting young daughter plants and propagating new plants from severed pieces. Use floating plants in spawning tanks to hide young fry.

One plant in particular, duckweed (*lemna*), multiplies so rapidly that your tank may look like the lights have burnt out permanently. Avoid buying duckweed unless you have time to prune it back. Another floating plant is the water lettuce (*Pistia stratiotes*).

Rooted plants

Rooted plants anchor themselves in the substrate and draw part of their nourishment through their leaves, and part through their roots. Rooted plants reproduce by creating runners (slender plant shoots) that branch off of the main stem. These runners eventually reroot and form new plants or sprout young shoots out of existing leaf surfaces. Many species of rooted plants can grow very large, so use caution when choosing the correct species for your particular tank.

Potted plants come with a small receptacle around the roots and are often raised in humid nurseries. With this type of plant, you have the option of submerging the entire basket in the substrate or removing the basket and planting the roots directly. If you leave the basket intact, the plant's roots will grow through the basket's holes and then anchor themselves in the substrate.

We remove the baskets so that they don't show above the substrate level when rooting fishes begin digging around them. Unless you have ten feet of gravel in your tank, these horrid baskets always seem to find a way to show off and emerge into the limelight.

Removing the basket often reveals several small plants combined into one tight group. Carefully separate each individual plant from the others around it. Plant each of these little cuttings in the substrate separately. Remember that these plants are not full grown, so you need to allow ample space for them to spread out.

Cuttings

Many varieties of plants are sold in aquarium stores as cuttings. Cuttings often grow very rapidly as they gather nourishment through their leaves. A group of small cuttings (plants too small to stand alone) can be bunched up together with aquarium weights (which you can purchase from your local fish dealer) and planted until they begin to root on their own. After they begin to grow a bit, you can separate them from each other.

Easy plant species

Some plants are a little easier to grow and keep than others. (You will find even more detailed information on plants, including some illustrations, in Chapter 17.)

The following are suggestions on freshwater plants that are good for beginners:

- **Dwarf swordplant (*Echinodorus tenellus*):** Use this in the front area of your tank to create a carpet effect.

- **Corkscrew val (*Vallisneria spiralis*):** Corkscrew val's light green leaves are twisted like a spiral staircase. Val needs quite a bit of light.

- **Hornwart (*Ceratophyllum demersum*):** Hornwart has very stiff leaves.

- **Hairgrass (*Eleocharis acicularis*):** Hairgrass resembles the grass in your yard but is longer (our house being an exception).

- **Amazon sword (*Echinodorus grandiflorus*):** Amazon sword has heart-shaped leaves and is very tolerant of beginner mistakes. This plant enjoys soft water.

- **Java fern (*Microsorium pteropus*):** Java fern has large leaves that form a point at the top and requires only moderate lighting conditions.

And if you decide to attempt a brackish aquarium, here are a few easy-to-keep brackish plants:

- **Green cabomba (*Cabomba caroliniana*):** A plant with soft leaves and foliage resembles feather wisps.

- **Mangrove (*Brugiuera species*):** Usually purchased in pots, this plant spreads out all over the tank.

- **Giant hygrophila (*Nomaphila stricta*):** A beautiful plant that produces a purple flower.

Maintaining Plant-Friendly Aquarium Conditions

To keep your plants healthy, you need to provide them with the proper temperature, nutritional food, proper substrate, good water conditions, and adequate lighting.

Temperature requirements

Plants have temperature requirements just like your fish do. Check each species' temperature requirements before you purchase them, so you know whether they're compatible with your fish's needs. A large majority of aquarium plants are tropical and need to be kept warm — they eventually die in cold water.

While you're checking out a shop's tropical plants, see whether they are being kept in warm tanks. If they're kept in cold water, they probably won't survive very long after you place them in your home aquarium.

Substrate for rooting

Live plants prefer a one- to two-inch deep substrate that consists of fine gravel or coarse sand (1/16 inch to 1/8 inch is great). This type of substrate allows water to move through plant roots so that they can gather nutrients. It also provides plants with the space they need for their roots to fork out as they grow.

Filtration

Clean water is very important for successful plant growth in your aquarium. Dirt and debris settle on the surface of the leaves and clog the plant's pores. Keep plant leaves clean by gently brushing them with a soft toothbrush that you keep for plant aquarium use only. If your aquarium water gets too dirty, the amount of energy-giving light is drastically reduced. Water changes and vacuuming the water help correct the problem.

Try to use filtration that doesn't pump tons of air bubbles into the water, which drives out the CO_2 your plants need. A power filter or canister filter would be the best bets for a plant-heavy tank setup.

Feeding

The tap water in your aquarium doesn't have the necessary trace elements and nutrients your plants need for proper growth. You can put tablets and liquid feeders (which provide nutrients, found at your local pet shop) in the gravel near the plant's roots for fertilization — best done after a water change. You can also place a single cutting in the center of a plug, which provides nutrition on a continual basis. You then bury the plug in the gravel. Here is a good site to take a look at plugs:

www.aq-products.com/Catalog/Plants/Plant%20Plugs.htm

Do not use household plant fertilizers in your aquarium because they contain extremely high amounts of phosphates, which are bad for fish.

Lighting

Tropical plants require a constant source of light during the day in order to grow properly. Most tropical plants should receive at least eight hours of light each day. Planted tanks require more intense lighting than fish-only aquariums, but your fish probably won't mind an opportunity to get a bit of an extra tan now and then.

On the other hand, some plants such as the Amazon sword and the Java fern prefer low lighting situations. Check the requirements of each species before you buy so you get plants that will survive under the same lighting conditions.

You can use a plant-growth light, which provides the proper light spectrum plants need. You can also control the amount of light your plants receive by using a simple timer on your aquarium light so that peak intensity remains the same each day.

One way to compensate for the different lighting requirements between plant species, if you choose to mix them, is to place taller plants so that they shade the shorter species that thrive in low-light levels.

Supplements

One of the most important supplements for plants is iron because plants use it to produce chlorophyll, necessary for photosynthesis. Make sure you get an iron supplement for your plant tanks. You can find them on most aquatic Internet plant sites and in some fish stores.

Purchasing and Transporting Your Plants

If you're fortunate enough to live in an area where the local pet shops stock a wide variety of live plants, you need to know how to get them home safely. If possible, always purchase your plants from a dealer (in town or on the Internet).

Taking from the wild

You *can* collect plants from small bodies of water, such as ponds, but take a few precautions if you choose to do this. Make sure the plants in your area match the water conditions that will be in your aquarium. Any plants you take from the wild must be carefully cleaned in clear, cool water with a toothbrush to avoid introducing disease and aquatic pests such as snails and parasites.

Before you go yanking up any plants at your local stream, make sure that their removal won't have any detrimental effects on the natural environment. You should also check with local authorities about endangered species and other regulations to ensure that your liberation of the plants doesn't cause your own removal from home to jail.

Buying from a dealer

Before purchasing any live plants, you should have a good idea of which types and sizes best suit your project. Write out a list that includes the total number of plants you need to reach the design effects you desire. It is possible that your local fish shop won't have all the plants you're searching for. Include substitute species on your shopping list just in case the shop cannot order them for you.

Start out by purchasing just a few of the plants on your list. Remember that plants usually grow very quickly. If you buy too many in the beginning, your aquarium may end up looking like an Amazon rainforest in a couple of weeks. If your gardener has to come in and trim your aquarium plants back so you can open your front door, you may want to thin them out a bit. One general formula to obtain the total number of plants for your aquarium is to calculate one plant for every six square inches of gravel area. Simply multiply the length of the aquarium by the width (in inches) and divide by six to get the number of plants you need.

You also need to use a little common sense when you buy your plants. Some species are naturally "fuller" than others and take up quite a bit more space. After you become familiar with a particular plant species, you'll have a better idea of how much room the plants occupy when they are full grown (see Chapter 17 for more).

Getting plants home in one piece

To maintain your plants' good health, you need to make sure that they don't dry out on the way home from the shop. Ask your dealer to bag your plants in water or carefully wrap each one in wet newspaper. If it's cold out, transport your new plants in a cooler so that the water remains warm.

Achieving acclimation

When you arrive home, place your plants in a pan of water that contains a 10 percent solution of potassium permanganate. *Potassium permanganate* is a substance that kills unwanted germs and disinfects plant surfaces. If you cannot find this solution in your local pet store, clean the plants under room-temperature water by gently brushing them with a soft toothbrush as mentioned previously. Trim all cuttings to the correct height for your tank and remove any dead or wilted leaves with a sharp pair of scissors.

Never pinch off or tear dead plant pieces with your fingers — you may damage the delicate tissues!

Plants need time to acclimate to their new home. Don't expect them to flourish in a day. Some plants may lose leaves and struggle before taking a firm hold in their new environment, so give them a month or so to make themselves at home.

Plant Problems

Even the best hobbyist's green thumb turns black once in a while. Hey, no one is perfect! Fortunately, plant diseases in aquariums are really rare, so don't get too worked up at the thought of all your beautiful sword plants kicking the bucket at the same time. If your plants are growing at a normal pace and are developing new shoots and buds, they're probably in good health.

Signs of poor plant health

Knowing how to recognize and cure foliage problems before they become too severe can help you avoid losing your new aquatic plants. Here are some warning signs to look for when carrying out your daily aquarium maintenance routine:

- **Your plants have holes in them.** This problem is often caused by fish nibbling on the leaves. If your fish are vegetarians, and you provided the plants as a food source, get used to losing plants. If your plants begin to fall apart after the holes appear, they may be suffering from rot, which is usually caused by excess nitrates in the aquarium. Water changes help correct this problem.

- **Your plants' leaves are turning yellow.** They may be suffering from an iron deficiency. Aquatic plant fertilizer with iron (such as Hagen Nutrafin Plant Gro Iron Enriched Aquatic Plant Fertilizer) solves this problem.

- **The leaves have turned brown or black.** This indicates decay, probably caused by too much iron. Water changes help this problem.

✔ **Some plants are dying, and some are surviving.** Hard-water plants are better able to extract CO_2 from the water, whereas soft-water plants have a harder time. Make sure you have enough CO_2 in your aquarium water for each type.

If you want to keep different types of plants together, try adding CO_2 (through water change or pressurized CO_2 equipment available at pet shops) to the tank. Different areas of the country have different amounts of CO_2 in the tap water. Note that adding CO_2 to the tank lowers the pH. Pressurized CO_2 systems are nice but can be expensive. To avoid this, keep plants with similar requirements together.

Algae

No matter what you do, you always have some type of algae in your aquarium system. Algae is often introduced into your aquarium by fish and live food. But, if you keep healthy plants in your system, algae doesn't stand much of a chance.

If your algae gets out of control, though, look out! Blue-green algae (caused by poor water conditions) can form a layer on all of your decorations and substrate, and if your fish stop swimming for a few minutes, they start to resemble a moldy cupcake. Red algae, which is caused by a lack of CO_2 in the water, is really nasty and hangs in threads all over your aquarium. Extra oxygen can be added to battle the red algae, but often a tank must be cleaned and restarted if it gets out of control. Brown algae (caused by inadequate light) forms huge brown layers in your aquarium. Green algae (caused by too much light) makes your aquarium water look like pea soup.

A good way to battle algae in your aquarium is to add algae-eating fish, such as the Siamese algae eater (*Crossocheilus siamensis*) or the bushy-nosed pleco (*Ancistrus sp.*). These fish help keep algae populations under control naturally. Don't depend on algae-eating fish to solve your problem alone, though. They couldn't eat that many algae in a million years.

Algae grows quickly in a cycled tank, but eventually the plants declare war on it and remove the nutrients that it needs to survive. Do not change your water when algae becomes very intense — that can lead to an even bigger problem. If your plants are in good condition, they will eventually win the algae war. Use algae-eating fish and keep your water conditions pristine. The combo will keep your tank looking great.

Medications

Aquarium salt, copper medications, and metal-based treatments can be very harmful to your plants. Make sure your new fish are quarantined so that you will not have to medicate them if they become ill after arriving home. If your fish do require medication, treat them in a separate hospital tank away from your live plants.

Planting Techniques

It is a whole lot easier to put live plants in your tank after you add the water. Arranging plants in a dry aquarium can be a very difficult job. All they do is look limp and fall over. Lock your front door until all the decorating is complete. That way, you can work undisturbed and then look cool when all is said and done. A full aquarium allows you a better view of the plants after they spread out into the water.

Don't push a plant into the gravel below its *crown* (the area between the plant's stalk and the roots). Space plants far enough apart so that they have room to spread their roots and grow properly. The distance between them should be approximately equal to the span of one leaf. A crowded tank causes the plants to wither and die.

One of the best strategies is to place all of your tall plants near the back of the tank. Fill the center of the aquarium with short or bushy plants. Use taller plants that spread out (such as elodea) to hide heaters, undergravel filter tubes, and other unsightly equipment. Place small plants near the front of the glass. Try to arrange your plants so that they don't look too symmetrical (the same on both sides of the tank) because they normally don't grow that way in nature.

Sketch a picture of how you want your tank to look before you start planting, so that you have a simple plan to follow. If you continually remove and replant the little shoots that grow out of a main stem, the parent plant grows faster.

Nothing is as astounding looking as an aquarium with live plants. If you have the chance to try out live plants, don't hesitate to add them to your aquarium. The benefits to your fish and natural underwater system far out weigh the slightly higher cost in terms of finance and time that are needed to keep plants healthy.

Chapter 17

Choosing Plant Species for Your Tank

In Chapter 16 we discuss plant types, the aquarium conditions required for live plants, how to purchase plants and transport them, and how to troubleshoot problems that may occur. This chapter covers different types of plants that you can put in your tank and maintain as a beginner.

Live plants add realism to your aquarium!

The species listed in this chapter are by no means all that are available. There are too many to name in one chapter, so we focus our attention on some of the really cool-looking ones that you can use to enhance your own special aquarium setup.

Don't be afraid to experiment with different types of plants to see what is most pleasing to your own eye. Purchase plants that you really like, but don't forget to make sure that they will work well with the aquarium conditions and habits of your aquarium fish.

As mentioned in the last chapter, live plants help enhance the natural beauty of your tank, reduce algae problems, improve the water quality, and provide your fish with places to hide and find shelter. Live aquarium plants are also a great way to help condition and nudge your fish into mating.

Don't overstock your tank with plants to the point that your fish have no swimming room! Overplanting causes stress and disease. If you want a good setup that looks natural, it should include a variety of plants and open spaces as well.

Aquarium lighting levels

So that you have a good idea what is meant by *low*, *medium*, *bright*, and *very bright* lighting, here is a guide:

Low: 1 to 2 watts per gallon

Medium: 2 to 3 watts per gallon

Bright: 3 to 5 watts per gallon

Very bright: 5 or more watts per gallon

Foreground Plants

All aquariums look good with *foreground* plants, and by that we mean smaller plants placed toward the front and middle of your aquarium. The last thing you want to do is have your tank look like it is just lined all around the outside with live plants. You need shorter plants in the front and center of the tank to compliment taller ones toward the rear and add variety to the aquascaped décor.

Cryptocoryne (Cryptocoryne wendetti)

This species is a beautiful plant that has long leaves resembling a garden trowel. The leaves are green with red-tinted areas. This plant is great for tanks that are cycled (see Chapter 14 for more on the nitrogen cycle). In the wild this plant grows on riverbanks and uses rhizomes for growth, so tie it off to driftwood or rocks with plastic gardening ties.

This plant requires a lot of nutrition. This is why placing this in an aged (cycled) tank will keep this species happy. Placing it in a new aquarium may cause it to die from lack of nutrition if you don't use any type of plant food supplement.

Don't be concerned if this plant looks like it struggling a bit and loses leaves when you first add it to your aquarium. That is normal in many cases. This plant tends to grow rather slowly and is great for smaller tanks.

Level: Easy

Temperature: 70–80 degrees F

Light: Bright

pH: 6.5–7.5

Placement: Foreground to mid-range

Baby tears (Micranthemum umbrosum)

Baby tears (Figure 17-1) is an amazing plant that is very fast growing and covers surfaces like a carpet. For this reason, it is recommended that you use it for larger tanks (over 30 gallons). In good conditions, this plant spreads like wildfire, so you will need to prune it back from time to time unless you want your aquarium to look like an uncut back lot or the front steps of a funeral home.

This plant also grows well if you allow it to float, and many species of fish just don't seem to like the taste of it, making it a good one to purchase if you have fish that like to nibble on foliage too much. Baby tears is also very hardy and seems to be able to put up with beginner's mistakes.

This plant has delicate little clusters of slightly round leaves (shaped, not surprisingly, like a baby's tear) that are a beautiful light green color. CO_2 addition is recommended for the best growth, but it will survive without CO_2 added.

Level: Easy

Temperature: 70–80 degrees F

Light: Bright

PH : 5.5–7.5

Placement: Foreground

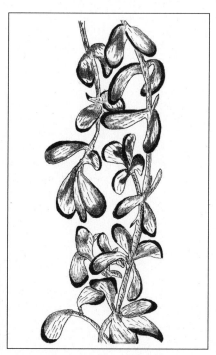

Figure 17-1:
Baby tears
grows very
fast.

Pearl grass (hemianthus micranthemoides)

Pearl grass is a very graceful-looking plant that is great for the foreground of your aquarium. This species is light green and has half-elliptical shaped leaves. As this plant grows, you will see it developing side shoots (in time you will come to think of them as runners) in all directions. You can easily prune this plant so it continues to grow and fill in the gaps that you want it to cover up.

Level: Easy

Temperature: 68–82 degrees F

Light: Medium to bright

PH : 5.0–7.5

Placement: Foreground

Brazilian micro sword (Lilaeopsis brasiliensis)

This South American plant is an interesting-looking species that resembles thick green grass. The thickness can be a problem, as it will encourage algae to grow all over it. The best thing to do is to thin the plant out by pruning interior leaves (the thick leaves inside the outer leaves) so that light and water can reach all of the plant's surfaces. Once you have thinned the plant out, carefully rinse it under room-temperature water to remove any excess debris before adding it to your aquarium.

One trick we use to keep this plant from becoming a big bound-up ball is to keep it in areas of the tank that have high circulation (near airstones or filter return water). This slow-growing plant does really well in fine substrate such as sand and eventually will look like you have a lawn growing in your aquarium.

Level: Moderate

Temperature: 60–79 degrees F

Light: Very bright

PH : 6.0–8.0

Placement: Foreground

Madagascar lace (Aponogeton fenestralis)

This species is dark green and has leaves that look like they are made out of a lace tablecloth. It is fascinating to watch this plant sway in a light water current. Because algae tends to gather in the latticework of the leaves, having algae eaters in your tank will be beneficial to this plant.

Once this plant gains height it can be moved to the back of the tank.

> Level: Easy
>
> Temperature: 60–75 degrees F
>
> Light: Very bright
>
> PH: 5.5–6.8
>
> Placement: Foreground to mid-range

Dwarf anubias (Anubias nana)

This is a wonderful plant for beginners because it seems to thrive even in less than perfect water conditions.

This slow-growing plant has broad green leaves that add a wonderful splash of color to any aquarium. It also uses rhizomes for nutrients and likes being tied to driftwood so that water can flow around it. It does not need to be embedded in gravel.

Make sure that this plant is not kept in direct sunlight or under strong artificial lighting.

> Level: Easy
>
> Temperature: 59–79 degrees F
>
> Light: Low
>
> PH: 5.5–6.8
>
> Placement: Foreground to mid-range on driftwood and rocks

Background Plants

Background plants are important for rounding out an aquarium aquascape. These plants can also help cover up unsightly filter tubes, airline tubing, and heaters in the rear of the tank. A spreading background plant that is placed in the front corner of a tank can also add an interesting aspect to the scene.

Experiment and see what looks good to you!

Hornwort (CeratopHyllum demersum)

Hornwort (Figure 17-2) is one of the most popular aquarium plants on the market. It does not have real roots, but can be planted in gravel. This fast-growing, beautiful plant has green featherlike appendages that reach skyward like upside down umbrellas waiting to catch the rain.

Figure 17-2:
Hornwort is very popular and grows in gravel.

This plants consumes a lot of nutrients and is an enemy to algae because it secrets a substance that is not good for its rival. It has bright green leaves that are stiff.

Level: Easy

Temperature: 50–80 degrees F

Light: Does well in any lighting condition

PH: 6.0–8.0

Placement: Background or can be used as a floating plant

Corkscrew val (Vallisneria spiralis)

Corkscrew val is a unique fast-growing Asian plant that resembles a corkscrew. There is no other plant that seems to stimulate the imagination like this species does when it is gently swaying in water current. Corkscrew val can be a bit difficult to keep alive when it is very small, so try to obtain larger plants with well-established roots if possible.

Level: Moderate

Temperature: 59–86 degrees F

Light: Does well in any lighting condition

PH: 6.0–8.0

Placement: Background

Elodea (Egeria densa)

Elodea (Figure 17-3) is great for beginners because it grows very quickly. This plant also secretes substances that help to discourage algae. Elodea grows very thick in bright light and is a good way to fill in the background. This plant can also float, removes large amounts of nitrates, has roots, and flowers under good condition.

Level: Easy

Temperature: 50–79 degrees F

Light: Bright

PH: 5.0–8.0

Placement: Background

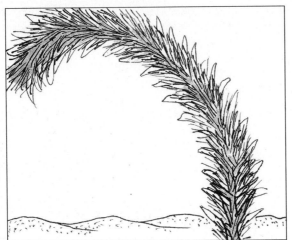

Figure 17-3:
Elodea is a
very good
choice for
your tank's
background.

Carolina fanwort (Cambomba caroliniana)

This species is a beautiful light green plant that has a feathery or wispy appearance. This is another great plant for hiding background spots, and fish seem to love to nibble on it.

The problem is, the leaves come off very easily, so if you have nibblers you may find an annoying number of plucked leaves floating all over your tank. These leaves will tend to clog up your filters as well.

This fast-growing plant loves soft, acidic waters and is stunning when planted in groups of three or more. Make sure you have enough gravel to keep it down, because this plant seems to float up quite a bit.

Level: Moderate

Temperature: 75–82 degrees F

Light: Very bright

PH: 4.0–7.0

Placement: Background

Giant anubias (Anubias barteri)

This slow growing plant (Figure 17-4) can grow up to 15 inches tall and makes a great background plant. This plant has very tough leaves and stems so it is a great species to use for cichlids and other plant aggressive fish. The rhizome should be above gravel, because it shoots down roots to grab nutrients from the substrate.

Level: Easy

Temperature: 59–79 degrees F

Light: Low

PH: 5.5–6.8

Placement: Background

Figure 17-4:
Giant anubias is tough and grows tall.

Red ludwigia (Ludwigia mullertii)

This beautiful plant has green leaves, with a slight tinge of red, and red stems. As it matures the red can spread to the leaf edges. Ludwigia grows very rapidly, so you will soon have a large plant even if you started with a smaller one.

This plant also grows side shoots, so you may have to prune it back if it gets out of control. It has very tiny flowers that can be difficult to see.

Level: Easy

Temperature: 64–77 degrees F

Light: Very bright

PH: 4.0–7.0

Placement: Background

Oriental sword (Echinodorus oriental)

This slow-growing plant (Figure 17-5) has broad red and green leaves that are shaped like the blade of a sword.

Level: Easy

Temperature: 68-79 degrees F

Light: Bright

PH: 5.5-7.0

Placement: Mid-range to background

Figure 17-5:
Oriental
sword does
best with
a rich
substrate.

Amazon sword (Echinodorus amazonicus)

This plant gets its name from the fact that it grows naturally in the Amazon, and the shape of its leaves resemble the blade of a sword. This amazing plant looks fantastic if you make it the centerpiece of your planted scheme. It will bloom, so if you can have the blooms above the water line you will be in for a really pretty treat.

This plant really should be provided with extra CO_2 and fertilizer if you want it to really flourish. The root system on this plant is quite large, so keep an eye on it to make sure it is not choking out your other plants.

Level: Moderate

Temperature: 72–82 degrees F

Light: Medium to bright

PH: 6.4–7.2

Placement: Mid-range to background

Red-stem milfoil (MyriopHyllum matogrossensis)

In our opinion, this is one of the coolest-looking plants you can buy. It looks like a winter tree that has lost it leaves, except that it is red and pinkish in color. It grows thickly, and often resembles seaweed with its three to five feathering leaflets around the stem.

Red-stem milfoil can be anchored to gravel or left to float. It will pretty much take care of itself, and is great for coldwater systems.

Level: Easy

Temperature: 60–75 degrees F

Light: Medium

PH: 6.4–7.2

Placement: Background

Stargrass (Heteranthera zosterifolia)

This fast-growing plant has bright mint-green leaves that grow on thick and numerous stems. Due to the rapid growth and fullness, you will have to prune it back periodically. The entire plant resembles an aquatic pine tree, and many aquatic species love to use it as a breeding ground.

Level: Easy

Temperature: 70–80 degrees F

Light: Medium to bright

PH: 6.2–7.0

Placement: Background

Floating Plants

Floating plants are important for aquariums that require dim lighting, because they block the light from above. They also provide a lot of place for small fry to hide and provide privacy for mating. Even in setups that don't require dim lighting, one small floating plant can give a realistic river or pond look to your aquarium.

Amazon frogbit (Limnobium laevigatum)

The frogbit plant grows into the shape of a rosette. It will then produce shoots that will form a tiny plant at the end. Once this end breaks off, it will become a new plant on its own. The leaves are waxy green and tend to resemble a pond lily. Although it is a floating plant, you want to make sure that the leaves do not get too close to the aquarium lights, because they are sensitive to burning.

Level: Moderate

Temperature: 64–82 degrees F

Light: Medium to bright

PH: 6.5–7.5

Placement: Floating

Duckweed (Lemna minor)

This is a wonderful fast-growing plant for ponds, because it blocks out a lot of harmful sunrays that can quickly overheat the water or produce algae.

This plant also provide shelters and is a great incentive for spawning among its numerous clusters of oval green leaves in an aquarium. You will have to prune it to keep it from getting out of hand.

Coldwater and pond fish love to eat this plant, and it provides good nutrition because it is high in vitamins and minerals. Duckweed is good for your pond's water, too, because it helps to absorb excess nutrients and ammonia.

Level: Easy

Temperature: 64–79 degrees F

Light: Medium to bright

PH: 4.5–7.5

Placement: Floating

Pond Plants

Pond plants are fun and add realism to any pond.

Water lettuce (Pistia stratiotes)

Water lettuce (Figure 17-6) is a plant that has soft, light-green, ribbed leaves that are large and round.

The leaves form a rosette. The long, thick roots provide an excellent hiding place for fish that like to swim near the surface of the aquarium, but it has to be pruned periodically or it will take over your entire tank or pond. This plant is also useful for filtering your aquarium water.

Level: Easy

Temperature: 65–85 degrees F

Light: Bright

PH: 5.0–8.0

Placement: Floating

Figure 17-6: Water lettuce provides lots of hiding places for your fish.

Water hyacinth (Eichhornia crassipes)

This plant grows very quickly and will become matted if not pruned.

The shiny green leaves are oval in shape. The plant stalk is thick and keeps the plant buoyant. It has beautiful purple flowers. This has a huge root system that fish will love to eat. Fortunately the roots grow faster than the fish can eat them.

>   Level: Easy
>
>   Temperature: 59–85 degrees F
>
>   Light: Bright
>
>   PH: 5.5–8.0
>
>   Placement: Floating

Keeping It Real

There are several reasons for keeping live plants in your aquarium. Live plants do all of the following:

- Provide natural shelter to make your fish feel safe and secure.
- Provide good places for aquatic species to spawn.
- Help keep light levels down in setups that require dim lighting.
- Provide a good food source for many aquatic species.
- Help to remove nitrates from your aquarium.
- Lend a more realistic look than artificial plants do.
- Reduce CO_2 and add oxygen to the tank for your fish.
- Help control algae by competing for the same resources.

Chapter 18

What to Do if Trouble Strikes

*E*ven if you are the world's greatest fish keeper, problems are going to occur.

No matter what you do, things will go wrong, and at the most inopportune times. Mother Nature does not always follow our timetable.

The best thing you can do if there is a problem is to have a handy solution at hand. That is what this chapter is for. We have tried to compile a list of the most common problems that can happen to or in an aquarium system. This handy little guide should get you and your aquatic pets through thick and thin.

Even if you are not having a problem, take the time to read through this chapter to get a good idea what to do if something goes wrong. Keep this chapter in mind so you can turn to it quickly if needed. We try to keep the solutions very short and to the point so you don't have to wade through a bunch of text in a time of need.

Problems have solutions, so don't sweat it! Things will go wrong from time to time, so remember to simply do your best to resolve the issue. Nobody can ask for more.

Fish Problems

Most fish problems can be cured if you take time to check your fish out on a daily basis in order to catch illness, aggression, equipment malfunctions and feeding problems early. Here are some common problems and what to do. Check daily to see if your fish have

- ✔ Torn, clamped or ragged fins
- ✔ Missing scales
- ✔ Cloudy eyes
- ✔ Unusual white spots or body fungus

These are signs that you need to take immediate action (see Chapter 11 for details on treating disease in freshwater fish).

What to do until the pet store opens

Put the ill fish in a hospital tank for treatment (see Chapter 11). If you don't have chemicals on hand, keep the lights on the hospital tank off to reduce stress.

Restoring your tank

Make sure your fish remain disease free for two weeks after treatment before returning them to the tank.

Separating fighting fish

There is no way to guarantee 100 percent compatibility between two fish until they are placed together. Spats do break out from time to time. If they happen too often, immediately remove the most aggressive fish by adding food to the tank to lure it to the top so you can net it. Another option is to have a Plexiglas insert handy to separate the two fish into opposite sides of the tank until one can be netted.

Looking at the injured

Check for torn fins or other bodily injuries such as missing scales after a fight. If they do, place them separately in a quiet hospital tank with a stress-relief formula and allow them time to heal. Check for disease that may develop from the damage.

Solving the aggression problem

As with people, some fish just can't seem to get along. Try these things:

- ✔ If possible, permanently move the aggressive fish to another tank.
- ✔ Rearrange aquarium decorations (rocks, plants, plastic divers) to break up established territories. Build caves from rocks and give all fish places to hide.
- ✔ Made sure your fish get plenty of food. Fish that are constantly hungry from lack of proper nutrition tend to fight more.

Correcting Feeding Problems

Often fish won't eat due to being stressed out from the trip to your home, or because of problems with other fish in the tank.

Getting your fish to eat

Fish can lose their appetites. Here are a couple ideas:

- ✔ Try giving them frozen brine shrimp or other appropriate aquatic treats to kick-start them into eating again.
- ✔ Rearrange the aquarium decorations to bust down territories that may be keeping some fish from getting their fair share.

Dislodging items eaten by your fish

Add 1 level teaspoon of Epsom salt for each 10 gallons of water in the aquarium.

Equipment Problems

If you want your aquarium to function properly, you need to keep your equipment running properly. Here are a few common equipment problems and their solutions.

Fixing a clogged filter

It's very important to have a clean filter. Be sure to do these things:

- If your filter uses pads, rinse them under used tank water that you have removed from the tank and placed in a clean bucket.
- If you are using an undergravel filter, vacuum the gravel.
- Clean all tubes with a filter-cleaning brush.

Analyzing heater problems

Heaters have a way of conking out: Here are some ideas for fixing them:

- If the tank is not staying the proper temperature, make sure you have enough wattage for your aquarium. (Quick rule of thumb: 5 watts per gallon.)
- If you have the correct wattage, make sure the heater is not covered by plants or other decorations that will stop the flow of warm water throughout the tank.
- If all else fails, replace the heater.

Lighting falling into the tank

You wouldn't believe how often this happens. Do this if it does:

1. Put on a rubber kitchen glove (kept in your fish kit!) and unplug the lighting.

2. Remove the lighting from the tank and allow it to completely dry before plugging it back in. *Never* remove a light that is underwater and plugged in!

Exploding light bulbs

Do the following:

1. Unplug the lighting system.
2. Allow the bulb to cool down completely before removal to avoid burning.
3. Gently remove the remaining part of the bulb by wrapping a kitchen towel around your hand. If the bulb cannot be removed, push a small potato into the broken bulb socket (screw in bulbs) to grasp and remove the light.

Flickering lighting

If a light is constantly flickering, replace the starter unit. If the bulb continues to flicker remove the light to make sure the metal connections are dry and replace. If this does not work, replace the bulb.

Tank Problems

Nothing is worse than a leaking tank. Fortunately there are solutions to this problem. The important thing to remember is to act quickly.

Checking for leaks

✔ Make sure the tank itself is leaking by doing an inspection. Sometimes what appears to be a tank leak is actually an airstone-driven decoration pushing water over the rim, or a leaking powerfilter.

✔ If the airstone is causing the leak, shift the decoration until the problem stops.

✔ If a powerfilter is leaking from being cracked, replace it.

Getting your fish to safety

If the tank is leaking, immediately remove the fish to another tank. If you don't have an extra tank, a large plastic bowl or clean aquarium bucket works. Add gravel to the bottom of the bowl or bucket, put a few floating plants in, add an airstone connected to a pump, and cover it with a plate to keep the fish from jumping out.

Repairing a small crack

Follow these steps to repair a small crack:

1. Remove *everything* from the leaking tank: water, gravel, and equipment.
2. With a safety razor, remove the old silicone from the whole side where the leak is occurring.
3. Wipe the area dry with a clean cloth.
4. Apply new aquarium sealer to replace the old sealer you removed.
5. Allow the sealer to completely dry (drying time will be listed on the sealer tube) before adding water.

When an entire side of your aquarium breaks

If the entire side of an aquarium breaks, get your fish into a hospital tank or aquarium bucket as quickly as possible.

If the fish are out of water, use a clean paper towel to gently pick them up, as the oil and other residue on your hands can damage their scales and fins.

Call a professional glass installer to have the side replaced. Replacing it yourself is dangerous and risks further leaking. You probably would not replace broken glass in your home's picture window, and aquarium glass is even more of a challenge due to the water pressure that is constantly on it. Let the professional glass installers handle it. They know what they are doing.

Water Problems

Problems with your water can lead to stress, poor health, and death for your freshwater friends. Here are a few of the most common water problems and solutions to get your aquarium back on track.

Solving green algae problems

Green algae — that cloudy green gunk — is a result of having too much light and dissolved waste in the water. Here's what to do:

✔ Cut back on the light.

✔ Do 10 percent water changes daily until the algae clears up.

✔ Purchase algae eating fish such as Siamese algae eaters.

Controlling chemical problems

If household chemicals are dumped or spilled into the tank by accident, do this:

1. Remove your fish immediately to a hospital tank.

2. Completely drain your main tank and clean the decorations, tank, and gravel with warm water before restarting your tank.

3. Replace any filter material with new material as you are setting up the tank.

4. Remember the tank will have to biologically cycle again, so keep an eye on the situation and add a couple fish for starters (hardy fish, such as guppies and swordfish) until it has established itself.

Cooling a tank that's too hot

If your tank gets too warm, follow these steps:

1. Unplug the heater and allow it to remain in the tank. Remove the hood and replace it with a mesh top (like the ones sold for the tops of reptile tanks.) Do not remove the heater before it cools down or it can shatter. Do not remove the fish or you will shock them.

2. If you don't have an *aquarium chiller* (a piece of equipment that can be added to your tank to keep the water cool), put ice into a plastic bag and float it in the tank to *slowly* lower the temperature. Never try to lower the temperature quickly as you will do even more damage to your fish.

3. Add an extra airstone to the tank to increase oxygen because the levels will have dropped with the higher water temperatures.

4. When the temperature is back to normal, reset your heater and monitor it closely to make sure it is functioning properly. If it is still not working correctly, replace it.

Warming a tank that's too cold

If your tank gets too warm, follow these steps:

1. Put a hot water bottle in a plastic bag and float it in the tank to warm it. Do not remove the fish or you will shock them.

2. Make sure the heater is functioning and slowly raise the temperature back to normal. (A couple degrees per hour is best.)

Part IV
Breeding and Other Fun Stuff

In this part . . .

Y
ou will find out about the exciting and rewarding
world of fish breeding, how to do it and what to
watch out for when your pets are spawning. In other
chapters here we fill in some of the other fun aspects
of fishkeeping, such as photographing your fish, competing in fish shows, and the enticing brackish and saltwater
worlds that may lie beyond for you.

Chapter 19

The Breeding Room

The first thing you need to know about breeding your fish is that there is no perfect way to breed any single species of fish. Sure, a lot of techniques are known to be successful, and a lot of aquatic breeding methods are steadfast and true — but, what one hobbyist finds to be a successful method, others may have no luck with. Better methods are waiting to be discovered, and there is always room for improvement and new ideas when it comes to breeding fish.

Many hobbyists have bred fish accidentally, just by having the right combination in their aquariums. Whether it occurs by accident or on purpose, breeding is breeding. Don't let anyone tell you any differently. (If they do, tell them to come see us.) When you're breeding your fish, take the time to observe everything:

✔ What are the spawning pair (male and female that you want to mate) doing about the other fish around them?

✔ Are there any changes in the pecking order?

✔ Have feeding patterns changed since the courtship started? Are the fish eating more or have they stopped feeding normally?

By making pertinent observations of all your fish's activities, you can gain a better understanding of how aquatic relationships work.

Keep a logbook so that you have a permanent record of your spawners' ages, successes, diseases, and brood sizes.

It's a great idea to exchange information, such as by calling other hobbyists on the phone and bragging, or writing an article and bragging. Only by sharing information can breeding methods be refined and perfected. Never adopt complete secrecy: You may hold the key to solving a very difficult puzzle for someone else! Also, by exchanging information or asking for advice, you can avoid breeding hazards and unwanted mutations (no one wants to produce piranhas the size of the Titanic).

Deciding to Breed Your Aquarium Fish

Aquarists, like everyone else, have goals for their hobby. One of your first goals as a fishkeeper is to maintain a healthy and successful aquarium. After you accomplish that, then what?

You may decide to try another type of system (such as brackish or marine) or investigate unfamiliar breeds. But when all is said and done as far as maintaining an aquarium is concerned, what does the future hold? (If you're like us, one answer is: a lot of bills at the local fish shop.)

Breaking new barriers

Breeding aquarium fish successfully is kind of like getting into a sport's Hall of Fame: There is no greater reward. So many species can be bred easily that you should have no problem getting into this fascinating and enjoyable aspect of the aquarium hobby. There are also many fish out there that have never been bred, which leaves the door wide open for you to become a pioneer. Just imagine what it would be like if you were the first person on earth to successfully breed a species. It can happen.

Gaining new knowledge and enjoyment

The satisfaction of accomplishing something new (and perhaps snagging a little fame and money while you're at it) is a good reason to start breeding fish. You can gain an overwhelming amount of wisdom, knowledge, and pleasure by partaking in this scientific aspect of the hobby. When you successfully breed a particular species, you also find out much more about that species than the average hobbyist learns in a lifetime.

And, above all, breeding fish is fun. Hey, if you think human courtship is a little odd at times, wait until you see your fish go a few rounds.

Conserving the environment

Probably the most important reason to breed fish is to contribute to the conservation (keeping species alive for future generations to enjoy) of our Earth's aquatic species.

At one time, freshwater fish were shipped from many countries around the globe so that the average hobbyist could enjoy them. Today, thanks to massive freshwater breeding programs, most of these species are captive-bred. If anything ever happens to them in the wild, aquarium hobbyists will be there to pick up the ball. Already, many home aquarists and organizations such as the American Cichlid Association have saved many fish species from extinction by breeding them when their numbers reached alarmingly low rates in their native environments.

You, too, can contribute to this aspect of aquarium fish breeding. We all have a responsibility to put back what we take from the wild.

We think every aquarist should attempt to breed some species. Don't concern yourself with wondering whether it's already been done — just go out and do it.

Choosing Your Equipment

Before you set up a spawning tank, decide whether you want to breed a few fish in your main aquarium (in which case you don't need a breeding room) or turn out fry faster than your local greasy spoon. (*Fry* is a technical term for baby fish, by the way.)

A large-scale breeding operation requires space. Easy-to-breed fish multiply very rapidly. You may end up living on the back porch permanently to make room for your new arrivals. To breed fish in a serious way — to develop new colors, sizes, and/or fin shapes — you need quite a *bit* of room. An extra bedroom or office offers the perfect solution. But if your house is the size of a small cabin, you may want to look into the possibility of a heated storage shed. Make *sure* you have plenty of room before you start, or you may end up hastily trying to bamboozle your local dealer into buying some fry off you. (When you sell fish to a dealer, don't look desperate or they will cut your profit margin because they think you need money.)

The aquarium

A 10- or 20-gallon aquarium is a good starting size for a breeding tank for small species such as guppies and platys. You don't want to use a tank that is too large, because you might lose track of your spawners and their fry. In order to keep up with everything your fish are doing, you have to spy on them frequently. A smaller tank allows you to remain in control of the action at all times, and is much easier to work with and clean. As with any aquarium, thoroughly rinse it with clear water before you use it.

Putting a lid on the whole thing

When your fish are ready to breed, they get a little excited. Excited fish tend to jump very high. High-jumping fish can end up as permanent decoration stuck on your room light or as an afternoon treat for the cat. A tight-fitting hood keeps your fish in the water where they belong, protects eggs and young fry from many unseen disasters, and keeps heat loss at a minimum. A good hood also prevents dirt and household chemicals (such as your daughter's hair spray) from entering the water.

Decorations

Plenty of places to hide, such as within and under rocks and plants, give your spawning pairs the opportunity to get used to being around each other before they start spawning. It's a fact of life; some couples just don't get along very well. If your breeding tank has no hiding places, the male of many species may have to kill or maim his mate out of territoriality or frustration before any spawning has an opportunity to take place.

Many species of fish like to breed on pieces of shale, rocks, flowerpots, or plant leaves. In Chapter 20 we discuss these decorating options in further detail.

Don't laugh, but many hobbyists mistakenly place two aggressive males together in a breeding tank (it's more difficult to determine sex in some species than in others), which leads to total disaster without places for them to hide. The loss of fish in these cases can be avoided with proper hiding places.

Substrate

Hobbyists disagree as to whether to use a gravel substrate in the breeding tank. We generally recommend using no substrate for several reasons:

- ✔ A tank with gravel or sand is much more difficult to keep clean.

- ✔ Most species are happy breeding in a tank that has no substrate and use rocks, plants, or flowerpots for protection and laying eggs if needed. Check the breeding requirements on your species, though, because some do require substrate for digging during breeding. (See Chapters 19 and 20 for more.)

- ✔ The newborn fry of *livebearers* (fish that bear live young) often sink down to the substrate after birth. We have seen many fry trapped by gravel too large for them to navigate around.

- ✔ It is really difficult for you and the parents to see and keep track of the fry's health and growth with substrate in the breeding tank. For example, a betta male gathers eggs that fall from the surface and spits them back into the safety of his bubble nest. If the bottom of the tank is covered with gravel substrate, the young fry may fall between the individual stones and become unreachable.

Many hobbyists argue that a spawning tank is not natural without substrate, but we have seen most species of fish bred without it. If you feel the need to use substrate for species that prefer to spawn on it (like some killifish), a thin layer of fine sand is a good choice.

Spawning grates

Once in a while, you run into a species that likes to eat its own young or eggs. To prevent this, lay a *spawning grate* (available at many pet shops) on the floor of the tank so that the young fry or eggs fall to the bottom through the holes. This allows you time to remove the parents before they can have their offspring for dinner. You can find woven lattice plastic mats that work well at most hobby or craft stores, and you can cut them to any shape you need. Just place the lattice sheet on top of small stones, and you have a made-to-order spawning grate for very little expense. Another option is to buy a *breeding trap*, which allows newborn live fry to fall safely between a slot underneath the mother.

You know those green plastic containers that hold strawberries? (Remember you unsuccessfully tried to turn them into a Christmas ornament?) Laid side by side with the open side down, they work well as a spawning grate. Sometimes a little imagination goes a long way.

Turning up the heat

Use a good quality heater in the breeding tank to keep the water from chilling. This is especially important if your breeding room is not insulated as well as the rest of your home. Besides, many fish require a small increase in temperature to prepare them for breeding. Although it's possible to control the water temperature with the heating system in your home, it doesn't work well because all home temperatures do not match species requirements, so this isn't a practical method. It's better to have a heater you can adjust as needed on each individual tank.

Filtration

Filters are important in breeding tanks, because they supply needed oxygen and produce the water movement that entices many species to mate. Filtration also keeps wastes that can destroy eggs and fry from building up.

A sponge filter is ideal for almost any breeding tank. This unit has a very simple design and is easy to use. A sponge filter provides simple biological filtration without the risks of mechanical filters (such as youngsters being sucked up in the intake tubes). A sponge filter creates current, but doesn't cause the excess turbulence often produced by larger power and undergravel filters. If your spawning fish are stuck together permanently due to excessive water waves, you may want to cut down on the current with a valve or a smaller filter. Heavy turbulence from an extra air supply (bubble disks or airstones) can damage delicate eggs or young fry.

If you decide to use a larger filter, make sure it runs slowly. If you use a sponge filter, you can always do water changes to remove any floating debris that is usually removed by a mechanical filter.

Plants for safety, spawning, and inspiration

Plants have a wide variety of uses in a spawing tank:

- ✔ Plants look cool.
- ✔ Plants are generally inexpensive.

- Plastic and live plants provide privacy and offer security.

- Several species of fish use live plants in the construction of their nests.

- Plastic and live plants serve as spawning sites for many species of fish.

- Live plants remove carbon dioxide from the water and replace it with oxygen.

- Live plants cut down on algae present in the water by competing for the same resources they require to survive.

- Live plants are a natural food source.

- A planted tank can make your fish think they're in a natural environment, which helps inspire and speed up their spawning plans.

- Plants can provide protection and shelter when a spawning partner becomes aggressive (and many do). You're wise to always have several thick plants on hand just in case the lovemaking reaches Round 15.

If those aren't enough good reasons to use plants for spawning, we'll never be able to talk you into it!

Thoroughly clean any plants with room-temperature water that you choose for your spawning tank before adding them to the tank. Plants often carry snails and small nematodes (worms) that can potentially harm eggs and fry. To be on the safe side, you can set up a separate tank to grow plants that can be used especially for spawning.

In case you're wondering what types of plants to use in your tank, we provide you with a list to get you started in Table 19-1. Remember that many freshwater plants have different pH and temperature requirements. So, check the list in Table 19-1 and match the plant to your individual aquarium setup accordingly. (See Chapters 16 and 17 for more on live plants and for explanations of the terms we use to describe these plants.) By the way, dH means degrees of hardness.

Table 19-1	Plants for Spawning Tanks				
Name	*Temperature Range (in degrees F)*	*pH Range*	*dH Range*	*Planting Method*	*Uses*
Amazon swordplant (*Echinodorus bleheri*)	72–83	6.5–7.5	2–15	Planted or potted	For species that prefer to spawn on large plant leaves

(continued)

Table 19-1 *(continued)*

Name	Temperature Range (in degrees F)	pH Range	dH Range	Planting Method	Uses
Cryptocorn (*Cryptocoryne affinis*)	72–82	6.0–7.5	3–14	Planted or potted	For species that spawn on leaves
Hornwort (*Ceratophyllum demersum*)	60–84	6.0–7.5	5–14	Anchored or	For almost every free-floating type of freshwater fish
Java moss (*Vesicularia dubyana*)	68–85	5.8–7.5	3–15	Anchored	For free-spawning fish (fish who let their eggs scatter anywhere)
Ludwigia (*Ludwigia repens*)	62–82	5.8–7.5	3–14	Planted or free-floating	For fish that like to spawn on leaves
Sagittaria (*Sagittaria subulata*) dwellers	68–83	6.0–7.7	2–12	Anchored, planted, or free-floating	For many varieties of bottom
Spiral val (*Vallisneria spiralis*)	60–85	6.5–7.5	5–12	Planted or anchored	For species that spawn on leaves
Water hyacinth (*Eichhornia crassipes*)	72–82 2–14	6.0–7.8		Floating	For bubble nest builders
Water lettuce (*Pistia stratiotes*)	72–80	6.5–7.5	5–14	Floating	For bubble nest builders
Water sprite (*Ceratopteris thalictroides*)	68–84	6.5–7.5	2–12	Anchored or free-floating	For fish that build bubble nests, such as bettas

Getting the Water Right

The water in your spawning tank must suit the species of fish you're trying to breed. Take a look at Chapters 12 through 14 for more info on getting the water right.

pH and dH control

You must keep the pH and dH (degrees of hardness) level of your water under control in a breeding situation. Changes in pH are very damaging to your fish, and the ill effects double in intensity during the breeding ritual. Eggs and young fry are especially susceptible to the smallest of fluctuations in pH level. A good pH test kit will allow you to monitor your water (see Chapter 12).

Water temperature

One important thing to keep an eye on, especially if you have *egglayers* (fish that don't bare live young, but lay eggs that hatch), is the temperature of the water. Eggs can be severely damaged in temperatures above 85 degrees F. You may end up with poached eggs. Higher temperatures also cause eggs to develop too quickly, which can lead to weak, deformed, or weird-looking fry. Research each species (Chapter 8, other hobbyists, your local dealer, the Web) that you want to breed carefully before starting out so that you know what their water requirements are.

Cleanliness

Young fry and eggs are much more susceptible than adults to problems resulting from too many nitrogen compounds (waste) in the water. Poor water conditions can destroy eggs or damage the growth cycle of newborns. Carefully change at least one quarter of the water each day in a spawning or growout tank and make sure you have some type of filtration.

To avoid fouling the water in a breeding tank, feed the fish small amounts of live foods instead of flake.

Conditioning the Love Birds

Many fish practically jump into the spawning tank from across the room in order to breed. Others, however, have a hard time adjusting to their new partners and your breeding goals. This section gives you some die-hard methods that you can try to help *condition* (get your fish in the mood to spawn) your aquatic lovebirds. (Don't bother with Mozart and a little wine in the water — we already tried that.) No lovemaking tricks are completely foolproof, but several tried over the years have proven to be quite reliable and accurate.

The way to the heart is through the stomach routine

Everyone loves to eat, right? (In the case of some teenagers we could name, some more than others.) Fish are no different. You probably already picked up on that last time they jumped out of the water and into the open food can in your hand. So, it is easy to turn the tables and take advantage of the fact that your fish are real gluttons most of the time.

One change that commonly occurs during the breeding season in a fish's natural environment is the sudden appearance and overabundance of live foods. When seasonal rainstorms sweep over ponds, lakes, and rivers, a large supply of live insects and fresh food drops onto the water surface. Offer your fish live foods such as brine shrimp and tubifex worms (okay, okay, so it's a bribe) to condition them for breeding purposes. Just remember to rinse all live food before feeding.

Fruit flies (Drosophila), mysis shrimp, and small earthworms also make great conditioning food.

The old fake rainstorm trick

Weekly water changes are very important to the health of your fish, and you can use them to aid in the conditioning process as well. In the wild, seasonal rains (you know, when you find your car has floated down the block) usually signal the start of the breeding system. Now, we know that it's not practical to run outside with your fish tank in your hands every time it rains in your neighborhood. The only other option is to create an artificial rainstorm.

In the home aquarium, you can duplicate a rainstorm to some degree by doing frequent water changes (about 20 percent per day in a breeding tank). Clean, demineralized water stimulates most species into entering their seasonal spawning cycle.

Another way to duplicate the rainy season is by showering the surface of the water in your spawning tank with drops of water. You can do this quite easily by using an inexpensive plastic watering can purchased at almost any garden shop. No, you don't have to stand there all day imitating a stone fountain. Just run one full can of water slowly over the surface each hour when you have time. (Don't forget to remove some water first!) You can also try pouring water slowly through a plastic fine-holed colander or fine plastic mesh.

The barometric pressure advantage

In the wild, an increase in *atmospheric pressure* (the weight of air as measured by a barometer) often makes fish more lovable and loving. Many hobbyists report that their fish breed more actively right before or during a rain or snowstorm. Follow the local weather conditions and you may be able to introduce pairs to the breeding tank during a barometric pressure drop and have a successful spawning.

The old change the temperature ploy

If you go backpacking out to your species' natural environment, you soon find that they do not live in an area that remains the same temperature 24 hours per day. (If you don't believe us, pitch a tent for a night out there.) Try fluctuating the temperature of the breeding tank overnight. Slowly drop the temperature 3 degrees at night by adjusting the heater, and then slowly raise it back up in the morning. Now don't get carried away and start tossing ice cubes into the tank or anything. All temperature changes must be done slowly!

The new guy next door approach

If you have a beautifully colored male that is being really stubborn and refusing to breed, you can always try introducing a second male (the meanest, ugliest one that you can find) in close proximity. This is kind of like sending your fish to a singles bar. Placing the rival male in a glass holding container near the spawning tank often inspires the stubborn spawner to breed when he suddenly realizes that there may be competition for his female.

The absence makes the heart grow fonder routine

If a pair is being outright stubborn about getting along, you can always separate the male and the female with a glass partition until they decide to either breed or die of boredom. (You know the old saying, "Absence makes the heart grow fonder.") This method is illustrated in Figure 19-1. While separated, keep feeding them small bits of live food until they shows signs of mating such as displaying brilliant colors or excessive contortions and body movement. This method works best when you only have one pair of fish in the spawning tank.

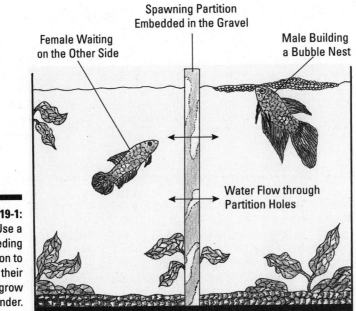

Spawning Partition
Embedded in the Gravel

Female Waiting
on the Other Side

Male Building
a Bubble Nest

Water Flow through
Partition Holes

Figure 19-1:
Use a
breeding
partition to
make their
hearts grow
fonder.

So What's Next?

This chapter goes into the equipment you need and how to condition your fish for spawning. In the next chapter, we examine individual courtship and breeding routines in more detail.

Chapter 20

Let's Spawn!

*B*reeding your fish is a great way to advance your fishkeeping skills. After you learn the basics and have successfully bred your first fish brood, there's no reason why you can't begin thinking about selling the excess offspring to a local dealer, trading them to friends, using them as feeder fish, or buying more tanks to house them. You may get lucky and find a dealer who needs a regular supply. This little bit of extra money can help offset some of the expense incurred with your hobby (and offset your spouse's financial wrath at the same time).

Simply ask your local dealer if he or she would be willing to trade equipment or purchase your extra fish at a cost that will satisfy both buyer and seller. You can also run an ad in your local newspaper and sell your fry to other hobbyists.

Before you actually sell your new fish, you should decide which ones you want to keep for further breeding. There may be a particular fish in the new brood that has a slightly different color or pattern that is pleasing to your eye. You usually have to wait for the fry to grow up a bit before they develop their colors and patterns. Make sure their markings are no longer changing before you make any final decisions.

Some fish breed in your community or species tank without any help from you. For example, if you have a bunch of male and female guppies in a community tank, chances are they will breed on their own, as long as the aquarium is clean and has good water conditions, without any extra work on your part. Some species are simply more willing to breed in captivity than others.

But if you want stay in control of which fish breed and when, set up a spawning tank (a tank designated only for breeding and raising certain fish at a certain time). That way, you can adjust the water quality and feeding schedule as necessary, as well as *cull* (separate the good from the bad) the fry of each species you're raising. Culling is simply the process of separating the fish you want to keep from the fish you don't. This ensures being able to breed individuals with the characteristics you want.

A good spawning tank is just a miniaturized version of the main tank. Make sure it has proper filtration, good water conditions, gravel, and plants to give your fish that "feel at home" sensation. A 5- or 10-gallon-tank makes a great breeding tank. Many hobbyists remove a majority of the decorations in a breeding tank, but we like to keep it as natural as possible. The final choice is yours.

Beginning a fish-breeding program brings with it some humane responsibility. Fish that you produce through breeding should, as they do in the wild, find their place in the biological ecosystem. Some species produce dozens or even hundreds of young. It's doubtful that you will want to keep every fish that your breeding pairs create. You should make every attempt to raise these fish, sell them, trade them, or give them away to good owners. If you think you cannot do these things, it may mean using excess fry to feed larger fish. Although this situation is found in nature, if you don't like the sound of you yourself doing it, then breeding is not for you.

Introducing the Bride and Groom

With most species, it is better to introduce the female to the spawning tank ahead of the male. Males are more aggressive, and putting the female in first allows her to establish a little bit of territory for herself. There are a few exceptions to this rule, so check the breeding requirements and strategies for each individual species by talking with other hobbyists who breed that species, attending fish clubs, talking to your local dealer, and researching species on the Web.

Give the female plenty of time to become comfortable in the new tank (at least a couple of hours, until she is swimming normally and not hiding in her new surroundings). When she looks like she has become queen of the hill, place her behind a clear tank partition (usually made of professionally cut glass, plastic, or Plexiglas) before you introduce the male. You can purchase partitions at pet stores or make your own. This "prenuptial" separation lets the male get accustomed to the sight of his mate and give him a chance to calm down a little bit before he actually meets her. Leave the partition up until the male seems like he is calm. You don't need to do this with all species, but it is usually the safest way to go.

Dealing with aggressive males

Some males are naturally more aggressive (actually *nasty* is the word we were looking for) than others, and it's difficult to determine an individual's habits before you see him in action. We've had very peaceful males of one species, only to turn around and end up with one of the same species that was ready to take on Mike Tyson. The only way to tell how aggressive a male is going to be during breeding is to keep a close eye on him once he is introduced into the spawning tank.

If your spawning tank is heavily planted and contains many safe areas where a female can hide, you may be able to introduce both partners at the same time. We personally do not use this method very often because we've seen too many females torn up by normally peaceful males that got a little too excited. Be safe and use a partition to allow them to get to know each other first.

Setting up the second date

If a spawning pair seems to get along well on the first date, it's probably safe to put them back into the same spawning tank at the same time. But fish in love can be very unpredictable, so don't bet the farm on their getting along again. It never hurts to use a partition more than once.

Yay, my fish really like each other!

If your fish are having a real romantic picnic, why spoil the fun? Let them continue to breed as long as they're in good health. If you don't want anymore newborns, keep them in separate main tanks.

Darn, my fish hate each other!

If your fish are throwing gravel at each other, they probably won't be in the mood to mate. Don't force something that isn't meant to be. Give them a little time away from each other and then try again. If they still try to kill each other, forget it and work with a different set of partners. We have witnessed a couple of instances where one male would refuse to mate with only one particular female out of a group of ten identical-looking fish! Why they seem to turn on one individual is unknown. A bit of fin nipping during spawning is normal in many species such as the beta. Just make sure they are not seriously injuring each other.

Following are a few physical reasons why fish won't spawn:

- Their water looks like a sewer.
- Their tank is too small.
- They need more fish (for example, neons mate more often in schools).
- One of the partners is cradle-robbing, or is older than dirt.
- The fish have not been fed live foods prior to spawning.
- The fish may be sterile.
- You have two females in the spawning tank (not good).
- You have two males in the spawning tank (even worse).
- They just don't feel like it.

If the problem seems to be mental, check out Chapter 19 for tricks to get your two fish to like each other. Unfortunately, there are no fish psychologists to help you along, so if these tricks don't work you may as well forget it and try another pair.

Understanding Breeding Types

Fish reproduce in one of two basic ways. *Livebearers* bear live young. *Egglayers* lay eggs. Each type of breeder has special requirements.

Livebearers

Livebearers give birth to free-swimming young that are fully formed and resemble tiny adults. A female livebearer is internally fertilized by her partner and carries the fry internally for about a month (called the *gestation period*) before birthing them. Immediately after entering this world, the young fry swim and search for food.

All livebearing fish are either *ovoviviparous* (the female produces eggs that contain yolk to feed the embryo) or *viviparous* (the young are nourished by the mother's circulatory system). Ovoviviparous females tend to lose their brood to miscarriage more often than viviparous ones.

How to tell male from female

A few well-known examples of livebearers include guppies, swordtails, mollies, and platys. Most livebearers are brightly colored and make great community fish. It is easy to determine the sex of most livebearers because the female is usually larger and more full-bodied than the male. Most males have a rodlike organ (developed from the anal fin) called a *gonopodium*. This unique organ is used to internally fertilize a female. After a single fertilization, a female can produce multiple broods (batches of fry) month after month without a male being present.

Except when they're in drag

In some livebearers, females can develop secondary male sexual characteristics. Where not enough males are present to ensure survival of the species, the female's anal fin may change into a gonopodium, and that fish will then carry on male duties!

The egglayers

Egglayers lay eggs (which usually range in size from 1.4 to 3 millimeters) that eventually hatch into newborn fry. The fry of egglayers are not as hardy and fully formed as those produced by livebearers. The babies of egglayers take much more time to mature. Popular egglayers include angelfish, cichlids, goldfish, and bettas.

When breeding egglayers, be aware of the following dangers to eggs:

- **Lack of oxygen:** The eggs in your breeding tank can be seriously damaged by lack of oxygen in the water. Without oxygen, their normal rate of cell division decreases. But you don't want heavy turbulence in the tank either. Hook up a small airstone or bubble disk (which splits the air into smaller bubbles) to a gang valve (which splits up an air supply to supply several pieces of equipment) so that you can adjust the oxygen flow. This setup provides beneficial aeration for the eggs without blowing the eggs into the next county.

- **Poor water conditions:** Dirty water can cause eggs to deteriorate. Make sure your water is clean and has the proper temperature and pH for your species.

- **Lack of vitamins:** Eggs can also be damaged if the mother lacks the essential vitamins needed to help them grow correctly. Diseased females can produce bad eggs. If the eggs from an unhealthy mother hatch, the young are usually defective and will produce deformed babies or none at all. Make sure that your spawning female is in good health before you attempt to breed her.

- **Intense lighting:** Light that's too bright can also damage fish eggs. Minimize lighting in your breeding tank.

Bubble nest builders

Bubble nest builders lay and incubate their eggs in a nest of bubbles that usually floats at the surface or is attached to plants. Bettas and gouramis are the most famous of these bubble nest builders. A male betta builds a floating nest that he carefully constructs from mucus-coated air bubbles he blows out of his mouth. Males often use plant debris as a "glue" to help keep the bubbles together. In some species, the entire nest has a foamy appearance.

Nests are built in different shapes and sizes, depending on the individual male. Some males complete a nest in a few hours, whereas others take their time and end up working several days to accomplish the same task. If excess circulation or other factors damage the nest, the male constantly repairs it as needed. Often males build more than one nest to impress a female and entice her into breeding.

The female should be removed immediately after spawning. If the fish do not spawn, she should still be removed so she does not get attacked by the male. The betta male cares for the eggs once they are laid and keeps them clean using chemicals in his mouth. Don't panic if he picks up eggs in his mouth and spits them back into the nest, because this is normal. After a few days the egg case will dissolve and the fry will emerge. This betta example is only one of the amazing things that you will see while breeding your fish!

Egg scatterers

Egg scatterers must hide their eggs because they do not take care of them after birth. These species scatter their eggs around decorations, rocks, plants, and gravel. During the courtship of these species, the male actively chases his mate and fertilizes her eggs as they fall freely into the water. They do this for large numbers of eggs at one time, ensuring that some survive by sheer numbers alone. A few common examples of egg scatterers are danios, barbs, rasboras, and tetras.

Substrate spawners

Substrate spawners lay their eggs in such a manner that the eggs attach to *one particular area* of rocks, driftwood, plants, or substrate. The male of the species fertilizes the eggs while the female lays them. Common examples of substrate spawners include some cichlids, catfish, and killifish.

Mouthbrooders have all the fun

Mouthbrooders are unique, because they incubate their eggs in their mouth until it is time for them to hatch. As the eggs are laid, the male fertilizes them. The parents (either the male or female) gather them up in their mouths for protection and incubation. Examples of mouthbrooders are some labyrinth fish and some cichlids.

Saving Everyone from Everyone Else

After spawning is complete, and the fry are produced, there may be a few problems between Mom and Dad; Mom and the kids; or Dad and the kids. (Hey, sounds like our family.) It is crucial that you keep an eye on everyone after breeding — this is when the third world war may break out among aggressive species. Let us put it this way: If fish had nuclear weapons after spawning, we would all be vaporized.

Saving Mom and Dad from Mom and Dad

Just because your fish had a great night out on the town doesn't mean that they like each other *now*. In fact, there's a really good chance that they want to tear each other fin from fin. No one seems to know why they get like that. Perhaps they're just really tired after spawning or are suffering from PASS (post aquatic spawning syndrome). Whatever the reason, many fish have to be separated after they spawn.

If you have a pretty decent-sized fish room, move the female to her own holding tank (as small as 4 gallons, depending on the size of the fish) and then move the male to his own quarters. It is not a good idea to move spawners back to a main aquarium with other fish. The male may still be aggressive because his hormones are as high as a kite on a windy day. He may look for his next victim in your community or species tank. The female may be torn up or worn out, and you should allow her to rest in a tank of her own for at least 48 hours to recover properly.

 The slime coat (coating on the body that helps to protect fish from disease) on a mating pair can be easily damaged during breeding. After you move the male and female to their own quarters for recuperation, add a little Stress Coat to the water to guard against bacterial infections.

Saving the kids from Mom and Dad

Many fish (such as cichlids) normally make good parents and perform tasks such as caring for their brood and defending their nesting spot. However, should this pair suddenly be upset by outsiders, they can turn from Ward and June into Bonnie and Clyde in a heartbeat. Unfortunately, the young fry or eggs suffer the most from their parents' newfound wrath.

One way to avoid this problem with aggressive species is to use a large tank equipped with many hiding places. Try to keep their breeding tank in a quiet, low-traffic area so that the fish aren't irritated by people walking by and making noise. You can also use a *spawning grate* (a plastic sheet with holes that allows the eggs to fall though) for protection (see Chapter 19 for more on spawning grates).

Livebearers (such as guppies) often eat their young. To prevent this, you can purchase a *breeding trap* to separate the young after birth. Breeding traps come in a few different designs. A net breeder, shown in Figure 20-1, is a simple rectangular device that floats in your aquarium, kind of a net shaped like a box. Put the female inside the net, so that her young are protected from other fish in a community tank. Unfortunately, the net trap does not protect the young from Mom. The advantage of the net breeder is that the net allows free water flow from the aquarium.

You can also put the expectant mother in a plastic breeding tank and float it in your larger aquarium until she gives birth. One advantage of this type of breeder is that after the fry are born they drop through a small slit and are separated from their mother and future tankmates. Unfortunately, the plastic breeder does not allow water flow to keep the interior clean and can foul rather quickly if birth is delayed.

Most breeding traps are too small to accommodate a pregnant female for any length of time. While under prolonged restraint, she may struggle to escape and damage herself or her unborn fry. Pregnant females should only be placed in breeding traps when they are ready to deliver. By becoming familiar with the species you are breeding, you learn to recognize when your fish is ready to give birth. This can vary from species to species, but it usually includes the mother looking complete bloated, constantly moving toward the bottom of the tank, or looking for cover.

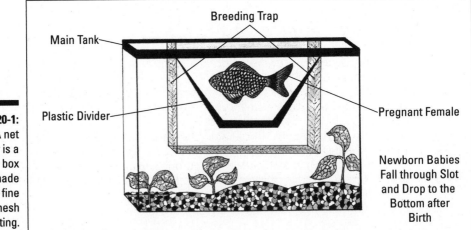

Figure 20-1:
A net breeder is a simple box shape made out of fine mesh netting.

Main Tank

Breeding Trap

Plastic Divider

Pregnant Female

Newborn Babies Fall through Slot and Drop to the Bottom after Birth

Saving the kids from each other

Fry eventually reach a stage where they are sexually mature. If you have a bunch of juveniles in a *growout* tank (a separate tank for the young fish so they won't be attacked by other larger tankmates), you should separate the males from the females as soon as you can determine their genders. If you don't, you may end up with a lot of unwanted spawning that interferes with your breeding plan. As the fry grow, you need to start *culling* (separate fish out that you want to breed again).

A problem with growing fry is that the larger ones (the males usually grow quicker) start eating the smaller ones. This is very common, even if they are fed properly.

Raising the Fry

After the fry are born, and the parents have been moved to a resting tank, you can begin feeding the babies. The fry (depending on the species) are usually very small and should be fed liquid foods or infusoria cultures through an eyedropper (to measure and add the food to the tank). Microworms are another good food choice.

Stepping up to brine shrimp

After a few weeks, you can begin feeding the fry baby brine shrimp — live foods help them gain maximum growth. Brine shrimp is a great choice because of the relatively low odds of introducing disease into the tank.

Giving them a real home

Be sure to feed your newborn fry small amounts 3–5 times a day to ensure maximum growth. Baby foods tend to foul water quickly, so change the water frequently in order to keep the tank clean. A well-planted aquarium allows them to mature more normally than a bare tank with no decorations does.

Check each species' specifications (see later in this chapter for a few examples of species specifications to get you started) before removing the parents! Some fry, such as discus, depend on their parent's slime coat for nourishment and may not survive if their parents are removed from the tank.

Picking new stock

When selecting future breeding stock from your own bred stock and new purchases, choose the most colorful, vigorous fish in the group and move all the females to one tank and the males to another tank. You don't want to rely upon chance sexual encounters or you may never be able to develop the strain you're seeking.

Understanding Genetics

A while back, a bored young monk named Gregor Mendel did a few experiments with peas in a quiet monastery garden. He selectively bred pea plants for certain characteristics and kept track of those characteristics. He was surprised to see traits (physical signs) not seen in either parent plant appear in their offspring. Everyone thought he was weird, but he learned a lot of cool stuff — such as, what you see is not necessarily what you get (he had discovered recessive genes). *Selective breeding* allows you to choose fish that have the characteristics you're searching for and breed them until that characteristic remains stable from generation to generation. And, like Mendel, you may end up with a few surprises to boot.

Choosing the best

To breed selectively, you need to choose a male that possesses characteristics you want to develop into a pure strain, so that generation after generation of fish display the same certain colors, fin types, and whatever other factors you isolate. Selecting a good female may be a little more difficult, because they usually do not carry as much color as the males. Just try to pick a full-bodied female in good health.

Obtaining variation the good way

Few *strains* (an entire breeding family tree) produce identical fish from generation to generation. If they do, it can take a very long time to develop fish that are identical in color and shape consistently by interbreeding them with each other . Because genetics are so varied, it is possible that you may end up with a brand new characteristic (not seen in the parents) within a few years. This occurs because of *recessive genes* (genes that are present but which are not "turned on" and thus don't show their traits in the physical makeup) which make an appearance periodically.

Obtaining variation the bad way

Another way you can obtain variation is when a mutation occurs. A *mutation* is a more radical change from one generation to the next and does not occur in increments. Mutations are not very common. The main disadvantage of a mutation is that many mutants are sterile or, if they're fertile, they may carry deformed genes that are not passed along to future generations. The odds of carrying a mutation long enough to make it pure are staggeringly long, to say the least.

Creating strains through inbreeding

The breeding process used to produce a "pure" strain of fish is known as *inbreeding*. After the first brood is born and raised, pick a healthy male and breed him back to his mother. From the next generation, select the best quality grandson (who displays the characteristics you want) and breed him with his grandmother. Keep repeating this process for successive generations. This helps solidify the characteristics you want by keeping unwanted traits from other fish out of the picture. This is perfectly normal as far as fish are concerned, because they would breed with each other anyway, and you are just pairing them up for the best traits.

As each new brood is born, check for males born with unique characteristics that you want to continue on with. If the females that you started with die, select a healthy daughter and continue on. This method of inbreeding is more effective than *line* breeding, which involves mating half-brothers and sisters.

Inbreeding in mammals causes genetic defects, and many people find it a distasteful topic generally. However, in the fish world it happens all the time. Sometimes survival depends on it. In our opinion inbreeding in fish should not be thought of in the same light as it is for higher animals. However, it's possible that no amount of evidence or argument can get you over that hurdle. If that is the case, then inbreeding to produce new strains of fish is not for you.

Choosing the Right Species for You

It's best to start out with a few of the easier-to-breed species so that you can learn the ropes. The following examples give you basic information on a few species that are relatively easy to breed so that you can get started on this fascinating adventure without encountering a lot of difficult problems off the bat.

Guppy (Poecilia reticulata)

The guppy is probably the easiest aquarium fish to breed. Guppies would breed in a puddle of water if given half a chance. Combine several males with a few females in a species tank, and within a year you will have to purchase a new aquarium to house all your new fish. Guppies readily breed in a community aquarium, species tank, or spawning tank. Males have a gonopodium and are more brightly colored than the larger-bodied females. The young fry are born fully formed and ready to eat food. Standard water temperature for breeding is 74–78 degrees F; dH 12; pH 7.

Convict cichlid (Archocentrus nigrofasciatus)

Breeding convicts is very easy. Because convicts who are breeding can be very aggressive toward their tankmates, put them in their own spawning tank with a few plants and rocks or a flowerpot turned on its side. The female is larger and shows much more color than the male. She also exhibits black and red bars during the breeding cycle. Water for breeding is 69–79 degrees F; dH 8; pH 7.2.

Convict spawning occurs very rapidly. They lay their eggs in a rock cave or in a flowerpot. Both parents help take good care of the young — unless they begin to quarrel. If the parents fight, remove the losing partner. The young eat readily and flee to the parents when they feel threatened.

Angelfish (Pterophyllum scalare)

Angelfish breed steadily when you provide the proper conditions. Angle a piece of slate (about 45 degrees), 2–3 inches wide, against the glass of the tank for your angelfish to lay their eggs on. The spawning pair will clean off the slate before using it. When the housework is done, the female lays her eggs on the slate, which the male then fertilizes. Angelfish often pair up, so the easiest way to start matching them with a spawning partner is to pay attention to who hangs out with whom. Male angelfish have a bump (common among cichlids) on the front of their heads. The genital area is round in the female, and pointed in the male.

After the eggs are fertilized, both parents use their fins to gently fan them with water and remove any infertile or damaged eggs. The eggs hatch within 48 hours, and the fry absorb their yolk sacs before searching for food. Some angelfish are carnivorous and eat their own eggs. (Angelfish also help their young emerge from the eggs by removing the case, so make sure you know what you're seeing before you do anything about it.) If the angelfish are eating their eggs, remove the piece of slate with the eggs on it and place it in another tank with an airstone. Water temperature for breeding is 75–78 degrees F; dH 7–16; pH 6.7–7.5.

A Few Final Tips

As we hope we've made clear, breeding tropical fish can be fun, educational, and profitable. Just remember the following few simple tips and you'll be on your way:

- ✔ Choose healthy fish to breed.
- ✔ Breed your fish in a special breeding tank to control your genetic lines. Make sure your breeding tank has the correct water conditions and hiding places.
- ✔ Research your species so that you can benefit from what other aquarists have learned about breeding that particular type of fish.
- ✔ Don't let your fish injure each other during the breeding process.
- ✔ Most important of all: Have fun and enjoy your new fish!

Chapter 21

Recording Data and Photographing Fish

*O*ne great way to enhance your fishkeeping hobby is by keeping a written log and taking pictures of your prize aquatic pets. Photos and logs are good tools for learning more about your fish, their breeding habits, environmental quirks, and natural social interactions. Photography is also a fun way to enhance your social standing by impressing your friends with your great pictures. Most of the equipment you need for fish photography and written logs are fairly inexpensive and can be easily obtained.

Keeping a Log Book

Keeping track of your fish's individual health, breeding schedule, and food preferences can be quite a difficult job, especially if you have a large variety of species, or more aquariums than the National Aquarium in Baltimore.

One good way to keep tabs on your aquarium fish is to use a written logbook. A complete record of each fish in your aquarium lets you monitor your pet's history, social habits, growth, water conditions, feeding habits, and spawning successes.

If you keep track of each new fish as you purchase it, you gain a better understanding of each species' needs, and that can be beneficial in decisions regarding purchases of future tankmates. For example, the "calm" oversized molly you bought a couple of months ago cleverly turns your community tank into a World Wrestling Federation battle royal, and you note its bizarre behavior carefully on your written log. On your next trip to the fish shop, this individual fish's rap sheet will remind you to run at warp speed past the giant molly section toward calmer waters.

Beginning a log is kind of like starting your first diary except you don't have to make up stuff. Keep a separate sheet for each fish. We suggest encasing each sheet in a plastic slip-folder and placing the individual sheets in a three-ring binder to protect the logs from water and moisture. To get you off on the right foot, the following list details the information we usually record in our own aquatic logs:

- Date and place of purchase
- Number and type of tankmates
- Monthly growth record
- Common and scientific names
- Sex, size, and color
- Preferred temperature, dH, pH, and lighting requirements
- Type of feeder and preferred diet
- Environmental distribution (for example, "found in Guatemala and Mexico")
- Social behavior (whether it gets along with other species or needs its own tank) and what type of tankmates it tolerates
- Spawning date and number of fry
- A disease record that includes the type of disease, date contracted, treatment, and how long the treatment took to work
- Date and cause of death
- Any personal comments

Photographing Your Fish the Old-Fashioned Way

Okay, just admit it, buried deep within your creative depths is a shutterbug itching to get the old, dusty, 35mm (millimeter) camera out of the attic and snap a few quick photos. Or maybe you're just an enthusiastic hobbyist like ourselves, continually searching for new and exciting ways to enhance your aquarium-keeping records. In any case, see this book's color section to get a sense of how beautiful and exciting aquarium photography can be.

Many hobbyists try their hands at selective breeding at one time or another. Have you finally succeeded in breeding the perfectly colored platy and now feel an overwhelming need to capture and preserve that beauty? Have you had a fish for a long time that has become very dear to you? Fish photography can offer a new challenge for you.

There are a variety of reasons for photographing fish: You may want to capture the beauty of your aquarium and email these aquatic treasures to your family, friends, and colleagues. Nothing compares to the pride you feel when others openly admire your aquatic and photographic creativity.

Another good reason to consider fish photography is that you can turn good-quality fish photos into extra spending money if you catch the right scene, interaction, or pose on film. Many aquarium magazines, stock photo houses, and publishers purchase photos to use in their articles. It takes time to build up a photo business, so don't quit your day job until you are established.

All types of fish photos are important resources for historical preservation. In today's world where once-abundant species are slipping into extinction at an alarming rate, photographs may become the only reminder to future generations that a particular species of fish once existed and is now extinct due to human carelessness.

Get to know the personalities and habits of the fish you're taking pictures of and make sure the fish are healthy and happy before starting your photo shoot.

After all is said and done, the most important rule of fish photography is *have fun*!

There are many places to practice your aquatic photography outside the home, such as zoos, aquariums, and fish shows. Check your local phonebook for great opportunities to try out your photography skills.

The camera

Almost any camera works well for fish photography. However, a *single-lens reflex* (SLR) camera has several options that other cameras lack:

- The picture you see through the camera lens on an SLR is basically the image that you see in the finished and developed photo.

- You can easily equip most SLRs with auxiliary wide angle, telephoto, macro, and zoom lenses.

✓ SLRs are capable of taking synchronized electronic flash pictures, which can help you capture the action of fast-moving pets.

✓ You can purchase a wide variety of cool attachments such as filters to help you make interesting shots and create different types of scenes.

✓ A 35mm SLR makes you look like a pro if you get a cool camera strap and have a bunch of accessories crammed into a stylish bag.

However, the most important thing is to get the shot. Start with a camera that is equipped with automatic exposure so you don't miss shots fumbling with numerous settings. Many SLRs, including digital SLRs, have a fully automatic feature, but some cameras are so complex that by the time you set up everything for your shot, your fishy subject has spawned several times and is about to collect Social Security. (If someone is watching as you, simply wipe imaginary sweat off your forehead, fiddle with all the camera buttons, and look relieved when the shot is over.)

Another good reason to begin with an SLR is that you can start with a 35 mm camera body and a standard 50 mm lens and then gradually add to the unit as your interests and experience expand. Inexpensive instamatic cameras usually have a fixed lens, and the quality of the picture compared to that of an SLR is the difference between a Rembrant and our son's attempt at finger-painting his bedroom walls.

Throwaway cameras are not great for fish photography either. With this type of camera, you shoot the film, take the camera in to develop the photos, and they throw the camera away. This type of camera doesn't take the best quality photos and is very limited to point and shoot type scenes.

Mount your camera on a sturdy tripod to help eliminate blurred pictures caused by camera shake. You can find cheap tabletop plastic tripods at camera shops that will work fine. If you don't have a tripod, support the camera on a table or firm surface.

The film

The simple fact is, if you want good-quality photos, you must purchase the highest quality film on the market. In our opinion, Kodak is the best film made and produces the truest color.

Cutting costs with inexpensive or low-grade film costs you much more in the long run (buying tons of film to get a good-looking shot on bad film) than if you had just spent a few extra pennies on a better quality roll. Ask any professional photographer, and she'll tell you the same thing. When you are first starting out, you can save money by purchasing rolls of film with more exposures (36 instead of 12 exposures).

Always choose the slowest-speed film possible to avoid the grainy pictures produced by faster films. Film speed is measured in numbers such as 100, 200, 400 and 800, and the lower the number, the slower the film speed and the higher the level of detail, but the more light you'll need to get good pictures (see later in this chapter for more on lighting). A slow, fine-grained film such as ASA 100 produces higher quality images that can also be enlarged with better results than does a faster film such as ASA 400, which often makes your pictures look as if they were taken during a desert windstorm. Increase the lighting before you attempt to increase film speed. Begin with a 100 speed film and work from there.

Make sure to have plenty of extra film on hand, because it may take several rolls to get the one perfect shot you're seeking. After you achieve lighting proficiency and mastery of the camera and lenses, consider using *slide* film (very slow film that offers bright, realistic color saturation,) which gives you the ultimate in color saturation and picture quality.

Don't overlook black-and-white film, either, which can be a simple yet exciting medium that adds artistic impact to shots of rugged fish such as a convict cichlid, and can show the delicate shades and fin details of a veiltail angel. Black-and-white photography is an art form in itself, and you can get even more creative with it if you decide to develop your own film in a darkroom.

Lenses

A standard 50 mm lens works great on fish longer than 5 inches. But when working with smaller fish, use a zoom, telephoto, or macro lens to help eliminate background material. A macro lens is designed for taking close-ups and offers a 1:1 ratio, which results in a large center-of-attention subject in the finished photo. A 105 mm macro lens works great for small fish such as a pencil fish. However, macro filters can result in decreased sharpness and depth of field.

A zoom lens allows you to change the focal length of your lens to capture different sizes of fish (and spy on your neighbors after the photo session). A 100–200 mm zoom lens is a good lens to use for most smaller fish.

Telephoto lenses enlarge images that are far away and provide you with the freedom to work at a distance from the aquarium. Taking photos from a healthy distance helps avoid the possibility of your fish going into cardiac arrest from fright during photo sessions.

The three disadvantages of telephoto and zoom lenses are as follows:

- Camera shake due to the larger size and heavier weight of the lens if you don't use a tripod

✔ A shallower depth of field (zone of sharp focus), which tends to blur out any background

✔ A slight loss of quality in the finished prints

Take time to experiment with different lenses to become aware of the advantages and disadvantages of each type. Look through photo magazines and books to gain new ideas on the various uses of each lens length. Talk to other photographers about their experiences using different lenses.

Black and white and the darkroom

Learning the art of developing black-and-white photos in a darkroom provides you with a good opportunity to display not only your fish photos, but your creativity as well. You can sandwich negatives to create double images, and enhance or darken certain areas of the photo to suit your needs. Manipulating photos in the darkroom also helps you cover up embarrassing mistakes before your friends see them. After learning a few tricks, you can even add a picture of a fish you took at a public aquarium to your photo just in case all of your real aquatic pets look boring.

If you're not familiar with darkroom techniques, your local college or photography shop can probably provide you with a course in developing your own photo prints. It's worth your time and effort to check out this exciting aspect of photography.

Photographing Your Fish with Digital Photography

Digital photography is growing in popularity and is now a good alternative to film-based cameras. Digital images are made up of small squares called pixels, which resemble a bunch of very tiny tiles laid out to make the image. Digital cameras are judged by their pixel count, which is represented in millions and abbreviated by MP (megapixels). So, a 3MP camera has 3 million pixels, or megapixels. The pictures are stored on small memory cards instead of on film. You then transfer the images from the card to your computer or a printer.

There are many digital cameras to choose from. Cell phones and inexpensive cameras typically offer 2MP. This is good for emailing photos, but not much else. The 3MP camera is good for 4 x 6 photos and is relatively inexpensive.

The 4MP takes close to photo lab quality pictures and is a good all-round camera. The 5MP+ cameras are great for outstanding photo quality, but can be very expensive. Generally, the higher the MP, the more expensive the camera.

There are many advantages to using a digital camera. Most digital cameras have an LCD (liquid-crystal display) screen, which allows you to see what the captured image will look like before you take the photo, and also let's you preview it after you take the photo to see if it's worth keeping. You can take hundreds of photos on a typical memory card and only keep the very best. Using a digital camera allows you to save on the cost of film that is often wasted on shots that don't come out well. And most digital cameras are very light in weight compared to many film based models.

Printing your work

Once you have taken your wonderful fish photos with a digital camera, you can print them out on your computer's printer or email them to friends. You can also scan film photos into a computer and print them out, too. For higher quality prints, most film development shops can print your digital photos directly from your memory card.

Computer-aided fish photography

In order to store your wonderful fish photos, you can turn to your trusty computer. The images from your camera (and scanned photos) can be transferred from your camera to your hard drive for storage. However, hard drives can get viruses and crash or die, so if you have a CD burner, you should transfer your images to a CD so that you have another copy.

Photos can also be altered and improved using different varieties of image-manipulation software, such as Adobe Photoshop (expensive) and Paint Shop Pro (not so expensive). Many digital cameras come with basic software for this purpose as well.

Aquarium webcams

Many digital cameras also allow you to take digital videos. Also, cheap "eyeball" webcams are now available at most electronics stores. This option is great for capturing an entire aquarium of fish swimming happily in their aquatic home. You could even make a Web site so that friends and family (and you) can see your fish from anywhere that has an Internet connection.

Lighting Techniques

The main hood lights on an aquarium usually do not provide sufficient lighting to take good photos. If your tank has fluorescent lamps, you may end up with a green cast on your finished pictures; if you use tungsten lamps, an orange cast may appear. You're much better off using electronic flash or strobe units that provide proper lighting and freeze motion.

Ideally, you place your photography tank (see later in this chapter for more on photography tanks) in natural sunlight, which far exceeds artificial lighting in terms of color, shadow, and mood. The disadvantage of natural lighting is that the direct sunlight can quickly heat up the water in a small tank to lethal levels and turn your fish into a broiled entrees. Take great care to ensure that the water remains cool until you're ready to start the photography session, and that you don't leave them in direct sunlight for too long. A large, thick towel to cover the entire tank and block out the heavy sunlight is a great tool to have handy if you need to take a short break.

Another factor to take into consideration is that the sunlight two hours after sunrise and two hours before sunset is generally discolored and should be avoided. Photos taken in natural sunlight during these times tend to have a yellowish cast unless you use special filters. It is much better to take photos in natural sunlight during the late morning or early afternoon hours when the sun is high in the sky.

In recent years, large flood lights have become quite popular in fish photography. Caution is advised when using these lights as they have the potential to quickly heat water. Always check the heat intensity of these floodlights before using them.

If you're using one strobe light, direct it at the tank from a 45-degree angle near the top of the aquarium. If you use two strobe lights, place them at the same angle on opposite sides of the tank.

The 45-degree angle offers these advantages:

- ✔ Shadows appear below the fish and give your photos a natural look. These shadows also possess a softer tone than those in photos using straight-on lighting and are more appealing to the eye.
- ✔ You avoid flash reflection off the glass, which can ruin an otherwise good shot. Another method to avoid excess reflection is to wrap a black-cardboard tube around the lens on your camera. This tube is known as a *mask*.

Strobe lights generally have a flash duration of $\frac{1}{1500}$ of a second and are very effective in stopping action if you are photographing a fast-swimming fish in a large tank that isn't equipped with restraining glass. (A *restraining glass* is an inserted piece of glass that is used in small photo tanks, usually 2–5 gallons, to gently pin the fish against the aquarium glass so that it will not move while its picture is being taken.) Strobe lights are usually powered either by electricity or rechargeable cadmium batteries.

If the subject of your photo session is a very dark fish, move the lighting closer to the tank to compensate. On the other hand, if the fish is white or of a very light complexion, move the lighting back from the subject.

If your pictures are too dark or too light, try adjusting the lighting before you start messing around with lens settings. For optimal results, take a series of pictures as you slowly adjust your lighting from near to far. You'll be rewarded with at least one picture with the best lighting possible. A series of photos can be valuable to your future shots, too. You can sit down and review different lighting angles and distances to see what worked. If you are using a digital camera, you will be able to get a good idea of how the lighting is going to work by using the LCD screen without wasting film. You simply follow the camera's instructions for erasing bad shots from the memory device.

Red-eye (also known as vampire syndrome,) is the common name for reflections caused by lighting placed very close to the subject. You can avoid it by working with the light adjustments mention earlier in this section. For digital shots, you can use image-manipulation software to remove most red-eye problems.

Another option is to aim your flash or strobes up at a mirror or white card suspended above the tank. The light reflects off the mirror or card and bounces back onto the subject, creating a softer look. This method is popular for delicate-looking species, such as angelfish and other long-finned tropicals. Make sure that the mirror and cards you use are clean and free of streaks.

If you're a fairly serious photographer, you can purchase a photographic umbrella to diffuse light. The manager of your local photo shop can make sure you get the proper piece of equipment for the job. Remember that a bounced flash loses up to half of its original intensity, so adjust your calculated exposure accordingly.

Focusing Techniques

The focus of a camera is determined by the aperture, or opening, of the lens, which decreases as the size of the image increases. The aperture itself is a hole in the lens which regulates the amount of light striking the film. The aperture is adjusted by a diaphragm inside the lens and is calculated in steps called *f-stops*. You can see the f-stops available on an SLR camera on the ring on the outside of the lens. The smaller the f-stop number, the less light required, and the smaller the depth of field, or zone of focus. With fish photography, you are usually working close up and with limited ability to provide a lot of light, meaning smaller f-stops.

To get a large amount of the background in focus, you need a larger f stop — or more light. The lens manufacturer usually supplies a table to help you determine the aperture you need for the magnification you want. Or set your camera to semi-automatic mode, if it has one, meaning you can set the shutter speed to, say $\frac{1}{60}$ of a second, and the camera chooses the correct aperture automatically.

If your calculations point to an f-stop of 11, take one photo at f 8, one at f 11, and another at f 16. This *bracketing* technique reduces your margin of error, maximizes the probability of a useable shot. Keep a log of each exposure and ask the developing lab to number your pictures so that you can gain a better understanding of how each aperture affects your shot.

Larger lens openings (f 2, f 1.4) have a narrower depth of field (how much area behind or in front of the subject will be in focus), which means you have to focus more carefully. Smaller lens openings (f 16, f 22) have a larger depth of field and require less focusing to get the correct image. Depth of field increases with distance. The farther your camera is from your subject, the greater the depth of field. Macro photos (extreme close ups of small objects) have little depth of field because the lens is so close to the subject.

If all else fails, you can always have a photo studio crop your picture, which entails having a professional cut out parts of the picture that don't appeal to you. Another option if you are not using a digital camera is to scan the image into the computer using a scanner and then adjust it in your software. What's left is usually the shot that you were trying to get in the first place.

Composition Techniques

You need to organize all the visual elements into a balanced and appealing scene in order to take good fish photos. All photos require a center of interest (which is usually the most important image in the picture).

Obviously, most of the fish that you take pictures of are of some interest, but other subjects in the aquarium can be accented by your aquatic pets. For example, a piece of driftwood with an unusual shape or a brightly colored castle can provide a center of interest that you can highlight by capturing a small school of fish swimming nearby.

Using the rule of thirds

One general rule of composition that always produces a pleasing balance is to place the subject at the intersection of imaginary lines dividing the entire scene into thirds, horizontally and vertically, as shown in Figure 21-1. This simple but effective placement of subjects, known as the *rule of thirds*, often gives excellent results. If there are other lines in the picture, try to arrange them in such a way that something about them leads the viewer's eye toward the main subject.

Panning the scene

To obtain unique photos that stand out from the rest, try taking pictures of interesting moments, such as mating rituals or feeding sessions. Another fun thing to experiment with is a specialized effect such as panning — following a fish with the camera as the fish swims: You simply continue moving the camera in the direction the fish is swimming as you depress the shutter. The effect is a fish that's mostly in focus but with a blurred afterimage and background that can be quite interesting as it captures motion over time. To get the most realistic photo, keep the camera on the same horizontal plane as the fish. (If you suddenly look down and can see the back of your knees, you probably tilted too far down.)

Figure 21-1: The rule of thirds is a time-honored way of achieving attractive composition in photography.

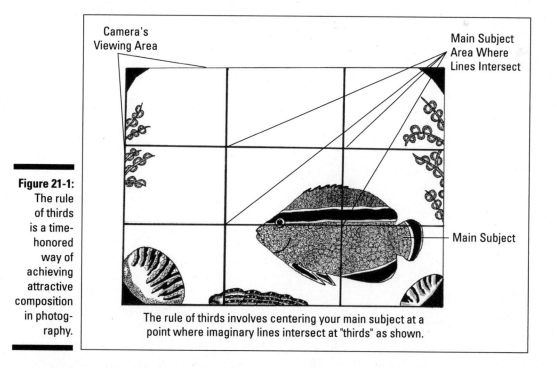

The rule of thirds involves centering your main subject at a point where imaginary lines intersect at "thirds" as shown.

Setting up for close-ups

For good close-ups, make sure your subject fills at least 75 percent of the frame — this keeps the background from overrunning or cluttering the shot. Focus on the best aspects of the fish (a beautiful flowing fin, for example).

The Photography Tank

Fish can be a difficult subject to catch on film, so you need to do everything possible to improve your odds of getting quality photos. If you plan to photograph your fish in your main tank, you must take a few important factors into consideration to insure good quality photographs.

- **Clear up the water.** Avoid glare (reflected light) by making sure that the aquarium's water is as clear as possible. Any debris or suspended particles (your toddler's uneaten lima beans from dinner) may reflect light and produce spots in your finished photos.

  It's a good idea to add extra mechanical filtration to the tank a few days before you take the pictures. Another effective process is to filter all the main tank water through standard floss (the same type you put in many filters and can be bought at your local pet store). The only drawback to this procedure is that it is quite time-consuming and can take anywhere from two days to five years, depending on the size of your tank.

- **Clean the tank itself and the decorations.** Remove all unsightly algae from the glass of the aquarium; otherwise your photos may end up resembling a bad still-life of chunky pea soup. Clean all plastic plants, rocks, and other artificial decorations before your photo session begins. The gravel in the tank should be vacuumed prior to shooting — a photographic lens does not miss nearly as much intricate detail as the human eye does.

- **Check the aquarium glass or acrylic surface for scratches.** The surface must be scratch-free to obtain the best photos. Several commercial scratch-removal kits on the market remove imperfections from acrylic walls.

- **Clean the lighting.** If you're using overhead or hood lighting in the photography session, make sure that the cover glass is clean so that it allows maximum light to enter. It is mandatory that the outer glass covering each light remains translucent and clean.

Shut off all tank lights at least thirty minutes before you clean, for safety purposes. (Photo lighting can be very hot and can cause serious burns if touched or electrocution if accidentally knocked into the tank while cleaning.)

Building your own photography tank

One of the easiest and most practical methods to insure great photos of your fish is to construct a miniature aquarium to use exclusively for photo sessions. This technique was founded by Dr. Herbert Axelrod and is an important part of the famous Axelrod technique of photographing fish. The Axelrod technique involves using a small photo tank with an interior restraining glass embedded in fine sand and angled from the bottom front to the back top of the tank. The angled glass restricts fish movement when the restraining glass is gently leaned forward.

A photography tank is much smaller than any standard aquarium and offers several unique advantages over a larger tank:

✔ Keeping the water in a mini-tank clean and clear for your pictures is easier in a small tank.

✔ Arranging plants, rocks, and other decorations is simple.

✔ Water changes are a snap for good photos.

Building a photography tank (if you don't choose to purchase a small aquarium) is something even a beginning hobbyist can do. It doesn't require much time, knowledge, or lessons from Bob Vila to complete a simple tank 7 inches high by 7 inches long and 2 inches wide. You can build tanks of other sizes to accommodate the size of the fish you're photographing and the materials at hand. The glass you use to construct your mini-tank should be thinner than standard aquarium glass to help promote good photos.

The four sides and the bottom glass of the new tank can be easily positioned using clamps and then siliconed with aquarium sealer or aquatic-safe cement to obtain a small rectangle. No frame or supports are really necessary if the glass you used in construction is thin. The newly siliconed sides should be allowed to dry for 48 hours before water is added or the tank is moved (unless you plan on checking out your new galoshes). This will ensure that the seal is tight and waterproof. A sixth piece of glass should be cut to size so that it fits into the tank like a partition. The glass should slide in easily without scraping the sides of the tank. The safest way to do this is to go to a glasscutter and have it done for you, because glass cutting can be very dangerous.

Gently place the fish you're photographing between the front glass on the photo tank and the restraining glass — which works like a cover slip on a microscope slide. (If your fish's eyes start popping out like Marty Feldman's, you might want to back off on the pressure a little bit.) Another advantage to this restraining technique is that you, the photographer, have the freedom to place the fish in creative arrangements that aren't possible in a larger tank. This glass restricts movement of faster swimming fish and keeps them safe during the photo shoot.

Using different backgrounds

Because flying off to the Cayman Islands or Cancun every time you feel the urge to photograph fish is not financially practical, you can use simple non-distracting backgrounds to allow the natural attributes and colors of your fish to capture center stage. Many materials found around the home — a towel, solid-color wrapping paper, and thick construction paper — make excellent backdrops.

When choosing a background, take into consideration the color of your subject. A darker background is appropriate for a light-colored fish, such as a glass catfish. On the other hand, you're better off using a light background for a dark-colored fish, such as a tiger oscar.

Try to avoid cluttering the tank or the glass with too many objects (three plastic divers, a shipwreck, and Donald Duck on a life raft is too many) — they may take away from the natural beauty of your fishy subject. Keep all decorations, such as gravel, plants, and rocks to a minimum, especially in a smaller photo tank. But these decisions are a matter of personal preference and ultimately rest with the individual photographer. Some of the best fish photos come about as a result of the trial-and-error method of artistic arrangement.

Displaying your work

Once you have taken a bunch of fish photos, you will want a place to store them. For printed out photos, you can use a photo album just like you would for family snapshots. Try to group shots of different species and aquarium backgrounds together if possible, so you don't have a large group of photos all showing the same fish. If you want to display your digital photos, many different types of photography computer software allow you to create electronic photo albums to display your shots.

Chapter 22

Competing in Fish Shows

*E*ntering a local, regional, or national fish show can be a great way to expand your fishkeeping hobby; win a bunch of cool prizes such as trophies, ribbons, equipment, and money; and display your aquarium-keeping and breeding skills.

Fish shows also offer quite a few other personal attractions worth checking out as well. For example, you often find people dressed up as fish, aquariums, and equipment at these shows because they are either promoting a product or attempting to get a little extra mileage out of their Halloween costumes. Either way, a full-grown adult trying to win a five-pound bag of gravel by walking around with a glass fish bowl on his head can be a real scream. It is also nice to be able to get a glance at new products that display stands have to offer.

Many other cool things go on at fish shows — like door prizes and special drawings. Just by showing up, you may have a chance to win neat fishkeeping supplies, such as heaters and filters. You also find many experts in the aquarium field waiting to answer any questions you may have concerning your hobby. These pros can be representatives of manufacturing companies, or hobbyists who have become experts in their individual fields.

If you finally decide to involve yourself in a little bit of friendly competition, your aquarium-keeping skills will steadily improve. After all, in order to display only top-quality fish at every competition, you will need to do lots of research on nutrition, water conditions, and other factors that influence proper growth, good coloring, and vibrant health.

Only through research and improving your aquarium-keeping skills can you consistently produce high-quality show fish. Sure it's possible to get lucky and purchase a guppy for a couple of bucks at a local fish store and have it grow into championship material. But this is the exception rather than the rule. So you need to do your homework.

Why Competing in Fish Shows Is Good for Your Fish

Participating in fish shows keeps your aquatic pets from becoming totally bored with their lives. (If you had nothing to do but swim back and forth in your bathtub all day, you'd probably be looking for a way out, too.) Fish are a lot like humans in that they need a little mental stimulation every once in a while.

In the wild, competing for food, avoiding larger predators that want to have them over for lunch (literally), and other factors such as unpredictable weather keep a fish's senses alert and stimulate it into constant action. After sitting in a home aquarium for month after month, most fish appreciate a change of pace, even if it means being carted off to a weird place where strange-looking people with large, distorted faces walk by and stare into the tank.

Despite the fact that most freshwater species are bred for the industry, their natural instincts and desires remain intact.

Getting to Know the Shows

The great majority of aquatic competitions are organized by aquarium societies. These aquatic societies can be international in scope, as is the International Betta Congress (IBC), or can be local groups in large towns and cities. The following is a list of the types of shows you're likely to encounter.

Small shows

Small shows (also known as *bowl* shows) are usually sponsored by local clubs and generally include all different classes of fish such as goldfish, cichlids, and tetras. Bowl shows are set up for only a few hours so that their paid members can exhibit their favorite wet pets. These shows are usually not open to the general public. So, to enter the competition, you must become a member of the society.

Regional shows

Aquarium societies often enter larger fish shows that cover a broad geographic area within a marked region that can include several states. In this type of competition, different societies compete against each other to see who is really the top piranha. A regional show forces you to become a team player, so make sure you have several good excuses ready, just in case your entry doesn't place very well.

Open shows

An open show is similar to a regional show, except that anyone can enter the competition — you don't have to belong to a particular aquarium society. These shows are cool because if you don't win, you can sneak out the back door without having to answer to anyone else. Or you can tell family members that you had a flat tire on the way to the show and missed the entire competition.

Exhibitions

One of the largest shows you can enter is known as an *exhibition,* or *aquatic convention.* These types of shows are generally put together by tropical fish magazines and international societies. Exhibitions are massive affairs, generally held in huge auditoriums and fancy hotels. Aquarium manufacturers are usually present to demonstrate their newest lines of tanks, food, chemicals, and equipment to people they consider prospective buyers. (If you don't want to spend the day listening to sales pitches, wear old clothes and look poor.)

Exhibitions are exciting and extremely important because they help to keep hobbyists informed on major new trends in the hobby. If you go to one of these shows, you will probably find a lot of excellent information on new equipment and fishkeeping procedures. Not to mention the tons of new ideas from other hobbyists you'll get.

Understanding Competition Classes

You need to learn a little bit about how fish shows operate so that you know what to expect when you enter your very first serious competition. True, fish shows have more rules than cribbage, but you can still go to a competition, have a great time, and pick up some important aquarium-keeping skills.

To make sure that the competition between individual fish is fair, you have to enter your contestant in a specific class. Classes are usually grouped by similar species. For example, if you have an oscar (*Astronotus ocellatus*), you don't want to place it in a livebearer class normally intended for guppies (*Lebistes reticulatus*) and mollies (*Mollienesia sphenops*). Your fish would be instantly disqualified simply because it was in the wrong class. Trying to convince a judge that your 11-inch oscar is really a champion guppy that has eaten too much usually goes over like a lead balloon.

Classes can also be divided into smaller sub-categories. For example, a guppy class may be divided into fantails, lyretails, and spadetails. So, before you enter your fish in any competition, check with the show's sponsors to make sure that you are placing it in the correct category. It would be a shame if your potential best of show was disqualified from the competition just because you mistakenly placed it in the wrong class.

Getting Your Fish in Shape for the Show

At competitions, you want your fish to make the best overall impression it possibly can. If your entry bolts for the corner of the tank when the judge comes up for her first look, your entry probably won't receive high marks because the judge didn't have the opportunity to look it over properly.

Swimming upright and smiling

A good show fish isn't shy around strangers and doesn't panic every time someone walks by its tank. There probably will be many visitors — competitors and other hobbyists — sneaking over to take a quick peak at your entry before the judging begins. You don't want a bunch of people hanging around your tank and spooking your fish while it is trying to remain calm after being transported from its home to the show.

If your fish happens to be shy, it most likely will be digging an escape tunnel by the time the judge gets around to looking in the tank. So a little training is in order. There is really no big difference between fish and other domesticated pets as far as training is concerned. Conditioning works well for your aquatic pets, just as it does for your four-legged friends. To keep your show fish from being easily frightened by the presence of strangers, you need to create conditions at home similar to those found in competition.

Placing your show fish's holding tank in a moderate traffic area gets your entry used to people passing back and forth. How your fish reacts to people socially is known as *deportment*. Make sure your fish is used to people being around its tank everyday, but don't overdo it.

Ideally, your fish should act naturally, be active and alert, and show no fear after being trained for a short period of time. Another trick you can use at home is to periodically shine a light into the water so that your fish is prepared for sudden illumination — just in case a judge uses a flashlight during observation. A bad show fish swims upside down and looks bummed out.

A poor show fish exhibits unusual behaviors such as hanging out in areas of the tank that it normally wouldn't. For example, if your cory normally lives on the bottom level of the tank but is trying to fly two inches above the water level, a judge probably will mark it down for its odd behavior. If your fish is floating upside down, or looks ready for the great fish bowl in the sky, then you need to reevaluate your strategies and goals for raising top-quality fish.

Your entry should always be in top physical form. Start with a good specimen and then make sure it receives proper nutrition by feeding it a varied diet consisting of commercially pre-manufactured flakes and different types of live food. The water conditions your show fish is raised in should always be optimal, with good filtration and the proper water chemistry for the species.

The holding tank

When you spend a great deal of time, effort, and expense raising a show-quality fish, you want to make sure it does not encounter any physical problems prior to a competition. For example, if you were a professional model, you probably would not begin taking karate or boxing lessons a week before a photo shoot — the results could be disastrous.

A small holding tank is a great (and inexpensive) way to keep your show fish healthy and free from physical harm in the month or two preceding its competition. A holding tank negates the possibility of other fish damaging your prize entry's fins or scales by not allowing physical contact, which in turn prevents untimely fighting or breeding.

Your holding tank should be free from large decorations (such as sharp rocks) with the potential to damage your show fish. A few floating plants and a couple of rooted specimens give your entry the security it needs to remain stress-free. A smaller tank also allows you to carefully monitor your fish's progress, and makes cleaning and frequent water changes a snap.

The smaller environment of a holding tank allows you to check for any disease that may manifest during this waiting period. Physical ailments can be treated quickly and easily in a smaller tank. Solitary confinement also keeps your entry stress-free and calm until it's time to enter competition and really show off. Being alone in a semi-bare tank prepares your pet for the same conditions it faces during an exhibition.

Exhibiting Your Fish Properly

After you find and train your show fish, you need the guidelines for exhibiting them properly. The following tips can help your fish put its best fin forward:

- ✔ Study the rules carefully before you fill out an entry form so that you have a good idea of the requirements for the individual competitions.

- ✔ Fill out all your paperwork properly and legibly and submit it on time.

- ✔ Get your show fish to the competition with plenty of time to spare. This gives your entry an opportunity to calm down and regain any color it may have lost during transportation to the show. (Fish lose color when they're distressed, and transporting them is stressful for them.)

Water conditions

Bring water with you so that your fish can remain in familiar conditions during the competition. Water supplies provided at the show may be very different from those at your home. Discontinue feeding your fish the night before the competition to avoid water fouling (remember, it's good for fish to fast one day a week) and change the water frequently to keep your show tank looking crystal clear. If possible, use water that is a couple degrees warmer than what your fish is accustomed to — this generally helps fish show better. Make sure to provide an airstone, if possible, to keep the water well-oxygenated.

Tank considerations

It is important to place your show fish in a tank that correctly matches its size. For example, a single guppy in a 10-gallon tank is dwarfed by the sheer water volume and tends to look rather miniscule. It's better to show this type of fish in a 5-gallon container. On the other hand, an eight-inch plecostomus doesn't look very good in a 2-gallon container. It doesn't have the room to display all its fins, or the other attributes that may make it a winner. If you have to use a shoehorn to cram your entry into its show tank, then the aquarium is probably too small, and if you need a telescope to spot your fish in its show tank, then the aquarium is probably too large.

To set up an exhibition tank properly, read the competition's rules. For example, some categories and competitions allow gravel and decorations, whereas others do not. If you use gravel, make sure it complements the fish you're showing. If you have a dark-colored fish, lighter gravel will show off its colors much more naturally than a darker-toned substrate. However, make sure you use the same color gravel you choose for the show in the fish's home tank for at least two weeks before a competition so that it feels safe and secure with that color.

Here are a few more tips for competitors:

- ✔ If the competition allows tank backgrounds, choose a solid-colored sheet over one with a pattern that takes away from the natural beauty of your show fish.

- ✔ When using plants for decorations, in such categories as community or species tanks, always use fauna native to the region of the fish you're showing. Take my word for it, judges do know the difference. A natural setup always scores higher points than one that is a mishmash of plants from completely different geographic regions. Use live plants if possible for a more natural look that most artificial plants cannot match.

- ✔ The tank or container you use to display your entry should be immaculate. The glass walls should be clean inside and out. Vacuum any dirt or debris off the bottom of the tank right before the competition begins. (Or avoid this problem by bringing extra water with you.)

- ✔ Make sure your show tank is well covered because you do not want your fish jumping out during all the excitement. A lid also prevents people's hands and foreign objects from getting into the water.

After you get everything set up, step back for a moment and take a good look at the overall picture. Does the entire tank look clean and well kept? Is the water crystal clear? Are the decorations in the tank placed so that your fish has the best chance to show itself in front of the judge? Does the tank look natural? Does your fish look calm and happy? Does your entry seem to be adjusting to its surroundings well? If you can answer yes to all these questions, your fish is ready for competition.

Judging Guidelines for Your Fish: Another Point of View

In most competitions, judging guidelines are very strict. Usually, contestants are not allowed to be present when the judging takes place. So, if you want to do a little brown-nosing, do it before the competition starts. For example, simply walk up to a judge, smile, and compliment him on how much he looks like Jacques Cousteau.

Each class usually has its own judge. The judge is supposed to mark your entry on its own merit, not compare it to the other fish in the competition. But judges are human, and an outstanding fish sitting in the next tank over may have a slight bearing on the outcome of your own entry's marks.

After all fish are judged, the "best of show" is awarded to the highest quality entry of all the classes combined. This decision is usually reached by a group conference — the individual judges all get together to vote for what they consider to be the best overall fish at the show. An important thing to remember is that the marks that your fish receives generally are from a single judge's point of view. So try to resist the temptation to verbally tear every judge limb from limb because of what you consider to be serious oversights and bad vision. Nobody likes a spoilsport, so keep your cool and just remember that you are enjoying your hobby at a new level.

To keep judging from becoming too personal, aquarium societies devised a set of standards that each individual fish in a competition can be judged against. The fish that comes closest to matching a set standard in each category is usually determined the winner. This policy keeps the fish from being judged on personal preference only. Judges come from a wide range of backgrounds and aquarium-keeping skill levels. Most are experienced hobbyists or dealers who complete special training at schools that teach them how to judge fish shows efficiently.

Each competition's evaluation system varies slightly, but most show fish are judged on a point system. A certain number of points are allotted for different physical traits, such as size and color. The fish with the most total points after the judging is complete is considered the winner. In the event of a tie, the fish are judged again, or a decision is made by all the judges together. Judges disagree quite a bit, so don't hold your breath waiting for a unanimous decision, or you may pass out from lack of oxygen.

Size and body weight

One of the main physical traits that consistently inspire judges to give a fish high marks is its overall size. Judges generally look for a fish that has reached its full stage of adulthood and is the maximum size for that particular species. In other words, the bigger the better. So an oscar, which should be 10 or 11 inches long, probably won't win if it resembles a minnow with anorexia. If you are able to raise a fish to achieve its full physical potential, a judge may feel that you are a responsible aquarium keeper who takes pride in his/her hobby.

Your fish's body is judged on several different criteria:

- ✔ To begin with, your entry should have all of its body parts intact.

- ✔ Your fish should not have any unusual growths, such as humps on the head (except in the case of some cichlids, where a hump is consider normal in the males of the species) or large unnatural bends in the back, which is considered a sign of old age in most aquatic species.

- ✔ The body of a good-quality show fish is free from deformities and is in correct proportions for its species.

Color and fins

A fish's body color is produced by pigmentation and reflected light. In the wild, fish use these colors for defensive and mating purposes. In competition, fish must meet the coloration standards expected of an aquarium-bred species. Especially in show species such as the discus (which is bred artificially to produce amazing colors like tangerine and numerous cobalt variations), color can be a major factor in determining points.

Fish have the ability to darken and lighten their colors or even change them completely, depending on their surroundings and the time of day. Moods such as fright, stress, and excitement, and other factors, such as illness, can change a fish's color quickly. Take all these variables into consideration while monitoring your candidate's color. (If your fish glows in the dark, it probably has sufficient color to sweep any competition.)

The color on your entry should be evenly disbursed, and it should not look faded or patchy unless typical for the species. The color itself should be very dense, not superficial, and your fish should not look as if it's been run through a chlorine cycle in your washer. The area where two colors meet should be distinct and well defined, not blurred or run together so that the fish resembles a tie-dyed shirt.

Recently, a few unscrupulous breeders started using enhancing devices to increase the coloration of their fish. As far as hobbyists are concerned, this practice is immoral. The artificial color fades in time and generally doesn't look natural at all. An artificially colored fish is similar to a studio's colorized version of an old movie. If you saw Humphrey Bogart running around in a shocking pink hat and purple trousers, you'd know that *Casablanca* had been colorized. The same type of color errors show up on your fish and are noticed immediately by the judges when you use color-intensifying foods (such as spirulina) or hormones to artificially enhance your fish's appearance.

Never attempt to dye your fish to increase their color for showing, or purchase artificially colored fish for showing. This practice consists of injecting colored pigments into a fish's body and is unethical. Some species such as the glassfish develop a disease known as lymphocystis that causes growths on their fins, so never put a fish's health at risk by partaking in cruel practices.

Fins are judged very strictly in a competition. Your entry should have all the fins that are standard for its species. If your fish should have one dorsal fin, one anal fin, two pectoral fins, one caudal fin, and two pelvic fins — then it had better have all seven fins. Some species of fish have an extra adipose fin. If your fish falls into this category, make sure it has one. If it doesn't, don't enter it. If your fish is missing its tail or dorsal fin, wait until the next competition, because this physical problem doesn't go over very well with judges.

All the fins on your entry should be in good condition. Make sure there are no frayed or ragged fins to detract from your fish's natural beauty. The fins should be erect and of good color, not clamped or folded. To keep a show fish's fins in top-quality condition, keep it by itself prior to the competition so that more aggressive fish don't get a chance to tear or damage its fins.

Other causes of poor-quality fins include inadequate water conditions, netting, genetic problems, disease, and breeding spats. Make sure the water conditions in your show fish's tank always remain optimal so that the fish doesn't contract a fungal disease that can easily damage its fins.

To avoid having your entry's fins destroyed by netting, always use a plastic bag or cup to capture your fish.

Genetic problems are permanent, and the only thing you can do when you come across a deformity is to weed out that particular fish from your list of candidates for fish show competitions. Often, certain species of fish damage their pectoral fins when they fan eggs during breeding. For that very reason, it is best not to breed your show fish before competition.

Fins are no different from any other physical attribute and are judged against an accepted norm. Many species of betta (*Betta splendens*) are bred for long-flowing fins, and judges expect fin lengths and sizes in the proper proportion to the fish's body size. All fins should have a symmetrical (even) look pleasing to the judge's eye. If one pectoral fin is quite a bit shorter than the other, your entry probably will lose some points for this deformity right off the bat.

It is important to check out the requirements and rules of every competition carefully ahead of time so that you know exactly what the judges are looking for. Talk to hobbyists who have entered competitions in the classes you're interested in. You can pick up a lot of interesting ideas and learn a few good tips by talking to seasoned pros who have already battled the "ins and outs" of many fish competitions.

Overall condition

Many physical factors can have a bearing on your entry's final point score. Judges look for an overall picture of perfection — a combination of many individual physical traits. Even minor blemishes or irregularities can lose points for your entry.

The scales on your fish's body should be intact and in excellent condition. In many species, scales form standard patterns. This must always be taken into consideration. Scales should lie flat against the body, have a proper mucus coating, and not protrude at odd angles. Gill covers should be straight and preferably red in color, which is an indication of good health.

Your entry's eyes must be clear and bright, and not clouded over or protruding abnormally from the sockets. (If your fish looks like it has a hangover, pack up and go home.) Your fish should be completely free from disease because any sign of parasites, fungus, or other illness is just cause for an immediate mark down on the judge's score sheet.

Transporting Fish to and from a Show

Transportation safely to and from a show is important for your fish's overall health. You want to avoid stressing out or physically damaging your entry on the way to the show so that it has the best chance of remaining happy and healthy and can display its beautiful physical attributes to the best of its ability.

The first thing to do when considering transportation is look at the distance between your home and the show area. You need to give yourself plenty of time so that you don't have to rush to the show and hastily try to set up your entry tank at the last minute. Always allow plenty of time in case something should go wrong. Any unforeseen delay can become disastrous if you're forced to rush your entry in right before the judging begins.

Drive your route to the competition ahead of time so that you know exactly how long it takes and what the road conditions are like. If the roads are rough, plan on adding a little more cushioning to your packing box. Check the predicted weather for the day of the competition, so that you're prepared in the event of heavy rain, extreme heat, frigid cold, or snow. These factors are especially crucial on longer trips.

It really doesn't matter if you plan to show one fish or several fish as far as transportation containers are concerned. You should always transport your fish in a proper carrying case or tank to make sure that their journey is as comfortable as humanly possible.

A good transportation tank can be a small plastic or acrylic aquarium that is insulated by a Styrofoam container. Or you can use a 5-gallon bucket with a tight fitting lid.

Place your transportation tank in something that will insulate it and absorb shocks while you're carrying it in your car. A homemade wooden case that you place in the back seat or hatchback of your vehicle works well. Try to avoid carrying your fish in the trunk or other uninsulated areas that can quickly overheat or chill the water during the trip.

Cover your containers with dark cloth to help calm your entry during transportation. You should always use a battery-operated air pump to keep the water aerated.

Remember to Have Fun

The most important thing to remember when you go to a fish show is to have fun. Take time to chat with fellow hobbyists so that you can make new friends, learn important aspects of fishkeeping from others, and catch up on the newest trends in the fishkeeping hobby.

If you win at a show . . . congratulations! If not, there is always the next show to look forward to. Enjoy the moment either way.

Chapter 23

For the Advanced Aquarium Hobbyist

*O*nce you become successful at keeping freshwater fish, you may begin to wonder what else is out there. Not all water is equal, as you learned in a previous chapter, and some aquatic bodies are *brackish* (slightly salty) or fully saltwater. Different fish, plants, and invertebrates live in these waters. Brackish systems are easy to set up. Marine systems are a little more difficult. *Saltwater Aquariums for Dummies, 2nd Edition* by Gregory Skomal (Wiley Publishing, 2006) walks you through the entire marine aquarium process.

Brackish Aquariums

Fish for brackish aquariums are often unavailable from local pet stores and are usually more expensive than freshwater fish. The water in a brackish aquarium lies somewhere between fresh and marine in salt content. Popular species include monos, archers, puffers, and scats. Mollies can also be kept in a brackish tank. Natural brackish systems fluctuate from season to season due to rains and evaporation, and brackish fish are well adapted to surviving.

The equipment for a brackish system is similar to that for a freshwater setup, but only specific plants can tolerate a brackish system. The salt content in brackish systems can be achieved easily using synthetic marine mix in a ratio of one gallon of saltwater to every two gallons of freshwater. Your tank will basically end up being one-third saltwater and two-thirds freshwater.

There are not as many choices in brackish fish as there are for other systems, because few species in the wild can survive in an environment that is constantly changing. The good news is that brackish fish are very hardy, easy to feed, and many are very exciting to watch due to their high activity levels. Several plants work well in the brackish tank, including hornwort (*Ceratophyllum demersum*), *Vallisneria gigantea*, and *Vallisneria asiatica*.

Saltwater Marine Aquariums

Marine or *saltwater systems*, not surprisingly, require saltwater. You see marine fish on scuba and underwater television programs. The most popular of these fish includes the coral reef species often found living in close proximity to various *invertebrates* (animals without backbones). Saltwater fish are often very colorful and beautiful. They can also be very expensive.

The saltwater in a marine system is obtained by mixing fresh water with a manufactured salt mix available at fish shops. A good filtration system is important in marine tanks to keep oxygen levels high and ammonia levels low. Marine fish have lower tolerance to ammonia than freshwater species do, and an inadequate filter soon leads to disaster in a saltwater tank.

Types of marine systems

There are three main types of saltwater aquariums:

- **Coldwater marine:** Many tanks of this type house animals such as lobsters and rockfish that are native to colder ocean areas.

- **Tropical marine:** These heated tanks generally contain fish native to coral reef areas, such as tangs, clownfish, and damsels.

- **Reef tank:** Some reef tanks contain only invertebrates, such as anemones and scallops and organisms growing on live rock. *Live rock* is rock that has live beneficial organisms attached to it that provide food sources for your fish and help keep the water clean.

You can set up a saltwater system in a variety of ways (see Figure 23-1 for one example). Invertebrates are a little more difficult to care for, so if you do set up a saltwater system you may want to start with a fish-only tank.

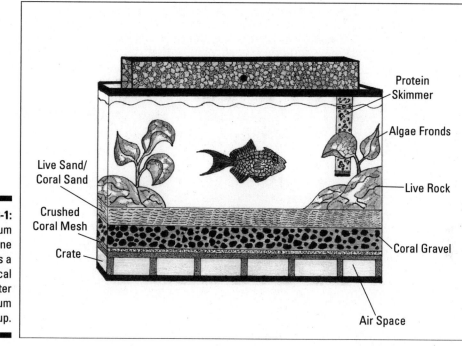

Figure 23-1:
A plenum marine system is a typical saltwater aquarium setup.

Protein Skimmer

Algae Fronds

Live Sand/ Coral Sand

Live Rock

Crushed Coral Mesh

Crate

Coral Gravel

Air Space

Gaining a little experience with a freshwater system is a great way to prepare yourself to enter the marine side. A beginner *can* maintain a successful marine tank, but the lessons you learn are expensive. We see many new hobbyists become disheartened because they start out with a marine setup that's too much to handle. If you have a friend experienced in marine systems, ask her for advice — she may be able to get you started successfully.

Many marine fish are social time bombs waiting to explode all over the other fish in your tank. In fact, saltwater fish can be down right rude. Most community freshwater fish have reached a state of enlightenment or something like that, and are pretty cool with each other.

Marine invertebrates

Invertebrates are animals that have no backbone. They are animals even though many of them look like plants of some sort. Invertebrates make saltwater aquariums look very cool. Invertebrates make up a surprisingly large number of the total animal population. About 2 million species of animals inhabit the earth, and roughly 97 percent of them are invertebrates.

Many fish and invertebrates do not mix well. Marine fish such as the parrot-fish enjoy eating several types of invertebrates. To set up an aquarium with marine fish and invertebrates that can live together in relative harmony without destroying each other, you will have to do a lot of research.

Comparing Freshwater and Saltwater Systems

There are a few pros and cons to marine and freshwater aquariums that you should consider.

Adaptability

Freshwater aquarium fish originally came from rivers and lakes that are constantly in motion and affected by changing temperatures and conditions.

A large majority of freshwater aquatic pets are bred for the fishkeeping industry, but they are still naturally resistant to fluctuations in their environment due to genetic adaptation. This does not mean you should keep freshwater fish in less than excellent aquarium conditions, but freshwater fish will generally be a bit more forgiving of mistakes than marine species.

Marine species are much more sensitive to even slight fluctuations in their aquarium conditions. This does not mean that they will automatically die the second your water temperature drops one degree. However, if the marine species tank does not remain consistent in temperature and *salinity* (amount of salt in the water), you could easily lose an entire tankful of fish.

Availability

It is generally much easier to find live plants for a freshwater aquarium than it is to find invertebrates for a marine tank in local stores. However, marine invertebrates can be easily purchased over the Intranet. You may have to wait for certain species of marine invertebrates and fish to become available as divers bring them in. Thankfully, more hobbyists and aquarium industry folks are beginning to find ways to breed more species of marine fish.

Cost

On average, marine fish are much more expensive than freshwater species. Compare a two-dollar guppy to a queen triggerfish costing several hundred dollars. A large marine tank could be *very* expensive to stock, and your wallet takes a huge hit if anything goes wrong. However, most aquarium hobbyists think marine species are well worth the extra money.

Beauty and friendliness

Marine fish are generally more colorful and larger than freshwater species. If you really like eye-popping colors in your aquarium, the marine side of the hobby will really dazzle you with brilliant yellow tangs, vibrant parrotfish, and many other spectacular species of saltwater fish. Generally you cannot keep as many marine fish in the same space as freshwater fish because the marine fish are larger and generally require more room to move around.

Equipment

Substrate and equipment are a bit more expensive for the marine aquarium. Freshwater gravel is less expensive than marine dolomite, and freshwater lighting costs less than the full-spectrum lighting of a marine reef system.

Many hobbyists are happy keeping only freshwater systems, whereas others plunge into the brackish and marine worlds. All the information you need is out there in books, periodicals, pet stores, and on the Internet.

Part V
The Part of Tens

The 5th Wave   By Rich Tennant

"Naturally we need to adjust the chemicals, but it seems to be the only thing that relaxes him after work."

In this part . . .

Every *For Dummies* book ends with top-ten lists, and we're not about to break the trend. This is where you can quickly check out some great gadgets for your tank, be warned about some of the most common problems beginners run into, and catch some of the lighter sides of the hobby with a Murphy's Law take on fish and a list of resolutions for you come December.

Chapter 24

Ten Cool Aquarium Gadgets

Aquarium Claws (Those Handy Picker-Upper Doodads)

An aquarium claw is really not as menacing as its name might imply. This little plastic claw (such as Aquatic Tongs) is a very handy tool for use in the home aquarium. It makes moving tank decorations as simple as spending mega bucks at the fish store. A button on the end of the handle closes the claw around an object as you depress it. After moving the item, simply release the button to release the grip.

The long handle on this device allows you to reach almost any area of a standard aquarium without getting your hands wet. Keeping your hands (which may be covered in germs, dirt, or household chemicals) out of the tank whenever possible is always a good idea. Other good uses for this tool include inserting plants into substrate, grabbing unwanted objects from the tank (marbles, plant debris, and so on), and removing dead fish. At an average cost of less than ten dollars, you really can't go wrong with this marvelous little gadget.

Never use a claw to retrieve live fish from your aquarium!

Algae Scrapers Are Fun to Use

One simple way to remove excess *algae* (the green, alien-looking glop that is blocking your view) from the aquarium glass is to use an algae scraper. There are several types to choose from, including a long stick with attached scrub pad/sponge that you simply slide up and down the interior glass; a two-way magnet system; and a "glove" type that fits over your entire hand. A real good version of this is the Kent Marine Proscraper 12-inch scraper. Personally, we think that the simple stick model works best, because the magnet version is difficult to work with, and the glove scraper can be quite messy to use.

Although algae can be beneficial as a natural food source, an overgrowth can quickly turn your crystal-clear water into mushy pea soup. Allowing a small amount of green algae to remain on rocks and decorations is okay, but a tank that is excessively overrun with "the green terror" is unsightly at best.

Why Owning One Net Doesn't Cut It

As you have already noticed, fish come in a wide variety of different shapes and sizes. Therefore, aquarium manufacturers were kind enough to create nets to match the individual physical characteristics of whatever uncooperative aquatic friend you happen to be chasing around the tank.

If you buy one of those complete aquarium kits in a box, it will probably come with a small net. After enjoying your aquarium for a few months, you will begin to get the idea that one net just isn't going to cut it. Owning one net is kind of like a fisherman who expects to catch everything with one size of hook.

Nets are one of the most inexpensive items that you can buy for your hobby, and they have the advantage of being very compact and easy to store. While shopping for nets, make sure to purchase one with fine mesh for catching fry, add a selection of small to large nets for different size fish, and, finally, include a few specially constructed nets for barbed and razor-toothed fish.

A Tool Box for Storing Stuff

If you're like us, your fish supplies are probably pretty well spread out along the entire length of the house, garage, and backyard. When your family starts complaining because they found fish food in the flour bin and airline tubing in their underwear drawers, then it is probably time to purchase a storage box.

A plastic tool container or tackle box works wonders for keeping aquarium equipment, fish food, chemicals, test kits, nets, and other supplies all in one neat little place. And you can carry it from tank to tank if you happen to have more than one aquarium. We prefer to buy waterproof plastic boxes that have removable trays on top. These trays can hold small items like thermometers, airstones, and medications while the bulkier items are stored underneath.

Depending on the supplies you have on hand, you may need to purchase more than one box. Most retail chain and sporting goods stores have a good selection in stock.

Extra Tubing for Emergencies

As standard air-line tubing ages, it may become brittle and split or leak. You should periodically replace the tubing that is attached to your equipment (unless you want a free water fountain to suddenly spring up in your living room).

Tubing is inexpensive and can be purchased in short rolls or by the foot. Whenever we find ourselves purchasing supplies, we always pick up a little extra air-line tubing because it never hurts to have it lying around. Tubing can also double as a mini siphon in case of emergencies. Stick one end in the tank, suck the air out of the other end until the water starts to rise, and quickly transfer the tube from your mouth to a bucket below tank level.

You can buy soft tubing that is light blue in color, which blends in well with your aquarium decorations. Soft tubing is easier to attach and bend than stiffer tubing.

Aquarium Sealer (Flood Insurance)

If you wake up one morning and find that your living room floor resembles a kiddy pool, then chances are one of your aquariums may be leaking. No hobbyist should be without a tube of aquarium-safe silicone sealer in case this catastrophe strikes. Besides, aquarium sealer is cool and squishy and fun to apply.

Unfortunately, in order to repair a leak, you must first drain and dry the tank to allow the sealer to set properly. But in the long run, it is also better to spend a couple of dollars on a tube of sealer instead of several hundred dollars on a new tank. Once in a while, factory sealer will fail due to age, weather conditions, and high or uneven water pressure. So make sure that you are always prepared. (Or buy extra flood insurance.)

Gang Valves to Hook Up Neat Junk

Despite the fact that as caring hobbyists we always strive to create a "natural environment" for our aquatic pets, we all fall prey at one time or another to the uncontrollable urge to buy those cool-looking plastic aquarium toys that do all sorts of wild and wonderful things.

As we move into our second childhoods, the colorful bubbling divers, scuba-diving cartoon characters, and sunken treasure ships that bob up and down become just too inviting to pass by. These toys are lots of fun to watch and can be very entertaining.

In order to hook up all this cool junk, though, you need a few gang valves. A *gang valve* works like a splitter. It redirects one main air supply via tubing into several outlets all at once. The flow of air to each outlet can be individually controlled by built-in valves. With this neat device, you can hook up many cool aquarium toys that will keep your kids (and yourself) preoccupied for several hours at a time.

Buckets to Slosh Around In

Buckets are beneficial tools to the fishkeeping hobbyist. Small, sturdy plastic buckets can be used to carry hoses and other equipment, transport water, move gravel, and temporarily hold fish. Besides, when everything in your aquarium has suddenly jumped out of whack, simply fill two buckets with cold water and stand in them. This procedure will help calm you down every time!

Remember to never use your aquarium buckets for other household chores, because residual cleaning chemicals left in the bucket can kill your fish.

Multi-Outlet Plugs

Many aquariums need electrical outlet space for one or two heater plugs, one or two light plugs, one to three air pump plugs, powerfilter or powerhead plugs, and more, depending on your setup. As you can see, an electrical setup can quickly outnumber your available wall plugs. A good multi-outlet plug or bar with a built-in circuit breaker can take care of this problem.

Razor Blades (the Miracle Cleaner)

After algae and water minerals have remained on aquarium glass for any length of time, they can be very difficult to remove and can make your tank look like an encrusted beach pier. A dirty piece of glass spoils the appearance of your aquarium and blocks out beneficial light that your fish and plants need to remain healthy and happy.

You can purchase single-edged razor blades with a safety handle at your local hardware store. This instrument will quickly remove build-up on glass and equipment faces. As with any other sharp object, extreme caution is advised.

Chapter 25

Ten Ways to Kill Your Fish Without Even Trying

In This Chapter

▶ Alerting yourself to things you shouldn't do to your fish

▶ Reminding yourself of things you need to do to your fish

*B*efore we go into discussing this, we want to mention one main thing to avoid if you want to keep your fish reasonably happy: Don't fuss too much and they will be much happier and healthier.

Go Away on Vacation and Forget Them

Okay, on your last day at Disneyland, you call your boss and sadly inform him that all of the airplanes in California have broken down, and you are being forced to stay for an extra week. No problem. But what about your aquatic friends?

Before going on vacation, make sure you have a reliable friend who can continue to care for your pets just in case you are gone longer than originally planned. Another option is to purchase from your local fish dealer tablets or automatic feeders, which dispense food to your fish while you are gone. Always leave enough food to cover a time period that is longer than your intended stay.

Play Doctor Without a License

Maddy once had an aunt who had a pill to cure every real or imaginary ailment known to man. The inside of her purse resembled a large pharmacy. As mentioned elsewhere in this book, when it comes to doctoring your fish, don't overdo.

Many new hobbyists tend to overmedicate their tanks at the very first sign of disease. This is a pattern that many people learned during childhood. If we thought chicken soup and aspirin would help cure our fish, we would probably dump that into the tank as well.

A large number of diseases can be avoided through good maintenance such as frequent water changes. Avoid the temptation to pour medicine after medicine into your tank in hopes you will find the right cure. Seek the advice of an advanced hobbyist or tropical fish merchant who can help you pinpoint your problem. If medication is necessary, always follow the manufacturer's instructions to the letter and use a hospital tank if possible.

Give Your Cat a Sushi Bar

Have you ever wondered why many cat foods are shaped like fish? Well, it's no accident. In your cat's tiny and distorted little brain, your new aquarium can be considered a free sushi bar. If your tank is not covered properly, your cat can sneak in for a quick snack while you wonder why his food is collecting dust in his bowl.

Take our word for it: No amount of pleading or yelling will keep some cats from this habit if they decide that fresh seafood is their favorite. Make sure that the hood you buy for your new aquarium fits properly and snugly. If you happen to own a particularly strong or fat cat, weigh the hood down with books or some other heavy objects so that it can't be pried or flipped up.

Stuff Your Fish with Seven-Course Meals

Many different varieties of fish food are on the market. A good combination of flake, frozen, and live foods help to promote good health in your wet pets. However, you need to realize that a fish's stomach is no larger than its eye, and overfeeding will rapidly foul the tank and eventually lead to disease or death.

Fish do not require seven-course meals each day to survive. If your fish are beginning to resemble the Pillsbury doughboy and are constantly getting stuck between rocks, then it's time to cut down on the chow.

Mix Apples and Oranges

While browsing your local fish shop, you find yourself suddenly becoming attached to a large cichlid who looks as if it has been feeding on "instant grow" flakes for a decade. You automatically figure that this toughie will provide leadership skills for your unmotivated guppies. Within an hour of adding your new leader to the tank, you are surprised to find that all of your guppies have vanished.

Mixing apples and oranges may be great for a summer fruit salad, but it doesn't work in the home aquarium. Check with your local dealer if you are unsure about the compatibility of any species.

Add Too Many Fish (the Shoehorn Syndrome)

It is really tempting to constantly add "just one more" fish to your home aquarium. All fishkeepers fall prey to this Shoehorn Syndrome at one time or another. If your aquarium resembles a phone booth-packing competition, then you have probably overstepped the capacity. Remember, overcrowding can be deadly.

Don't Do Your Homework

If you want to learn more about any subject, you need to do a little research. Skilled fishkeepers do their homework before setting up a new type of system and they investigate specific habitat requirements prior to purchasing unknown species of fish. Isn't that one of the reasons that you bought this cool book?

The Internet, a local library, and tropical fish magazines can provide you with a lot of extra good information that will keep you informed about the newest developments in the fishkeeping hobby as well.

Let the Neighbor's Nasty Kid Play with Your Fish

A mischievous kid can be every fishkeeper's nightmare. This is the same kid who always shows up at dinnertime, skateboards through your petunias, and in later years, escorts your only daughter to the senior prom.

A home aquarium is often a prime target for the neighbor's nasty kid who will drop all sorts of interesting objects into the tank, such as your cat, coins, sticks, and peanut butter sandwiches. These offerings will not be appreciated by your fish and can prove to be lethal as well. It is always best to prohibit young children from touching your aquariums, and to quickly check your tank for foreign objects at least once a day.

Become a Hypochondriac Hobbyist

It does not take long for a new hobbyist to get emotionally attached to their fish. The more we bond with them, the more we tend to overpamper them. Checking in on your fish every 30 minutes, constantly fiddling around with the equipment, and rearranging the decorations in order to achieve the perfect environment just isn't good for the fish. Maintain your aquariums, enjoy your fish, but don't fuss too much.

Buy Used or Cheap Equipment

Always test used equipment before purchasing it if possible. When buying new stuff from a local dealer, make sure to purchase the best equipment that your budget allows. Poorly made or worn-out equipment will inevitably lead to disaster down the road.

Be wary of old electrical aquarium pumps, hoods, and heaters at the neighbor's garage sale that look worn or have frayed wires. Don't get us wrong; we have purchased some good aquarium equipment at garage sales, but as the old saying goes, in most cases, you get what you pay for.

Chapter 26

Ten Scientific Fish Laws

In This Chapter
▶ Becoming aware of the way things sometimes happen with no warning
▶ Figuring out what to do when these things happen

From time to time during your wonderful adventures as an aquarium hobbyist, you may notice strange phenomena in and around your fish tanks that cannot even be explained by modern science. Seasoned hobbyists learn through experience that these strange occurrences actually have very simple explanations. Here are some examples of those strange fish laws that plague us all from time to time.

The Fish Law of Thermodynamics

The fish law of thermodynamics states that all heat in a house will flow directly into your aquarium at all times. Window light will be absorbed by your overheating tank immediately so that the remaining sections of your house will convince the local astronomer that there is a black hole in the neighborhood.

To take care of this problem, you need to make sure that your aquarium is placed in an area that has plenty of air movement and a consistent room temperature. Check to make sure your aquarium heater is functioning properly, and do not set your aquarium up near doors or windows. Remember that extreme temperature fluctuations can cause illness and death.

The Fish Law of Metamorphosis

The fish law of metamorphosis states that any fish in your tank, when given the right opportunity, will be able to instantly morph into any shape necessary to escape from the aquarium. Our own fish have morphed into the shape of a French fry in order to squeeze through an air-line hole.

The second part of this law states that after escape, this same fish will morph into either a carpet dust ball or a kitty snack. To fix this problem, make sure that all holes in the top of the tank lid are completely covered, especially if you have species of fish that are especially prone to jumping out of aquariums.

The Fish Law of Motion

The fish law of motion states that any sluggish or ill-looking fish will instantly be able to dash madly at twice the speed of light when a net is inserted into the aquarium. The fish will always move directly at right angles to the net's strategic placement — a maneuver which will leave you with wet clothes, a lot of frustration, and a torn-up tank.

To avoid this problem, try adding a little food to coax your fish up to the top of the tank when you need to catch one. Gently lift out large aquarium decorations, such as rocks, before you attempt to capture your fish. This will provide you with more space and maneuverability.

The Fish Law of Anti-Matter

The fish law of anti-matter states that fish are the only animals on earth that are capable of hiding their own body matter after death so that they can never be found. On a good day, Sherlock Holmes would not be able to find a dead guppy in a 1-gallon bowl because of this law.

It is important to have good filtration in your tank and carry out frequent water changes because of this unusual problem. If a dead fish cannot be located, then a build-up of waste will occur and cause water fouling and disease.

The Fish Law of Nutrition

The fish law of nutrition states that your fish will eat all food that is unfit for aquatic consumption, so make sure that you routinely check your tank for foreign objects that may have fallen into the water. The second part of this law states that any uneaten food will fall directly into an area that cannot be seen by the human eye. Because of this problem, it is important to feed your fish small meals several times per day, instead of dumping half a can of flake food into the tank all at once.

The Fish Law of Company

The fish law of company states that all aquarium fish will lethargically lurk in a corner or disappear behind decorations at the exact moment when your visitors arrive to see them. The fish will return to their normal activity level after dark, even if they are not nocturnal.

If you want to successfully show your fish to your company, arrange to have your friends come over at a time when you would normally give your fish a special treat. This will allow your friends to get a glimpse of your prize pets.

The Fish Law of Potential Energy

The fish law of potential energy states that a fish's energy can be stored indefinitely and will only be released when the aquarium hood is opened and a direct escape route is in sight. To avoid this problem, make sure that your aquarium hood fits securely.

The Fish Law of Psychic Felines

The fish law of psychic felines states that any cat within a hundred miles of your aquarium will be able to zero in on, sneak through an open window or door to get at, and physically engulf any fish that has jumped from your tank — before you can cross the room to save it. Your fish are fair game, so make sure to keep a distrustful eye on any other pets that are living in the same household or neighborhood.

The Fish Law of Aggression

The fish law of aggression states that any two fish can show aggression toward each other without just cause at any given moment of time. For this reason, it is vital that you keep track of your fish's social habits to make sure that a minor scuffle does not end up turning into a major war. Rearranging a few tank decorations every few months helps break down pre-established territories and reduce potential aggression.

The Fish Law of Time

The fish law of time states that a fish will be prone to contract an illness the day before your vacation starts, or at the beginning of a holiday weekend when all of the pet shops are closed. That is why it is important to have extra medication on hand for such emergencies. Training a friend, neighbor, or relative in the basics of fish disease and treatment comes in handy if you happen to be on vacation when disaster strikes.

Chapter 27

Ten Aquatic New Year's Resolutions

● ●

In This Chapter

▶ Promising to renew your dedication to your fish
▶ Declaring your commitment to the world

● ●

"**I,** (state your name), promise to do the following in the new year:

Feed the Fish

I promise to feed my fish properly and throw away the cans of food that have been in the attic since World War I.

Clean the Tank

I promise to clean my tank regularly and maintain it properly with frequent water changes and an aquarium vacuum on a regular basis.

Reduce Celibacy

I promise to buy my male swordtails several females and keep the correct mix of males and females (with standard exceptions, such as the betta).

Remove Algae

I promise to remove excess algae from the aquarium glass once a week and to maintain good water conditions and proper lighting.

Change the Filter Pads

I promise to replace clogged filter pads and change or rinse them monthly.

Turn on the Lights

I promise to turn on my aquarium lights daily and to slowly increase the room lights before switching the tank light on.

Use My Test Kits

I promise to brush the dust off of my test kits and use them once a week. I will regularly test for nitrates and ammonia and keep an eye on pH.

Pay Attention to My Fish

I promise to spend more quality time with my fish, such as wiggling my fingers near the glass. I will acknowledge my fish's presence at least twice a day.

Change the Airstones

I promise to change the aquarium's airstones when they clog so my fish aren't living in a stagnant rice paddy. I will check the airstones weekly.

Redecorate the Tank

I promise to rearrange the tank decorations at least twice a year and add new plants now and then. Then my fish won't look bored or spit gravel at me."

Appendix

Tank Figures and Facts

Maddy's math teacher once told her that she looked exactly like a zombie from a B horror movie when mathematical equations and formulas were presented to her in test form. Let's be honest: Numbers can be more boring than your neighbor talking about his last round of golf. But the fact remains that numbers are important in the aquarium hobby. Numbers tell you how big your tank is, how much it weighs, and how many fish you can safely put into it during one shopping spree.

So in order to preserve your mental health, we have included a few tables to help you get a better idea of just how much room your aquarium really has.

How Big a Tank Should I Get?

You want to make sure that when you set up your mega-aquarium that it does not end up in the apartment downstairs. Don't laugh, because this has actually happened on numerous occasions! If you live in an upstairs apartment, you probably don't want to place a 200-gallon tank directly over the downstairs resident's bedroom. Homes with older floors my have weak spots that cannot be seen. Always use common sense when choosing an aquarium size to match the home you live in.

In order to give you a better idea of what an aquarium weighs when it is full of water, and also empty, we provide Table A-1. All weights in the table are accurate to within a few pounds, depending on what equipment you use, the amount of gravel in the tank, and other factors such as the weight of decorations.

Table A-1	Tank Measurements		
Tank Size	*Outside Dimensions (in.)*	*Weight Full*	*Weight Empty*
10 gallon	20¼ x 10½ x 12⁹⁄₁₆	111 pounds	11 pounds
10 gallon long	24¼ x 8½ x 12⅝	116 pounds	16 pounds

(continued)

Table A-1 *(continued)*

Tank Size	Outside Dimensions (in.)	Weight Full	Weight Empty
15 gallon	24¼ x 12½ x 12¾	170 pounds	21 pounds
15 gallon high	20¼ x 10½ x 18¾	170 pounds	22 pounds
20 high	24¼ x 12½ x 16¾	225 pounds	25 pounds
20 long	30¼ x 12½ x 22¾	225 pounds	25 pounds
29 gallon	30¼ x 12½ x 18¾	330 pounds	40 pounds
30 gallon	36¼ x 12⅝ x 16¾	343 pounds	43 pounds
30 gallon high	24¼ x 12½ x 24¾	340 pounds	41 pounds
38 gallon	36¼ x 12⅝ x 19¾	427 pounds	47 pounds
40 gallon breeder	36³⁄₁₆ x 18¼ x 16¹⁵⁄₁₆	458 pounds	58 pounds
40 gallon long	48¼ x 12¾ x 16⅞	455 pounds	55 pounds
45 gallon	36¼ x 12⅝ x 23¾	515 pounds	66 pounds
45 gallon long	48¼ x 12¾ x 23¾	510 pounds	60 pounds
50 gallon	36⅞ x 19 x 19⅝	600 pounds	100 pounds
55 gallon	48¼ x 12¾ x 21	625 pounds	78 pounds
60 gallon	48⅜ x 12⅞ x 23⅞	710 pounds	111 pounds
65 gallon	36⅞ x 19 x 24⅝	775 pounds	126 pounds
75 gallon	48½ x 18½ x 21⅜	850 pounds	140 pounds
90 gallon	48½ x 18½ x 25⅜	1,050 pounds	160 pounds
110 gallon high	48⅞ x 19 x 30¾	1,320 pounds	198 pounds
120 gallon high	48½ x 24¼ x 25½	1,400 pounds	215 pounds
150 gallon	72 ½ x 18½ x 28½	1,800 pounds	338 pounds
180 gallon	72½ x 24½ x 25⅝	2,100 pounds	368 pounds

Conversions (and Other Useful Data)

If you were bad in high school math like the rest of us and spent most of your time sleeping near the window in the back of the classroom, then you might find the following simple tables quite helpful. (Saves on calculator batteries, too.)

Many tropical fish magazines and books use different types of systems to get their mathematical points across. One publication may choose to use the metric system, while another will crank out figures that would give Albert Einstein an embolism. The following information allows you to sort through the numbers game to come up with information that you can actually understand and use to your best advantage.

1000 cubic centimeters = 1 liter

1 liter of water = 1 kilogram in weight

1 cubic foot of water = 6.23 imperial gallons

1 imperial gallon of water = 10 pounds in weight

1 U.S. gallon = .8 imperial gallons

1 imperial gallon = 4.55 liters

Water hardness

1 English degree of hardness = 14.3 ppm (parts per million) of calcium carbonate

1 French degree of hardness = 10.0 ppm of calcium carbonate

1 American degree of hardness = 17.1 ppm of calcium carbonate

1 German degree of hardness = 17.9 ppm of calcium oxide

One liter = 0.26 gallons

One gallon = 3.78 liters

1 inch = 2.54 centimeters

One foot = 30 centimeters

One yard = 36 inches

One meter = 39.4 inches

Once ounce = 29 grams

To convert centimeters to inches, multiply by 0.40

To convert inches to centimeters, multiply by 2.54

To convert kilograms to pounds, multiply by 2.2

To convert pounds to kilograms, multiply by 0.453

Temperature

Celsius = (Fahrenheit − 32) × 5/9

Fahrenheit = (Celsius × 9/5) + 32

Volume = Length × Width × Height

Aquarium weight

1. **Determine capacity.**

   Capacity in gallons = (Length × Width × Height [in inches]) divided by 231.

2. **Use capacity to determine weight.**

   One gallon of fresh water at 4 degrees Celsius = 8.57 pounds of weight.

How Many Fish Can I Put in the Tank?

It is very important to remember that fish need space in order to be healthy. (Think about it, would you want to live in an elevator with ten other people?) A crowded tank that has exceeded its stocking limits leads to poor water conditions that can adversely affect your fish's health. Overcrowded tanks are low in oxygen levels and pollute quickly — much more so than the filter medium or biological bacteria can handle efficiently.

Table A-2 gives you an idea of how many fish can safely be put into a tank with the given dimensions.

The first column is simply the length of the tank multiplied by the width. This can be measured with a yardstick or measuring tape. The second column tells you the total surface area of what you measured. The third and fourth columns give you the total length of all the fish, in inches, that can be safely put in that size tank, depending on whether they are freshwater or marine fish. (This is a handy table to have if you decide to enter the marine side of the hobby later on as well.) Remember that the total length of the fish is measured from the snout to the beginning of the tail fin, and all the fish lengths are added together. Also remember that fish grow!

Smaller tanks (under 36 inches in length) are not recommended for saltwater, except when being used as a hospital tank.

Table A-2	How Many Fish Can Fit in a Tank		
Tank (L × W)	*Surface Area*	*Freshwater Fish (in.)*	*Marine Fish (in.)*
20 x 10	200	16	4
24 x 12	288	24	6
30 x 12	360	30	7
36 x 12	432	36	9
48 x 12	576	48	12
48 x 18	864	72	18
72 x 18	1296	108	27
72 x 24	1728	144	36

How Much Gravel Can I Put in the Tank?

In order to determine the approximate number of pounds of gravel that will be needed for a rectangular aquarium, you can use this formula:

Length (in inches) × Width (in inches) × desired gravel depth (in inches) × .05 = pounds of gravel

Index

SPORTS, FITNESS, PARENTING, RELIGION & SPIRITUALITY

0-7645-5146-9

0-7645-5418-2

Also available:

- Adoption For Dummies
  0-7645-5488-3
- Basketball For Dummies
  0-7645-5248-1
- The Bible For Dummies
  0-7645-5296-1
- Buddhism For Dummies
  0-7645-5359-3
- Catholicism For Dummies
  0-7645-5391-7
- Hockey For Dummies
  0-7645-5228-7

- Judaism For Dummies
  0-7645-5299-6
- Martial Arts For Dummies
  0-7645-5358-5
- Pilates For Dummies
  0-7645-5397-6
- Religion For Dummies
  0-7645-5264-3
- Teaching Kids to Read For Dummies
  0-7645-4043-2
- Weight Training For Dummies
  0-7645-5168-X
- Yoga For Dummies
  0-7645-5117-5

TRAVEL

0-7645-5438-7

0-7645-5453-0

Also available:

- Alaska For Dummies
  0-7645-1761-9
- Arizona For Dummies
  0-7645-6938-4
- Cancún and the Yucatán For Dummies
  0-7645-2437-2
- Cruise Vacations For Dummies
  0-7645-6941-4
- Europe For Dummies
  0-7645-5456-5
- Ireland For Dummies
  0-7645-5455-7

- Las Vegas For Dummies
  0-7645-5448-4
- London For Dummies
  0-7645-4277-X
- New York City For Dummies
  0-7645-6945-7
- Paris For Dummies
  0-7645-5494-8
- RV Vacations For Dummies
  0-7645-5443-3
- Walt Disney World & Orlando For Dumm
  0-7645-6943-0

GRAPHICS, DESIGN & WEB DEVELOPMENT

0-7645-4345-8

0-7645-5589-8

Also available:

- Adobe Acrobat 6 PDF For Dummies
  0-7645-3760-1
- Building a Web Site For Dummies
  0-7645-7144-3
- Dreamweaver MX 2004 For Dummies
  0-7645-4342-3
- FrontPage 2003 For Dummies
  0-7645-3882-9
- HTML 4 For Dummies
  0-7645-1995-6
- Illustrator cs For Dummies
  0-7645-4084-X

- Macromedia Flash MX 2004 For Dumm
  0-7645-4358-X
- Photoshop 7 All-in-One Desk
  Reference For Dummies
  0-7645-1667-1
- Photoshop cs Timesaving Techniqu
  For Dummies
  0-7645-6782-9
- PHP 5 For Dummies
  0-7645-4166-8
- PowerPoint 2003 For Dummies
  0-7645-3908-6
- QuarkXPress 6 For Dummies
  0-7645-2593-X

NETWORKING, SECURITY, PROGRAMMING & DATABASES

0-7645-6852-3

0-7645-5784-X

Also available:

- A+ Certification For Dummies
  0-7645-4187-0
- Access 2003 All-in-One Desk
  Reference For Dummies
  0-7645-3988-4
- Beginning Programming For Dummies
  0-7645-4997-9
- C For Dummies
  0-7645-7068-4
- Firewalls For Dummies
  0-7645-4048-3
- Home Networking For Dummies
  0-7645-42796

- Network Security For Dummies
  0-7645-1679-5
- Networking For Dummies
  0-7645-1677-9
- TCP/IP For Dummies
  0-7645-1760-0
- VBA For Dummies
  0-7645-3989-2
- Wireless All In-One Desk Reference
  For Dummies
  0-7645-7496-5
- Wireless Home Networking For Dumm
  0-7645-3910-8

HEALTH & SELF-HELP

Diabetes FOR DUMMIES
0-7645-6820-5 *†

Low-Carb Dieting FOR DUMMIES
0-7645-2566-2

Also available:

- Alzheimer's For Dummies
  0-7645-3899-3
- Asthma For Dummies
  0-7645-4233-8
- Controlling Cholesterol For Dummies
  0-7645-5440-9
- Depression For Dummies
  0-7645-3900-0
- Dieting For Dummies
  0-7645-4149-8
- Fertility For Dummies
  0-7645-2549-2

- Fibromyalgia For Dummies
  0-7645-5441-7
- Improving Your Memory For Dummies
  0-7645-5435-2
- Pregnancy For Dummies †
  0-7645-4483-7
- Quitting Smoking For Dummies
  0-7645-2629-4
- Relationships For Dummies
  0-7645-5384-4
- Thyroid For Dummies
  0-7645-5385-2

EDUCATION, HISTORY, REFERENCE & TEST PREPARATION

Spanish FOR DUMMIES
0-7645-5194-9

The Origins of Tolkien's Middle-earth FOR DUMMIES
0-7645-4186-2

Also available:

- Algebra For Dummies
  0-7645-5325-9
- British History For Dummies
  0-7645-7021-8
- Calculus For Dummies
  0-7645-2498-4
- English Grammar For Dummies
  0-7645-5322-4
- Forensics For Dummies
  0-7645-5580-4
- The GMAT For Dummies
  0-7645-5251-1
- Inglés Para Dummies
  0-7645-5427-1

- Italian For Dummies
  0-7645-5196-5
- Latin For Dummies
  0-7645-5431-X
- Lewis & Clark For Dummies
  0-7645-2545-X
- Research Papers For Dummies
  0-7645-5426-3
- The SAT I For Dummies
  0-7645-7193-1
- Science Fair Projects For Dummies
  0-7645-5460-3
- U.S. History For Dummies
  0-7645-5249-X

Get smart @ dummies.com®

- **Find a full list of Dummies titles**
- **Look into loads of FREE on-site articles**
- **Sign up for FREE eTips e-mailed to you weekly**
- **See what other products carry the Dummies name**
- **Shop directly from the Dummies bookstore**
- **Enter to win new prizes every month!**